PART ONE

The Well-Kept Garden

*"No occupation is so delightful
to me as the culture of the earth,
and no culture comparable
to that of the garden."*

Thomas Jefferson
1743-1826

CHAPTER 1

About Your Garden

The circumstances of each family have a direct bearing on the size and nature of its garden. For example, one family may be renting an allotment on a year to year basis, while another may own property and be able to plan years ahead. Suburban or country gardens will usually have space for a large sunny plot, while city gardeners may have to settle for a smaller, partially shaded one. Because each case will be different, the suggestions contained in this book may not apply in every respect to your particular gardening activities.

The art of vegetable gardening is to aid nature in the production of healthy crops. If the environment is hostile, it makes your job that much harder. Our gardening practices have, by and large, proven to be successful, and I hope that those who are able to follow them through this book will have equal success.

It is certainly true of gardening that "the best laid schemes of mice and men go oft awry". While general timing can be planned ahead, nature has a way of throwing timetables off schedule. The very weekend you plan to transplant seedlings a heat wave may arrive, or a snow storm, or failing this, a family crisis is sure to arise. You must therefore be very flexible, attending first to the most important jobs that time and weather permit.

When faced with spring work, it will seem to the novice gardener that he cannot possibly get around to doing all the necessary jobs. It may be better for that reason not to be too ambitious the first year. Start small, and allow the size of your cultivated area to increase along with your skills. Practical experience makes for lighter work.

Gardens require attention throughout the growing season, not just in the spring and fall. If you are planning a vacation during the summer, try to select crops that will not mature during your absence. Bear in mind that when a vegetable is at its prime, it should be harvested. A good neighbour on these occasions is invaluable, and often you can return the favour.

The list of jobs is never-ending, and no gardener ever completes them, nor does he expect to. This is one of the "joys of gardening"; we are working with nature and every living thing in the garden changes with each passing day. A row of seeds may emerge; the first tomato may set fruit; and white butterflies may be fluttering among the cabbages.

We are never sure what jobs we are going to do on any given day until that day has dawned and we have some idea what the weather will be like. Spring and summer rain does not stop work outdoors. On the contrary, it provides ideal conditions for such jobs as transplanting. A warm light rain is nature's way of helping young transplants to suffer as mild a set-back as possible. A soft rain is far more beneficial than any watering that man can do. Not only is the rain's temperature warm, but it also contains valuable nutrients which aid the growth of the young plants. So on a rainy day I may transplant or, if the seedlings are emerging in the row, I may weed down the rows.

Another rainy day job is maintenance of equipment and tools. Blades constantly need sharpening and oiling, and there are always flower pots and flats to be washed and disinfected.

Hot, dry sunny days are for lawn mowing and hoeing. Hoeing has a very high priority in our garden, and my aim is to never let the weeds grow more than an inch or two in height, and never go to seed.

Larry and I have made a practice of wandering through the garden and grounds after we have finished work in the evening. This is a leisurely stroll, a pleasurable one, when we take time to enjoy the surroundings we have helped to create. We also observe more closely the different plants, and if we notice anything amiss, like caterpillars or a wilt, we know we will have time to remedy the ailment before it gets out of hand. Sometimes all that is required is to remove and burn the offending material. Tent caterpillars are one example.

A garden is never dull, nor is it truly quiet. Although to city folks it would seem that we are alone most days, we are never lonely. Apart from the dogs which are excellent company, and very good at controlling groundhogs, the whole garden is alive with activity. We encourage birds and have quite a wide variety including a number of hummingbirds. Insects are always numerous, the "good guys" as well as the bad. Birds and insects are fascinating to watch, and I sometimes find myself diverted from my job as I watch a bumble bee pollinate a squash or a hummingbird gather nectar. There are many occasions when it is well into the afternoon before I realize it is long past lunch and high time we took a break and had a bite to eat. With a hobby like mine, I am never bored, and find there are never enough hours in the day to complete all I want to do. The hard work of the garden does not bring mental strain; instead, it supplies a rather pleasant form of physical fatigue.

As you read further, you'll also notice that although we do work long hours in the garden, we ease our labour by organizing the sequence of our tasks carefully; this is the secret to maintaining a garden as large as ours.

Zone

Unlike our ancestors we North Americans are a very mobile people. Most of us move to a new location several times during our careers.

Having lived in a wide range of climates (or zones) we have learned to adapt our gardening to the prevailing conditions. This is really quite simple. Wherever we settle we look around and observe the trees, shrubs, plants, vegetables and crops growing there. We find out what zone we are in and what type of soil we have. Most garden catalogues carry a zone map. The map should be used only as a guide-line especially when purchasing rooted stock. Many factors such as altitude, soil type, moisture, exposure and so on, can cause variations within that specific zone.

This book is written in a zone which, under average conditions, is frost-free after May 24 and where frost can be expected anytime after September 5. If the dates in your area are different, adjust your planting out and seeding times accordingly, but remember, there will always be seasons that are exceptions to the rule. Newcomers to an area will have to determine the frost-free dates for their garden. The most reliable source for this information is often the neighbour with the best garden.

Some readers will have a far longer frost-free season than others, enabling them to harvest such crops as tomatoes, peppers, and eggplant for possibly six to eight additional weeks. When this is the case, fewer plants need be grown to produce the equivalent crop. Where the season is shorter, the opposite would be the case.

An example of how the length of the frost-free season can vary throughout a small area is well known to gardeners around the Great Lakes. The gardens near the water will have cooler temperatures throughout the summer allowing certain crops, especially the Brassicas, to thrive. Those further inland will have higher temperatures so essential for the maturity of tomatoes, peppers, eggplant and corn. Gardens close to the lake will also have several more frost-free weeks than those inland.

We have now lived at Evergreen Farm for more than twenty years. During this time we have found that the squash grown behind the garage always survives the early fall frost, whereas the cucumber and beans growing in the main garden, only a matter of a hundred feet away, are blackened. These light early frosts are very localized, and after working in a garden for a number of years, you will learn where the warm and cold areas lie. Many vegetables are improved by light fall frosts, and it is sometimes possible to grow these crops in the cold, lower areas.

In our area early fall frosts are often followed by a long frost-free Indian summer. By protecting the frost-tender crops during the chilly nights, we frequently extend the growing and maturing period by several weeks. We protect tender crops against these early frosts by covering them with floating cover (Remay or plant protector), old sheets, or whatever is available. A special misting attachment for the garden hose can be used with great success. This must be switched on before the temperature drops below the freezing point, usually sometime around midnight.

Sunshine

To help determine the area to be allotted to a vegetable garden, the most important factor is sunshine. In our short growing season, vegetables require all the sunshine possible. A limited few will tolerate partial shade, but most need at least six hours of sunshine a day, longer if possible. The shady areas of the garden can be allotted to certain flowering plants, lawns or ground covers that thrive only in shade.

Because a garden lacks the perfect amount of sun does not necessarily mean that vegetables cannot be grown. The leafy crops, such as lettuce and spinach, will do well in partial shade, and it is well worth experimenting with others to find out which can be grown successfully in your particular area. If you must decide between morning and evening sun, choose the area with morning sun; it is more beneficial to the crops. Try to avoid locating the plot too close to large trees or hedgerows which would shade the area and sap valuable moisture and nutrients from the soil. Generally speaking, the roots of trees grow below ground to the same extent as the branches above; you can tell, therefore, whether the roots are likely to interfere with cultivation, or deprive the crops of nourishment.

In a small property several areas can be allotted to vegetables. There may be corners with plenty of sunshine suitable for tomatoes or peppers; a fence for beans, peas or squash to climb upon; a more shady area for lettuce and other leafy vegetables; and sunny flower beds which can be interplanted with several crops. As an example, beets and burgundy or rhubard chard have very colourful foliage and can be used as a contrast in a flower bed. Parsley and other herbs can be used to edge borders, and scarlet runner-beans are a colourful climber that produce very tasty beans for "frenching". However, when space permits it is more convenient to have all the vegetables in one area.

Drainage

Good drainage is essential. If the proposed site remains water-logged late into the spring, or if the water does not seep away rapidly after a heavy rain, drainage conditions are poor.

Vegetable crops will not succeed in water-logged ground. The roots will be deprived of oxygen and, although the plants may survive, their growth pattern will be permanently damaged, and the resulting crops will be poor. In the majority of gardens this condition can be remedied.

Often a simple ditch is all that is required to drain water away. In our garden the drainage was very poor during the first couple of years of cultivation due to the hardpan, and in some places sheet rock, about 3 feet below the topsoil. Hardpan is a cement-like layer of subsoil through which water penetrates very slowly. To remedy this, we hand dug the entire area very deeply, breaking up the subsoil, and at the same time taking care not to incorporate it with the topsoil. Fortunately, our area of sheet rock is not extensive, and we have learned to live with it, though occasionally it prevents us from driving stakes deeply into the ground.

After the initial digging we used the rotary cultivator to work in plenty of compost, well rotted manure and other organic material that was available. All this work has permitted the spring "run-off" to soak in more rapidly, allowing us to work the garden much earlier than in previous years. The ground also warms up faster, and drainage after a heavy rain is no longer a problem.

In a limited space where the gardener has been unable to overcome the drainage problem, raised beds may be the only way to have a vegetable garden. Raised beds can be made by tilling the ground and then shovelling out pathways between the beds. If more permanent beds are preferred, each bed can be surrounded by either boards or railway ties. The choice is up to the gardener.

The major expense for completing raised beds is the purchase of the best quality topsoil available. Time spent in checking just what type of soil is delivered is time well spent. I have seen a load dumped at a friend's house that was little better than fill, and contained clods of quack grass and weeds. Be sure you are at home when the load arrives; check it before it is dumped; and make sure it is dumped in the most convenient spot. You are going to have the job of carrying it to the bed in a wheelbarrow. Garden areas are rarely accessible to trucks.

No vegetable garden can be truly successful without good drainage. Time spent correcting this condition will amply reward the gardener.

Water Supply

Access to water is another factor to be considered. Most homes nowadays have one or more outdoor taps. With sufficient length of hose, watering the garden should not present a problem. But moving the hoses around the garden is time-consuming, especially in hot, dry weather. After several years of dragging the hose around, we decided to install outlets in more convenient locations. This proved to be remarkably simple and surprisingly inexpensive. We did the job ourselves, and the main work was in digging a trench approximately 18 inches deep. In it we laid a plastic pipe leading to various outlets in the garden.

Heavy plastic hose is available at hardware or plumbing supply stores. It is easy to install and will not be damaged by frost in winter if the water supply is turned off inside the house, and the outdoor taps are opened and drained. We now have several taps in the garden which save many hours previously wasted shifting hoses around.

Another very important source of water is salvaged rain water. We collect it in 45 gallon drums, located beneath all the downpipes from the house. In households with small children it would probably be advisable to put some form of lid over the top of the drum to avoid accidents. The lid must be detachable to permit the gardener to collect water in a watering can.

We always keep a plastic garbage can filled with water from the tap in the vegetable garden. Left standing overnight, it allows the ice-cold well water to warm up. We use this to give individual plants a good soaking or maybe some liquid fertilizer which we have added to it. This is especially good for newly bedded plants. Being plastic and light, the garbage can is easy to move from one place to another. During dry hot spells, when there is a possibility of water

Throughout these pages you will find references to keeping the soil moist. We frequently experience hot drying winds in the early summer and the soil has a tendency to bake and dry out. Make sure that there is no place in the vegetable garden that you cannot reach with the hose. Hoses should be stored neatly when not in use.

Rainwater collected from the roof in barrels or 45 gallon drums provides water at atmospheric temperature for watering young plants. In periods of drought this emergency supply is invaluable.

scarcity, keep the drums filled from the tap and water plants individually. The use of sprinklers during a water shortage is often banned and water barrels are a tremendous asset during these periods.

Always remember that when watering plants it is best to water a few thoroughly, that is, make sure the moisture goes beneath the root system, rather than giving a large number of plants a light sprinkling. In dry conditions roots will search for water, and if only the top of the soil is wet, the roots will reach upwards to obtain it. When this occurs, the root systems of plants are weakened and permanent damage is done. Although the plants may live, the size and quality of the crop will be poor.

When watering a garden, whether it is the lawn or the vegetable plot, always make sure that sufficient water has been applied, and that the water has indeed gone deeper than the root systems of plants or grass. I use a fork to check the depth of moisture. Remember, it is far better to water thoroughly once a week, than to give light daily sprinklings.

Access to the Garden

The lack of a convenient access to the vegetable garden is most frustrating. Whether the garden is large or small, there is frequently a need to bring in equipment, manure, fertilizer or lime. In a large garden the access should permit a truck or tractor to enter; in small gardens the gate and path should be wide enough to accomodate a wheelbarrow or garden cart. When landscaping the property, this is an important feature to bear in mind.

Hedges, Fences and Intruders

Wind can cause severe damage in the garden, especially to newly set out transplants. Many city gardens are protected by tree and shrub plantings or by fences which divide one property from another. They give privacy, muffle the sound of traffic, and help protect the family from highway fumes. Rural vegetable gardens are sometimes very wind-swept and exposed, and farm gardens often form part of a ploughed field, convenient for the farmer to do the spring cultivation with the tractor, but inconvenient for the family to maintain.

When properties are situated very close to roads that are salted freely in winter, there is sometimes a problem growing any plant material near the road. The owner can do little except dig a ditch to carry the spring thaw away, build a wooden fence, or erect a plastic barrier for the winter to try to protect the plants.

We prefer to give the vegtetable garden a permanent location, convenient to the house and protected from prevailing winds. Far more rewarding results will be achieved if the garden "climate" is conducive to the vigorous growth of crops.

We have planted cedar hedges around our vegetable garden, giving the area a "walled-in" look. A wide patch of grass divides the plot from the hedges, allowing plenty of space for the roots of the cedars to feed without robbing the crops of valuable nutrients. The mown grass space is also sufficiently wide for the garden tractor to operate and the hedge does not shade the garden plot. A hedge also acts as a barrier against airborne weed seeds and harmful insects that lurk in weeds growing in nearby uncultivated areas.

Many city gardeners use fences to grow climbing vegetables such as pole beans, cucumber or squash. This practice not only provides space for useful crops, but the fence also acts as a wind break.

Fences, gates and hedges can also be good aesthetic additions to the landscape. The gates can be rustic, formal, or whatever fits

The accesses to our garden are wide enough to permit the entry of a small trailer. Each entry can be closed with a wooden gate, and the hedge provides protection against the wind.

The vegetable garden at Evergreen Farms.
Cedar hedges separate the vegetable from the
ornamental garden and provide a windbreak. Grass
paths and wide gates provide easy access. The tool
shed, frames and compost heap are within easy reach.
The exposure allows for full sun throughout the
growing season. We have piped a water supply to
the garden.

the landscaping scheme, and should be wide
enough to allow equipment to enter.

Fences also protect the garden from
assorted strays. In rural areas cattle, sheep or
goats can be the offending animals, but for
city dwellers it is usually dogs, cats, or people. Nothing is more annoying than to find
your garden a neighbourhood shortcut. The
only way to prevent this is with some form of
barrier.

We have attempted to train our dogs not to
run through the garden beds, not too difficult
a task if you train the dogs when they are
young. Rabbits and groundhogs can be a
serious problem, and they must be prevented
from entering the garden. The best method is
to partially bury a narrow strip of poultry
netting along the base of the fence, hedge and
gate. Alternatively, you may prefer to keep a
dog or two, as we do, to help keep the rabbits
and groundhogs away.

Birds are sometimes a nuisance. They may
eat the heart out of newly planted Brassicas,
damage growing crops such as peas and
corn, or eat fruit just as it is ripening.
Scarecrows are often effective in deterring
the birds and are fun for children to make.
Aluminum pie plates can be strung across
the beds to glitter and flap in the wind.
Homemade streamers or anything similar
that will frighten the birds away can also be
used.

Raccoons can devastate the corn just as it
is ripening. Uncannily, they *know* when it has
reached its peak. A friend of ours has overcome this problem by setting a radio in the
corn patch and playing music all night.
Another friend hangs a lightbulb in the corn
patch as well. After a time, however, the raccoons come to appreciate lights and good
music while dining.

CHAPTER 2

Garden Tools and Equipment

The really necessary tools for a small home vegetable garden are few in number. As the result of good advertising, I have several tools that are seldom used. So for the sake of one's pocketbook, buy only good quality tools that will last a lifetime, know which tools are essential, and learn how to use them for the least expenditure of energy. As with any hobby there are always plenty of gimmicky tools and machines ready to tempt the unwary. The enthusiastic gardener is especially vulnerable early in the season.

Most garden tools are a combination of hardwood and steel, both of which suffer when exposed to the elements. To get the best value out of them, they need proper care and maintenance. This means keeping them under cover when not in use, cleaning and oiling both the wood and the metal and, where appropriate, sharpening the cutting edge.

It is both painful and dangerous to get a splinter in your hand from badly maintained tools. In our garden, we keep the tools in a shed adjacent to the plot, and always try to put them under cover after work. If they are very dirty, they should be washed off with the hose or, as we often do, rinsed in a convenient rain-water barrel.

All good quality garden tools come in different sizes and weights. Larry digs with a long handled shovel, I dig with a light fork. The result, in both cases, is pretty much the same.

For someone starting to garden, my advice is to purchase only the essential hardware.

First in this list would be a garden spade (not to be confused with a shovel), followed by a digging fork, a rake, one or more hoes (garden, draw, Dutch, or stirrup), a trowel, a sharpening file or stone, a watering can (plastic), a garden line or cord, and finally a garden hose. With these tools you can get your first garden under way and soon you will have become acquainted with other gardeners and their tools. Later on you will be able to judge what else you might need.

Shovel

The shovel is not primarily a digging tool. It seldom has a tread, and is meant to be used flat, to scoop soil, sand, manure and other materials as required. For example, the shovel will scoop out soil after sod has been removed. We find it essential, however, for large jobs that the spade cannot cope with, such as digging large holes for trees and fence posts. It is an important item for the tool shed.

Spade

A good garden spade is absolutely indispensible. It has straight sides, a tread on the upper edge and a sharp cutting edge for easy penetration of the soil. Most spades are short handled with a grip at the top. The digger's ease of work will be governed in part by the size and weight of the spade, as well as the sharpness of the cutting edge.

Most home vegetable gardens are of a size that can easily be dug by hand. Digging is

Above: 1. Shovel 2. Garden rake 3. Grass rake
4. Stirrup hoe 5. Garden fork 6. Spade 7. Grass edger
Right: The tool shed is handy to the garden. The
tools hang up allowing one to see at a glance what is
missing.

excellent exercise that can be spread over days or even weeks in the spring and fall, and the resulting condition of the soil and the digger will be well worth the effort. When you dig by hand, you maintain an even depth, breaking up the soil and thereby permitting the roots of the crops to penetrate more deeply. Working the soil also allows moisture and oxygen to circulate freely.

Garden tools should be washed down and wooden handles treated with linseed oil during and at the end of the season.

Digging Fork

The digging fork is straight with four round or flat tines. The tread is wide as with all tools intended for digging. The fork can often be used instead of the spade, particularly when digging clay or other heavy ground, or breaking up surface clods after digging. It is also handy for spreading and incorporating compost and manure, picking up garden refuse, and harvesting many crops.

Forks come in a very wide range of sizes and weights. One standard sized fork is all that is needed to start working a garden plot, but most gardeners find as their gardening interest grows, so does their interest in acquiring the garden implements that will save time and energy for certain jobs.

We have three different forks: my small, light digging fork with rounded prongs; a medium-sized flat pronged fork for general use such as spreading compost and stacking the bonfire; and a large, flat pronged fork which we use for digging potatoes, parsnips and other root crops. The wide, flat prongs of this fork are less likely to damage the tubers. Forks do not need sharpening, but the prongs must be kept clean and smooth in order to penetrate the soil with the least expenditure of energy on the part of the gardener.

Garden Rake

A metal-headed garden rake with a long handle is in constant use in our garden. After the ground has been worked in the spring, the rake is used to pulverize the soil, level the surface and make it suitable for the "seed bed".

I often use the end of the handle to make a furrow in which to sow seed. After seeding I rake soil over the seed and, finally, tamp or press the seed row with the prongs flat on the ground. A garden rake is essential to make a good seed bed.

Another use is to rake up weeds and garden refuse before removing them to the compost heap. Rakes come in different widths,

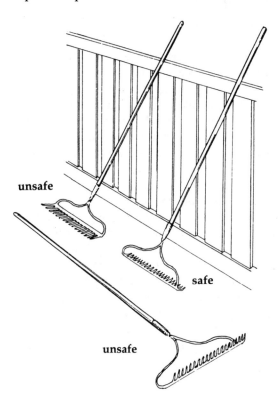

unsafe

safe

unsafe

the small ones being suitable for cleaning up hoed weeds between narrow rows. One standard sized rake is all the average gardener requires and is the main one I use. Make sure you do not leave your rake in a position where it can cause injury.

We recently acquired a rubber-pronged garden rake and find the flexible teeth do an excellent job cleaning up an area, without disturbing the roots of plants or grass.

Hoes

The garden hoe comes in a variety of types and should be one of the hardest worked of all tools in a garden. Before mulch is applied, the hoe is used to annihilate weeds which rob soil of food, harbour insects, and compete with crops for space, light, air and nutrients.

Hoeing loosens the surface soil and permits air, warmth, rain and sunshine to enter. If the hoe is used correctly and at the right time, many hours of unnecessary weeding labour are eliminated. A hot, dry, sunny day is ideal for hoeing; as soon as the hoe disturbs the weed, the sun shrivels it up. It is a waste of time to hoe when warm, humid conditions prevail, as the moisture permits the weeds to re-establish themselves. Constant light hoeing is the best, killing the weeds as they

A selection of hoes used in our garden.
(Left to right): Collinear hoe, Garden or draw hoe, Dutch hoe or scuffle, Oscillating or stirrup hoe.

emerge through the soil. Never permit weeds to grow to any size and never, never let them go to seed.

Although I say this, I know that even in the best kept gardens there are weeds that escape the eagle eye of the gardener, especially those weeds that germinate in the rows of vegetable seedlings and have to be pulled by hand. When I am wandering around my garden just looking things over, I often take a hoe with me and hoe down any odd weeds that have previously escaped my notice. The hoe is a constant companion and if used continually when the weeds are just emerging, very little expenditure of energy is required to control them.

You need a little general information before purchasing your first hoe. Consult with friends who have garden hoes, and maybe watch a demonstration as to how to use them. Note that with some hoes you walk forward over the ground you have just worked. With others, you walk backwards, hoeing the ground in front of you. Some hoes can be used both ways.

Collinear hoe: This hoe is extremely lightweight with a thin blade designed for cutting weeds, not moving earth. The blade is offset so the bottom edge is in line with the bottom edge of the handle (hence the name collinear). The long handle permits the gardener to hoe with a straight back: makes light work of hoeing.

Garden or draw hoe: Work walking forward and "chopping" at the ground with the draw hoe. This hoe is often effective where the "Dutch" hoe fails. The garden or draw hoe is useful in making furrows in conjunction with the garden line before seeding. It is also used for hilling up potatoes.

Dutch hoe or scuffle: This hoe is a great favourite of mine. Work walking backwards and cutting or disturbing the weeds just under the soil surface. Care must be taken not to scuffle too close to rows, thereby damaging

Using a stirrup hoe between rows of emerging seedlings. The hot sun will shrivel up the weeds.

the roots or stems of crops. The blade should be kept sharpened to make work lighter. We have two sizes, a wide one for use between rows and a narrow one for work between and around certain plants, for example, onions, cabbage and beans.

Oscillating or stirrup hoe: An excellent all-purpose type of hoe also in constant use in my garden. It has a cutting blade on either side of the "stirrup" and is easy to use. It can be worked in any direction, but is particularly useful for hoeing weeds close to crops. Use a "pulling" action towards you, thereby running no risk of damaging the plants, always a possiblility with the Dutch hoe. Keep the blades sharpened for easier work.

Sharpening File or Stone

This is an extremely important item of garden equipment; no serious gardener is without one. The time and energy saved by keeping equipment sharp cannot be overestimated. Many old-time gardeners always carry a stone in their pocket to keep cutting edges sharp.

I keep referring to timing. Ten minutes

spent maintaining the edges of garden tools before starting a job can not only save the gardener time needed to complete his project, but allows him to do the job with far less expenditure of energy. You will find that most well-maintained gardens will also have well-maintained garden equipment.

As our garden increased in size we found it necessary to purchase an electric sharpener, enabling us to keep not only the garden tools sharp, but also the blades of the lawn mower. Blunt lawn mower blades put extra strain on the motor, damage the grass and leave the lawn an ugly, untidy mess.

A hand-sharpening file or stone is still needed, even if the gardener has an electric sharpener.

Trowel

A small garden trowel should not be confused with the flat-bladed type used by plasterers. The garden trowel is scoop-shaped and is used to dig small holes in the soil. It is in constant use in the spring when bedding out transplants. Purchase a good-quality trowel; cheap ones are likely to rust and soon need replacing.

Watering Can

We prefer plastic watering cans to metal ones because they are so much lighter to carry. A watering can is especially important during seeding and transplanting times. They come in several shapes, and the better-quality ones have different sizes of "roses" which deliver various intensities of spray depending on the direction in which they are turned. The less expensive one is perfectly suitable for most gardening needs.

Spray Equipment

There are a number of insect and disease controls on the market now, that are safe to use, causing no harm to the environment or the consumer. If you intend to use liquid spray

A wide assortment of spray equipment is available. For a small garden the hand triggered plastic containers are all that are needed. For larger properties a hand pumped pressure tank will be required.

you will need some form of equipment. A small hand sprayer is handy for small gardens, but a pressure tank is more convenient when there is a large area to be covered.

We have a small (3 gallon) pressure tank that is designed to be carried over the shoulder. I find it rather heavy and cumbersome, so I have devised a more convenient homemade method. We have replaced the short hose with a much longer one, so that when I climb a ladder into a tree, I do not have the problem of carrying the tank with me.

Always carefully wash spray equipment after use; good maintenance is essential. We also find the washers frequently need replacing.

Hose and Sprinkler

These items are essential for all gardens. Since coming to North America in 1949, we have not known a season when we did not need them. It is false economy to purchase poor-quality hoses and sprinklers. Both these items should last for many years if well maintained and stored under cover when not in use. Quality rubber hose will not deteriorate when exposed to sunlight as will the cheap plastic ones. The same applies to sprinklers.

All garden hoses should have standard size fittings, so that when replacements are needed there is no problem fitting new hoses onto old ones. However, the 5/8 inch hose will deliver 50% more water than the common 1/2 inch one. Standard screw-on couplings are fitted on all garden hoses and attachments. We find it very tedious and time-consuming connecting and disconnecting these couplings when moving the hose around the garden. The answer to this problem is simple: attach "spring couplings", which are available through certain mail order catalogues and at some garden centres, to all the connections. They screw into the standard coupling and when you wish to change the attachment, you have only to pull the spring back to release the coupling. They provide a quick, easy, nonleaking connection and are made of stong-quality material which will not break if accidently dropped on a concrete surface.

Sprinklers are sold in a wide range of styles. Study them carefully and find the one best suited to your individual needs. You may end up with both a sprinkler and a seepage hose.

There are several types of seepage hoses, which have tiny holes along their surface, but their ends are closed. They allow varying intensity of seepage, controlled by water pressure, and are excellent for soaking a row of vegetables individually. They also conserve water in time of drought or shortage.

Garden Line or Row Marker

This handy gadget is a boon to vegetable gardeners. Most gardeners have , for years, tied string between sticks to mark the rows. Our new string-line has a built in reel and the 50 foot cord is strong, highly visible and weather proof. It can be locked at whatever length we require. This is not an essential, but a wonderful convenience when putting in the vegetable garden.

Wheelbarrow or Garden Cart

As the garden develops, the need soon arises for taking all kinds of things from place to place. Each time I set out to work in my garden, I go first to the tool shed and load up my garden cart with all the equipment I may need. This probably includes garden tools, a basket with stakes, twine, scissors, a knife, some diatomaceous earth and sulphur, as well as other extras such as garden labels and markers. You soon learn what you need, and

Right: The garden cart is well balanced and light to use.
Below: The spring couplings about to be attached.

save time and energy by loading the cart before you begin your gardening.

We do not like the wheelbarrow with a single wheel in front. We used to have one but found it heavy to use and tippy to manoeuver. For the past few years we have had a well-balanced two-wheeled garden cart and find it a joy to work with and well worth the extra initial cost. Wheelbarrows and garden carts are available in several sizes, materials and weights. Do not rush into this purchase. The initial expenditure can be quite considerable and you want to be quite sure you are buying the right model for your needs. A good-quality wheelbarrow or garden cart should last many years.

Grass Rake

The grass rake may be metal or bamboo. As the name implies, it does a much more efficient job than the garden rake in cleaning lawns. It is used to rake leaves in the autumn, to clean the lawn in the spring, and to tidy up the grass after work has been done in the adjoining beds. Unlike the garden rake, the grass rake, being flexible, is used in a light "sweeping" motion which "flicks" rather than drags. Therefore, it can be used effectively in the spring on perennial crops to remove leaves or mulch.

We use the grass rake constantly throughout the gardening season. When working in the garden I have a habit of throwing weeds and garden refuse onto the mown grass surrounding the vegetable plot, then raking them up and carting them away to the compost. The grass rake is light in handling and leaves the grass clean and tidy. We have found it false economy to purchase any but the best-quality metal grass rake. The cheap metal or bamboo models do not last even one season.

Grass Edger

Many vegetable gardens are surrounded by lawn and may be close to the flower garden.

It is visually much more attractive if these lawns are kept well manicured by cutting and edging. This also prevents the grass from encroaching into the vegetable plot. The grass edger is the tool for keeping edges neat and straight. It consists of a short, wooden handle with a hand grip at one end and a metal banana-shaped blade at the other.

Some gardeners prefer to use a spade. Whichever is used, the blade must always be very sharp to make a clean cut, and also lessen the work. Never cut edges when the ground is dry. The edge will only crumble and fall away.

After edges are straightened in the spring, they can be maintained throughout the season with a string-trimmer. With a little practice the operator of this mechanical device, either electrical or gas powered, can keep the edges trimmed in very little time.

Shears

The garden shears have innumerable uses in keeping a garden in shape. Their main job is to clip hedges and trim around trees and shrubs, so they are always among the tools loaded into my garden cart. Because their use requires considerable expenditure of energy, often under difficult circumstances, great care should be taken to select good-quality light weight shears. They should be kept well sharpened and oiled.

Pruners or Secateurs

Pruners, or secateurs, are a small scissor-like tool used for pruning. It is wise to purchase top quality pruners; guard them carefully and they will last a lifetime. We prefer the scissor cut to the anvil cut type. It seems to cut more cleanly and evenly. Fruit trees must be kept shaped and under control, allowing light to enter and air to circulate. Raspberries must be thinned and dead canes removed. Good quality pruners make a clean cut, reducing the likelihood of disease entering the plant's wound. Keep them well oiled and under cover when not in use. Being small, they can be lost in high grass and rust in no time. Tie a brightly coloured ribbon to the handle to make them conspicuous.

Rotary Tillers

A rototiller is a major garden expenditure, and the need to own one will depend on the size of your garden.

If the garden is small, it is more practical to rent one for the few hours a job may take in the spring and fall. Between times, digging can be done by hand. For larger gardens it is more convenient to own your own machine. You can use it on and off throughout the season cultivating between rows, after early crops have been harvested, and before late crops are planted. The rotary tiller works up the ground in preparation for planting.

Some models have the prongs in front of the engine, others behind. It might appear at first glance, that having rear prongs so close to the operator would involve some risk, but this is not the case. We have used both types and find that the latter are the easier to use. Try both types before making a purchase.

Depth of tilling can be adjusted. The action of the rotating prongs pulverizes and aerates the soil. This leaves an excellent seed bed, but in a dry season care should be taken not to overwork the soil, permitting it to dry out too rapidly.

When tilling in the fall, the ground should be left "rough", that is, no raking or levelling should be done. This subject is discussed in more detail in the section on "Putting the Garden to Bed".

A word of caution: as with all power tools, care must be taken, particularly when children are around. If the motor is left running, the rototiller can very easily be put into gear and started up when least expected. Observe all the warnings given on the machines.

Lawnmower

The lawnmower is another major expenditure for gardeners, and therefore a good deal of research should be done before making a purchase.

For a small lawn area, we would recommend a push reel mower. Not all push mowers work well. Look for quality. We use the Traditional hand mower made by the

Below: Spring cultivation using a 3½ hp Bolens rotary tiller with prongs in front. *Right:* A Troy-built Pony Rototiller with prongs behind engine.

A light, modern reel mower shears blades of grass rather than tearing them.

American Lawn Mower Company for all the small areas in our garden. It is very light to push and the reel blades do a superb cutting job. These new models are a far cry from the heavy old monsters of our grandparents' day. An added feature is - no noisy engine to break down, and very little sound when operating it.

With power mowers there is a very wide selection from which to choose. The size of the property will play a large part in the decision, as will the price. Grass cutting with power equipment can be hazardous, and safety precautions must be observed. Leather shoes should always be worn. The risk of stones being picked up by the mower and thrown at high speed at a bystander is also a real possibility.

Pocket Knife

This is an indispensible part of the gardener's equipment. I have found it necessary to attach a long piece of string and/or brightly coloured ribbon to the knife. Knives had a habit of getting lost in my garden, and this trick has helped enormously in avoiding this problem.

Scissors

Scissors are often very useful, but not essen-

tial if you have a knife. Tie a ribbon to the scissors too.

Finding Your Tools

A friend of ours has solved the problem of tools being left out in the garden overnight by grandchildren and other enthusiastic "helpers". She paints a bright red band around each tool, which makes them conspicuous when she is packing up for the night.

Distinctive bands of bright paint will also identify tools borrowed by neighbours. Avoid painting the part generally held in the hand. A band of flourescent tape makes tools visible at night.

Garden Clothing

The photographs in this book will reveal that, while gardening, I am not one of the ten best-dressed women in the world. Garden clothing should be functional, comfortable, have plenty of pockets for putting things into, and be easy to wash.

Garden mail order houses carry clothes specially designed for gardeners. These clothes take into consideration the fact that gardening involves bending, kneeling, squatting, crawling, stretching, and carrying a wide assortment of items.

Pants with special pockets for knee pads take away the discomfort of strapping on the pads and also create a nice soft kneeling surface. Garden clogs keep feet dry in wet weather and insulated in warm or cold temperatures.

Hats are now a must. Gardening gloves provide protection from cold and wet during spring and fall. Leather gloves are needed when tackling thorny jobs.

When working around power tools, such as a lawn mower or rototiller, I wear leather shoes. An added safety precaution is to avoid clothing which could get caught up in machinery. Jackets should always be fastened and neck ties and scarves avoided.

CHAPTER 3

Soils

Often in my reading I have become confused over the complexity of soil, what with micro-organisms, carbon/nitrogen ratios and other such terms. With time and experience I have come to understand that this wonderful material need not be an imponderable mystery. "Soil-building" is a necessary part of garden soil management, and in the next few pages I will "build" the picture of soil and explain how an appreciation of the way it works clarifies so many other mysteries and makes an understanding of plants and how they grow so much clearer.

Soil Formation

Soil has developed over the millenia, and continues to develop from the breaking down of solid materials, primarily rock, during various physical processes, such as expansion and contraction, that occur continually. This action gradually forms smaller particles of varying sizes. Depending on the type of rock, these particles contain a variety of chemical minerals which can be described as *chemical properties*. Physical weathering of this now superficial material is followed by the natural invasion of living organisms; soil formation has begun. With time and weathering the chemical minerals in the soil change form, usually very slowly. Depending on the amount and activity of the soil organisms, the soil begins to "build". An environment that is now capable of supporting plant growth is developing, and the subsequent cycles of growing, then dying and regrowing of plants over the seasons build the *physical characteristics* of the soil. Organic materials or *humus* increase as the soil activity develops. This is an extremely variable process, explaining why soils differ so greatly from one area to another.

Soils that have formed from rock formations with adequate minerals and enriched with an abundance of organic life will naturally develop into the best growing environment. As the acids produced by the breakdown of the organic matter in turn break down the mineral particles, nutrients are released.

I have mentioned both *physical* and *chemical* properties which I shall elaborate upon.

Physical Properties of Soil

Such characteristics refer to the consistency of the soil that can be seen and felt. This soil will be a combination of particles from very fine grade clay to coarse sand and decaying organic matter or humus.

Texture refers to the actual particle size, the smaller the particle, the tighter the soil and the less space for oxygen and water. This explains why clay-type soils are often poor drainers, crack during the summer and present quite a challenge in growing some plants, particularly root crops. Silt and sand are the progressively larger particle sizes; the latter is coarse and well-drained but with the disadvantage of drying out quickly and retaining nutrients poorly.

When describing a soil, an equal amount of these major ingredients listed above is called *loam* . As these ingredients are rarely found in equal proportions, the terms sandy loam, clay loam, etc., are often used, indicating which particle size predominates.

A typical soil sample will, when put in a glass jar, mixed with water and shaken, settle out to show the various layers of different particle sizes. Although not very scientific, this method does serve as a basic way for the home gardener to evaluate the type of soil in his garden. Any humus will, of course, float on the surface, and the sand will sink.

Humus is produced from the decomposition of animal and vegetable matter. Aside from its nutrient value, it helps to retain moisture and air and also to bind smaller particles together in developing the "crumb-structure" that is often talked about.

Virtually any soil type can be made productive with modification to its texture. The addition of coarse sand and organic matter to a clay loam will improve drainage and aeration. Similarly, the incorporation of organic matter to coarse, sandy soil will increase moisture retention and its ability to retain nutrients. Very few people are fortunate enought to begin with an ideal soil, but much can be done with the most hopeless looking land.

In addition to the soil modifications, soil texture can be improved by using nature and its methods. Clay soils, deeply and roughly dug in the fall and allowed to weather, will have developed a noticeably improved tilth, or working quality, in the spring. The incorporation of materials such as leaf mold, compost, ashes and manure will quickly result in an improvement. A sprinkling of gypsum also helps.

You can check the texture of the soil by taking a handful of moist soil and squeezing it tightly in one hand. If it can be compressed into a thin thread without breaking, you have a very heavy clay soil. On the other hand, if the soil falls apart as soon as you release your grip, it is very high in coarse particles. A loam soil will retain its form but break up when touched lightly.

The other extreme would be a soil from almost purely organic origin such as peat (also called "muck" soil) which is primarily organic matter. Its moisture retention is very high and it is frequently acidic. When altered with some "substantial" ingredients it may produce an excellent medium for growing vegetables. In its raw state it is unlikely to be highly productive.

Chemical Properties of Soil

As I mentioned previously, chemical minerals are released as the solid particles break down. This is usually a slow process, and although often adequate in nature to support annual growth, in the home garden some nutrient management becomes necessary. First, it is advisable to identify what the soil contains in the form of minerals. These are usually referred to as the *major* or macronutrients, and the *minor* or micronutrients. All are essential, but the plant relies more heavily on the three elements of *nitrogen* (N), *phosphorous* (P), and *potassium* (K), than it does on the others. These elements are present in varying amounts in most organic manures and form the basis for commercial-type fertilizers.

Nitrogen (N) is important for the healthy growth of leaves and stems. All leafy vegetables require nitrogen, but too much will cause excessive growth and delay flowering and setting of fruit in fruiting crops.

Phosphorous (P) is essential for the formation of flowers, fruit and seed. It is also necessary for the development of a strong root system. Watering with a cupful of high phosphorous transplant solution is beneficial when setting out young plants.

Potassium (K) is necessary in the development of strong roots and stems. It also aids cell formation. All root crops require an adequate supply of potassium. Wood ash is a source of potash.

When present in an organic or natural

form, the minerals are released slowly; their availability depends to a great extent on the rate of organic matter decomposition. The formulation of commercial fertilizers and particularly their solubility will dictate the rate at which they break down and become available to plants. Remember, plants can only absorb nutrients when the nutrients have become soluble (or dissolved) in the soil water.

We can now see that soil is quite simply a combination of solid particles, organic matter, air spaces and moisture containing minerals which dissolve as they are released. Most important in maintaining the smooth operation of this mechanism is the pH or acidity of the soil.

The Importance of pH

The availability of nutrients and the activity of small soil organisms is dependent upon correct acidity. This in turn, when adjusted, influences the release of certain minerals for specific crops.

---

pH Effect of Nutrient Availability

pH

The chart (lower left) shows how all the major elements are made available when the pH is neutral, that is at 7. Extreme variation on either the acidic or alkaline side reduces their availability.

The pH level can be checked with a simple test kit which should be a part of every home gardeners' equipment. This will also enable a check to be made of the elements N, P, and K, and fertilizer applications adjusted accordingly.

Adjusting the pH

Most vegetables prefer a pH of around 6.5, except for the Brassicas that do best in a pH level of 6.8 to 7.5. The following table shows the pH preferences for the vegetables and fruits that are of concern to us.

pH 5.0-6.0	pH 6.0-6.8	pH 6.8-7.5
Blueberries	Beans	Asparagus
Eggplant	Carrots	Beets
Peppers	Celery	Broccoli
Potatoes	Corn	Brussels sprouts
Raspberries	Cucumbers	Cabbage
Squash	Leeks	Cauliflower
Strawberries	Lettuce	
Tomatoes	Onions	
Turnips	Parsley	
Watermelon	Parsnips	
	Peas	
	Radishes	
	Rhubarb	
	Spinach	

When the pH is out of balance, various methods of correction may be tried. The acidity may be increased (the pH lowered) by the addition of organic matter such as natural peat moss, which is usually quite acidic. Large quantities are necessary to change the pH even a small amount, so for larger adjustments the addition of sulphur or iron sulphate will help.

To lower the pH by 1 point:
Spread sulphur or iron sulphate at the rate of
2 lb. per 100 square feet.

Where large adjustments are required, it is best to spread the applications over two or more years so as not to disturb the careful balance of other soil ingredients.

The pH may be raised (alkalinity increased) by the application of lime, usually in the form of ground limestone.

To raise the pH (sweeten the soil) by 1 point:
Spread finely ground limestone at the rate of
5 lb. per 100 square feet on sandy loam,
7 lb. per 100 square feet on loam,
8 lb. per 100 square feet on heavy clay.

It will take several months for the effect to become apparent. Although many gardeners still practice "liming" as an annual fall routine, it is best to check the pH level first. Do not use lime in conjunction with manure or commercial fertilizers.

The soil structure and texture will, when suitable, assure good aeration, drainage and root development. Good roots mean that the plant can make the most use of the nutrition that surrounds it. Now, for supplying that nutrition, there are various methods.

Fertilizers

Fertilizers fall into two groups, inorganic, (chemical) fertilizers, and organic, (natural) fertilizers. Both types can be purchased in packaged or bottled form at garden centres.

Chemical fertilizers are either mined or produced chemically, sometimes as a by-product from industrial processes. Both the organic and inorganic forms of fertilizer supply plants with the essential elements needed for good growth: nitrogen, phosphorous, potassium, and trace elements. Many organic gardeners believe chemical fertilizers cause disease in humans and animals, and refuse to use them. Scientists are still divided as to the accuracy of that claim.

When the novice gardener visits a garden centre to purchase fertilizer, he finds a large selection of bags, bottles and tins to choose from. The price tags will vary considerably. I have heard people claim that fertilizers were far cheaper at certain stores. When I investigated, I discovered that they did not understand that the contents of the fertilizer containers varied greatly too.

For example, a 100 pound bag of 10:10:10: has only half as much fertilizer as a 100 pound bag of 20:20:20. The rest is fill. The three numbers on the bag denote nitrogen (N), phosphorous (P), and potash (K), always in that order. The numbers refer to the percentage of each element contained in the bag. Therefore it will require two bags of 10:10:10 to do the same job as one of 20:20:20. A bag of 20:0:0 contains only nitrogen, and one with 0:15:10 contains no nitrogen, only phosphorous and potash.

A complete fertilizer contains all three elements. Experienced gardeners often take soil tests to ascertain what ratio of N:P:K their garden requires. A soil test is the only way to be certain of your garden's nutrient deficiencies.

In spring, if necessary, you might apply a correctly balanced "slow release" fertilizer in granular form to the whole vegetable garden. This can then be tilled into the soil at the same time as the manure and compost.

Slow release fertilizers have been manufactured to release their contents over a period of time rather than all at once. Although more convenient in that they may be applied just once for the season, a soil analysis must be made before adding the nutrients. Some slow release types may have just their nitrogen content in a form that dissolves gradually. This type of fertilizer is beneficial for crops such as tomatoes and peppers which need nitrogen throughout the season.

We prefer to feed the crops individually with liquid fertilizer. We mix the solution in a plastic garbage can which is easily moved around the garden, and add water to it from the garden hose.

Nutrients in *liquid* fertilizers are immediately available to plants. They can be applied to the soil around the plants and some are suitable for foliar feeding. The directions given with each product should be followed carefully to prevent fertilizer burn. Overfertilizing is a common error and will damage plants.

There are many brands of liquid fertilizers on the market, and many are suitable for foliar as well as root feeding. The purpose of foliar feeding is to bring nutrients quickly and directly to the plants through their leaves rather than through the roots. It cannot replace root feeding and should only be treated as a supplement to it. Foliar feeding is a quick way of correcting minor nutrient disorders such as a boron deficiency. We have never considered it necessary to foliar feed our vegetable garden, but we have friends who consider it a good practice. Dispensers, which can be attached to the garden hose, are available at garden centres for applying either water soluble or liquid fertilizers.

On the other hand, some gardeners prefer to apply a light application of granular "quick release" fertilizer by hand along each side of the rows or where plants (cauliflower, cabbage, tomato, squash, etc.) are widely spaced, in a circle around each plant and about three to five inches from each stem. The fertilizer can be worked into the soil using a hand cultivator and then watered in with a garden hose. Do not allow the granules to fall on the foliage of the plants as this will damage the tissues.

Overapplication of any fertilizer could cause root damage and kill the plant or severely set it back. Always make certain that the soil is moist and that fertilizer is not applied to plants that are wilted. (Probably all they need is a good drink.)

Often the directions on the manufacturers' package may be reduced; it is better to apply a weaker solution and then follow up later with another similar quantity. Dry fertilizers are best applied just before rainfall or watering, and great care must always be taken to spread them evenly.

Because home gardeners grow a wide range of vegetables in their garden plot, one ratio of fertilizer is unlikely to suit them all. With an ample quantity of humus in the soil, and the advantage of being able to fertilize each vegetable according to is specific needs, the home vegetable garden can produce many types of crops, all of superlative quality.

Organic Fertilizers and Animal Manures

Until recently it was the common practice for people to buy all their plant food in the form of chemical (inorganic) fertilizers. We have nothing against these fertilizers, but feel that they should only be used when necessary, and in addition to manures, compost and humus, not instead of them. For our garden, we consider both organic and sometimes inorganic fertilizers to be necessary for maintaining a constant supply of nutrients in the soil. A combination of the two is far better than a chemical fertilizer alone. Inorganic fertilizers become rapidly available to the plants, but can be leached, or washed, out of the soil during heavy rains, particularly in light soils. Organic fertilizers, in the form of manure or compost, are more slowly available to plants, contain trace elements (micronutrients) and add humus to the soil.

Animal manures are often scarce and expensive, but whenever obtainable are the best form of humus. Next on the list as a source of organic nutrients is compost, which every gardener can make at home and has the great advantage of being cost-free. Many organic materials that are commonly discarded can be recycled in the compost heap. (See page 25 for instructions on composting.)

Other forms of humus such as peat moss and sawdust improve the texture of the soil but have little food value, though in combination with manures they are very beneficial. Mushroom compost, when available, is an excellent weed-free source of both humus and nutrients. It is made from hay, chopped corn cobs, chicken manure, gypsum, and a specially prepared high protein fertilizer.

Approximate Nutrient Values of Some Organic Fertilizers
(% on dry weight basis)

Fertilizer	Nitrogen (N)	Phosphorous (P)	Potassium (K)
Blood	13	1.5	0
Fish Scrap	9	7	0
Seaweed	1	0.5	9
Bone Meal (raw)	4	22	0
Bone Meal (steamed)	2	27	0

The foregoing organic fertilizers may be purchased at garden centres, and applied to the garden in the amount required by that particular garden soil.

Wood ash : N:P:K; 0:2:6 (this may vary depending upon the kind of wood burned). Keep the ashes dry until needed, then work sparingly into the surface of the soil before sowing or planting. Wood ash is a free source of potash. Avoid using it where you plan to plant potatoes; it could cause scab. Too heavy an application will raise the soil pH.

Approximate Nutrient Values of Some Manures

Fertilizer	Nitrogen (N)	Phosphorous (P)	Potassium (K)
Cattle	0.5	0.3	0.5
Chicken	0.9	0.5	0.8
Horse	0.6	0.3	0.6
Sheep	0.9	0.5	0.8
Pig	0.6	0.5	0.4
Mushroom compost (spent)	1	0.5	1

The readings are only given as guidelines.

The nutrient value of all manures and composts will vary considerably depending upon the amount, quality and type of feed given to the animals. (You will note from the chart that sheep and chicken manures are particularly high in nutrient value. Care should be taken in their application and the directions on the bag followed carefully.)

Unless you have your own livestock, manure may be purchased from local farmers. Most manures are low in fertilizer value and can be used in relatively large amounts to improve soil structure. Damage may occur if the manure is too fresh; also weed seed will be brought into the garden. We prefer to "compost" our manure before incorporating it into the soil. The heat generated destroys most of the weed seeds. Manures also provide micronutrients which may be lacking in chemical fertilizers. For city gardeners, obtaining fresh manure is often impractical and a satisfactory solution is to purchase bags of dried manure at garden centres.

Liquid Manure

All animal manures can be given to plants in liquid form in spring and summer, but not to plants still in the seedling stage. Healthy plants benefit from a boost every two or three

Liquid manure made by filling a small sack with manure and immersing it in a garbage can of water.

weeks, but never apply liquid manure when the soil and roots are dry. Wait until after a rain or watering before fertilizing, and remember not to overfertilize.

To prepare, put the animal manure in a sack or an old cloth bag and suspend it in a barrel of water. Allow it to soak for several days, poking the bag occasionally with a stick. The solution should be the colour of weak tea. If it is too strong, dilute it with water before soaking the ground alongside the rows of vegetables. As the liquid is removed from the barrel, replace it with water until the richness is exhausted; the barrel contents will become increasingly clear.

The manure left in the bag can be emptied alongside any vigorously growing crop, such as rhubarb or asparagus.

Compost

Compost is another source of nutrients and organic matter which should be used and understood by all home gardeners. The materials you can put in your compost heap are listed below. The N:P:K ratio of compost varies according to the materials composted. It represents an excellent source of free humus and micronutrients when worked into the ground in spring and fall. The value of a compost heap in every garden, large or small, cannot be overestimated. It is simply a matter of collecting and subsequently returning to the soil much of the "goodness" that previous crops depleted.

Contents of the Compost Heap	
Leaves	Manure
Garden waste -weeds	Wood chips
Grass clippings	Hay-spoiled
Household vegetable	Straw
and fruit scraps	Earth
Coffee grounds	Newspaper-crumpled
Tea leaves	Rags-shredded
Sawdust	Eggshells
Hair	

What to Avoid in the Compost Heap	
Diseased garden waste	Glass
Plastics	Meat
Synthetic materials	Fat
Metal	Cat and dog feces

All healthy garden and organic household waste should be composted. Even if it is not scientifically perfect compost, it will so improve the texture of the soil that this alone will produce better crops. Cooked vegetables are of little value as compost as they lose much of their structure during the cooking process, but may be used in small quantities. Do not use any meat-type materials; they will certainly attract vermin.

In our garden, we try to make composting as simple as possible. The actual "making" of the compost does not have to be a high priority, but collecting all the refuse does. We now use a "Compost Aerator" to drive holes in the compost heap allowing moisture and air to enter. This simple tool, used frequently throughout the summer abolishes the need to turn the compost. It also helps speed up decomposition and eliminate odours.

Leaf mold: We prefer to compost leaves separately because we like to have leaf mold on hand to use when re-potting plants or to add to the soil mix for potting some transplants. Leaf mold also makes an excellent mulch.

To make leaf mold, use the same technique as you would for making compost: a layer of leaves then some soil. If the leaves are shredded, they decompose rapidly.

In every garden there should be an area allotted for compost. In a large garden like ours, this is relatively easy. The compost heap is contained in a temporary enclosure of wire and boards out of sight behind a hedge. Ours does not have to look neat and tidy all the time, but in a city garden this aspect may have to be considered.

For a city garden lot a "compost bin" can

be purchased at a garden centre. It takes up very little space, has a neat appearance and, in addition, will not attract flies, dogs or rodents. We use a compost tumbler for all our household waste. Every three or four weeks we add the partially composted material to the main compost heap. By then, it is no longer attractive to dogs or rodents. The tumbler is in constant use.

Our compost heap is usually enclosed in old wire netting or snow fencing. Throughout the season we throw in all the refuse, adding soil between the layers. It is most important that air can circulate through the heap to keep the beneficial bacteria active and prevent the "anaerobic" bacteria from forming and causing the often objectionable odour. Each heap contains one season's garden refuse. The following season we use the freshest heap of compost on which to grow our cantaloupe and squash. After two years the compost is well-rotted and ready to be returned to the garden.

Homemade bins for making compost.

1	2	3

Bin 1: Freshly collected organic debris.
Bin 2: Contains materials from previous year turned from bin 1.
Bin 3: Contains ready-to-use compost turned from bin 2.

The "pit" method can be used in large or small gardens. You simply dig a hole or pit in the ground into which you dump all compostable materials. The depth of the pit depends to a certain extent on the depth of the top soil in your garden. An area of about 3 feet by 3 feet is sufficient for most city gardens. Do not dig out too much subsoil. This will later be incorporated into your compost. The soil you remove will become the walls around your pit and will be added in layers to the refuse as the pit is filled up. Eventually, all the soil from the walls is added to the refuse and the height of the compost will be two or three feet above soil level. Try to keep the centre of the compost heap lower than the sides to retain all moisture possible. Apply a high nitrogen fertilizer to each layer, together with a little ground limestone. These assist the rotting-down process and increase the nutrient value of the mass.

To allow for better seepage, punch a few holes with a compost aerator around all surfaces of the heap. Also, it may be necessary to water the compost heap if there is not sufficient rainfall. Do not saturate because this slows down the decompostition process and leaches away valuable nutrients. This mass of compost will take a couple of years to rot, but once the pit is dug there is relatively little work until the compost is ready to be dug into the garden. This organic matter is of such value for enriching the soil that it more than repays the time and trouble taken.

The "bin" system makes excellent quality compost but requires some labour. The technique for making the compost is identical to the pit method, but first the bins must be very strongly built. Old lumber can be used and the size will depend on whatever space is needed to accommodate the amount of refuse your garden will produce. The bins will look like three small stalls and the partitions between them should be of such a height that it is easy to move or turn the contents of one bin into the bin beside it. To accelerate the breakdown of the materials,

Above: Compost will break down naturally when aerated by this tool. *Right:* The compost drum is especially good for household waste. We use it in conjunction with the large compost bins, emptying the drum into the bin every 3 or 4 weeks. By this time the contents of the drum are no longer appetizing to dogs or rodents.

Left: Spreading well-rotted compost in the fall on areas of the garden after crops have been harvested.
Below: The temporary enclosure has been removed from a two-year-old compost heap to allow easy access.

you should always move compost; the micro-organisms in the fertile soil need both moisture and air. There are a number of commercial compost activators on the market, but as we have never used any of them we cannot give a personal opinion. (I consider them an unnecessary expense.)

You can speed up the breakdown of organic wastes by using a specially designed rotating compost drum, that is turned, manually, once a day. It is designed so that the tumbling action breaks up the clumps and the mix is highly aerated allowing the oxygen consuming bacteria to hasten the decomposition process. It is our experience that during warm weather drum composting takes two to three weeks, but in cold weather, considerably longer.

The economic value of a drum composter will depend largely on the length of the warm season in your particular area. Drums are odourless and do not attract flies, dogs, or vermin, and are ideally suited to city and suburban gardens.

Green Manure

Another method of putting humus and nutrients into the soil is called "green manuring". This is the practice of growing certain grasses and legumes especially for turning into the soil to improve the tilth and fertility. This method of improving the soil has been practiced for centuries, but fell into disuse when chemical fertilizers became cheap and easily obtainable.

In colder, northern areas green manure crops are usually sown in the spring or summer and dug in before going to seed. In warmer areas green manure crops may be seeded in the summer or fall and turned under in the spring.

I would suggest to anyone planning to improve their garden soil with green manure that they inquire from the local agricultural representative as to which crops are recommended for their location and soil conditions. The legumes or clovers are generally consid-ered the best crops, because of their ability to add nitrogen to the soil. A mixture is often recommended.

I would like to add that legume seed that has been inoculated with nitrogen-fixing bacteria can be of particular benefit. These legumes take nitrogen from the air and when used as green manure crops will incorporate this valuable element into the soil at the same time. This practice is excellent for gardeners with sufficient space to permit them to rotate their plot, placing one-quarter or one-third in green manure each season. Green manure is a time honoured method of improving the soil.

Sphagnum Peat Moss

Peat moss is naturally occuring organic matter which is excellent for amending soil. It is both weed free and highly water retentive. When worked into sandy or clay soil it greatly improves tilth. It may be purchased in bales at garden centres and is clean and easy to handle.

Most peat moss in North America is found in Canada where 25% of the world's supply is located. It is a renewable resource and is harvested under strict guide lines self imposed by the industry. After a bog has been harvested it is then returned to a functioning wetland.

The Importance of Micronutrients

We have now discussed common methods of applying nutrients to the soil and particularly organic nutrient replacement. The object of manuring or composting the ground is to replace some of the plant food, especially the micronutrients, that all crops need in very minute amounts and extract from the soil. If they are not available, the plants may be stunted or starved, whereas an excess of some can be toxic.

Micronutrients are not generally a problem to the average home gardener who regularly uses manure, compost and/or green manure crops. However, constant crop production without such additions will eventually cause micronutrient deficiencies. It is next to impossible for any gardener, especially a home gardener, to know whether micronutrients are lacking in the soil unless he were to have a complete soil analysis.

If the vegetables in the garden are not growing healthily, and the reason not readily apparent, a nutrient deficiency in the soil may well be the cause. Many of the symptoms of these deficiencies are very similar, and it is only through a professional soil analysis that the situation can be remedied. As this is an area so often overlooked, I have listed the symptoms of specific micronutrient deficiencies. If these occur, they can be corrected by the application of sprays or by soil treatment.

Boron: This is perhaps the micronutrient most commonly deficient among garden vegetables. Boron deficiency causes cracked stalks of celery and discoloured patches on cauliflower heads. It is also important to apples (Cork disease), broccoli (Brown rot), cabbage, beets (Heart rot), tomatoes and turnips (Brown heart), though boron deficiency may occur in many plants and is often confused with other problems. Our garden had a boron deficiency, which we have remedied. We are now able to produce excellent celery.

Borax, available in supermarkets, drug stores or garden centres, can be applied to the soil at the rate of one tablespoon per 100 feet of row. Only a small excess of boron is toxic to several plants, especially beans and cucumbers, so the borax must be applied very evenly. It may be thoroughly mixed with fertilizer or with sand before spreading along the row. Raking is an additional help to even distribution. It can also be applied in a liquid solution. For heavy clay soils the amount of borax applied may be increased up to 3 tablespoons per 100 feet of row. In general, because of possible toxicity, it is safer not to add boron to a soil that has received frequent applications of manure or compost.

Emergency spray treatment can be effective if the symptoms are recognized very early in the crop year. Garden centres have preparations for this purpose; since compositions of various boron preparations differ, follow the directions on the label.

Iron: Iron deficiency frequently causes chlorosis (yellowing), especially in the tissue between the veins of young leaves. Again, a professional soil analysis is usually the only certain means of accurately identifying the problem. Various iron preparations are sold under differing trade names. Some are appropriate for application to the soil, some as foliar sprays. Each should be used as specified on the label.

Magnesium: Plants growing in a magnesium deficient soil are usually a pale greenish-yellow, although in some plants the leaves may be purplish-red with green veins. Magnesium deficiencies rarely appear, except in soils receiving very little organic matter. Where the pH reading indicates liming is required, available magnesium can be assured over a long period by using dolomitic limestone. A simple short-term treatment can be given by adding magnesium sulphate (Epsom salts) as a soil treatment applied as described for boron. The rate should be 1/2 a cup per 100 square feet for sandy soils, or 1 1/2 cups for clay soils. My method is to add the Epsom salts to a barrel of water and soak the rows of plants.

Sulphur: When sulphur is deficient in the soil the plants are often yellowish and stunted. This is seldom a problem, as sufficient sulphur is usually dropped by rain.

Molybdenum: This micronutrient is rarely deficient in soils that contain organic matter. Molyndenum seems to be involved primarily in the regulation of various physiological activities within the plant, as are manganese, zinc and copper.

Manganese: To treat chlorosis (yellowing) that suggests a manganese deficiency, spray with a one percent solution of manganese sulphate or apply manganese sulphate at the rate of one tablespoon per 100 square feet of soil.

Zinc: Zinc is rarely deficient in gardens of eastern United States and Canada, although this condition has occasionally occurred in sweet corn and in very wet soils. Treatment is as for manganese deficiency, but using zinc sulphate.

Copper: Copper deficiencies are also unusual except in peat soils newly placed in cultivation, or in sandy soils that have been subject to leaching. The crops grown in these soils display similar symptoms to those of iron deficiency. You can correct this by adding 2 to 4 tablespoons of copper sulphate to peat soil or 1½ teaspoons to sandy soil for 100 square feet of garden.

A Warning Note: It might seem to be much simpler to use a "shotgun" approach in supplying micronutrients. Indeed, preparations have been marketed which do include all of the micronutrients mentioned above. But persistent addition of all of them to soils suitable for vegetables could lead to an imbalance or excess causing toxic effects. Advice from experts in any locality where deficiencies are encountered is preferable to guessing.

Earthworms

I have always associated earthworms with good soil conditions. Somehow, where there were plenty of worms the soil was bound to be good for growing things. My research has led me to understand that earthworms are seldom present in soils that are not rich in humus; but soil which is devoid of earthworms is not necessarily low in nutrients.

In temperate climates earthworms may burrow to a depth of 6 or 8 feet below the surface of the soil, aerating the soil and allowing for better drainage. Their burrows also make it easier for the roots of plants to penetrate the soil.

Earthworms swallow soil as they burrow, and deposit it in casts on the surface of the ground. Only the humus encountered in the soil is used as food. In land with a healthy worm population, many tons of valuable nitrogenous fertilizer per acre can be brought to the surface annually.

A high organic content in the soil automatically encourages an increase in the earthworm population. The humus makes for better soil aeration, and the combined benefits of organic matter and earthworms increases the soil fertility.

Certain disease-producing bacteria only thrive in soil conditions where there is no oxygen. With a healthy worm population, soil conditions remain aerobic, consequently keeping the undesirable bacteria under control.

Worms are bisexual and all produce egg capsules which must be fertilized by another worm. The eggs are laid in sacs beneath the surface of the soil. Mating takes place twice a year, but in rich soil it can be more frequent. To increase the worm population in your soil, instead of buying them, establish "breeding boxes" containing kitchen garbage, manure and green matter. Personally, I rely on keeping the garden soil amply supplied with well-rotted manure and compost. This keeps the worm population happy.

Earthworms are very sensitive to chemicals, so use the latter selectively to maintain the benefit of a thriving worm population.

So, what type of soil do you have in your garden? Is it *really* hopeless? Probably not. A systematic approach to building up the soil to a good level of humus and nutrient content and then maintaining it is not an impossible task. But I should point out that it is not a "one-time" project either, and once the soil is understood and has become productive, the upkeep becomes essential if the garden is to *continue* to be productive.

CHAPTER 4

How Plants Grow

A plant is a carefully balanced mechanism which requires specific physical and chemical conditions to keep it healthy and functioning correctly. Each part of a plant plays an individual role and contributes to its overall development, which we call growth. The process of growth is controlled by *photosynthesis*, which in the presence of light is the manufacture of carbon-containing compounds which may be used by the plant. This process requires light, carbon dioxide and water, and occurs in all green-pigmented tissue.

By a process which we call *osmosis* roots absorb water and nutrients which are transported to the stems and leaves by conducting vessels called *xylem* (see illustration). Manufactured compounds are then moved within the plants by the *phloem*, which are also conducting tissues.

The leaf is the work centre of the plant with its continuous manufacture of compounds and their subsequent distribution within the plant for storage or use in the many biochemical processes which occur. It is designed to absorb light, exchange gases of oxygen and carbon dioxide, release excess moisture, and control excessive moisture loss during periods of stress such as drought. These processes take place in the leaf through structures called *stomata*, or "pores". The opening and closing of the pores is controlled by the guard cells and is dependent upon environmental conditions. As their name implies, they are protective mechanisms that prevent excessive stress on the plant during unfavourable weather conditions.

The green pigment within the leaves and some stems is *chlorophyll*, an essential requirement of photosynthesis. Chlorophyll contains carbon, hydrogen and oxygen, as well as nitrogen and magnesium. Deficiencies of various mineral elements inhibit chlorophyll synthesis and cause the development of *chlorosis* (yellowing). In the absence of normal amounts of chlorophyll, the upper leaves quickly become yellow and photosynthesis is reduced.

The utilization of the manufactured carbon-containing compounds (sugars) is called *respiration*, which takes place at all times within the plant, but the rate varies with temperature. The higher the temperature, the more rapid the rate. Oxygen is essential for respiration, which yields carbon dioxide, water and energy. The energy may be released as heat or as chemical energy which is important in causing cell division, absorption of minerals, movement of nutrients and the synthesis of amino acids and proteins. Photosynthesis and respiration are controlled by favourable environmental conditions. Good soil drainage and aeration, sufficient nutrients of the correct kinds, optimum soil moisture and an abundance of sunlight result in growth.

The plant roots absorb nutrients primarily in a soluble form. Commercial fertilizers are usually water soluble, at least in part, and are therefore immediately utilized. Organic fertilizers are not soluble and must first be broken down by soil micro-organisms. The chemical minerals will then be released and become soluble in water. By the time the

shoot

sugars (for fruit development)

Photosynthesis:
sunlight + water + CO_2 in
presence of chlorophyll makes
carbohydrates (sugar, starch)
and O_2

water lost by transpiration

oxygen

(respiration day and night)

CO_2

energy released for development

epidermis layer

phloem conducts food materials
for use

phloem

(in spring for development) ↑
(in fall for storage) ↓

xylem conducts water and
nutrients in solution

storage of carbohydrates in root crops

root hairs take in water and
nutrients in solution

root hairs

root cap

Diagram showing simplified plant processes.

minerals reach the roots, both the manufactured (synthetic) and the organic fertilizers are identical.

The acidity or pH of soil plays an important role in the availability of nutrients as it affects the activity of the micro-organisms. Most minerals, if present in the soil, are available to the plants when the pH is in the 6 to 6.8 range. When a soil analysis has been made for a home vegetable garden, the recommendations are based on bringing the pH to an optimum level.

A plant grows as a result of an increase in size or number of cells. Cell elongation takes place in many parts of the plant; cell division, or *mitosis*, occurs in certain areas called *meristems*, the most important being the shoot, root tips, lateral buds and the cambium layer.

These meristematic tissues are very delicate and sensitive to physical damage, pests and diseases. Stress conditions, which may result in an imbalance or disruption of cell growth, can cause increased vulnerability to disease.

Thickening of stems is the result of the continuously accumulating xylem tissue. The cambium layer surrounding the xylem is increasing by cell division as the stems develop. This can be seen on woody perennials such as the stump of a tree as annual growth rings. Certain cells eventually die but they are continually replaced. In vegetable plants that are growing for only one season, this process is not apparent, whereas in woody plants such as trees and shrubs these cells become support tissue.

CHAPTER 5

Planning Your Vegetable Garden

The size of your plot will govern the type and quantity of crops that can be grown, whether annual or perennial. A very common error, especially for beginners, is to order far more seed than they can possibly use.

Working Plan for Row Garden

Before ordering seed, we make a rough diagram marking the rows at 18 inch intervals. This is the standard distance between crops such as carrots, beets and lettuce. For larger plants like tomatoes and cabbage the rows can be double spaced. Vine crops, like cucumbers, need plenty of room and in small

gardens a bush variety should be grown.

The rows are best when they run north to south, but this is not essential if all the crops grown are of the same height. Tall crops such as pole beans or corn should be planted at the north side of the garden. Vegetables need plenty of sun, and care must be taken to make sure taller vegetables do not shade the smaller ones.

We like to make two plans for the garden for each season; the first one shows the early crops; the second shows the main and late crops. The first example we give here is only a guide to help beginners get started. No two garden plots are the same, and the vegetable preferences of individuals vary greatly. The

This plan for a 9 by 12 foot garden should provide a family of four with fresh salad vegetables during the summer months.

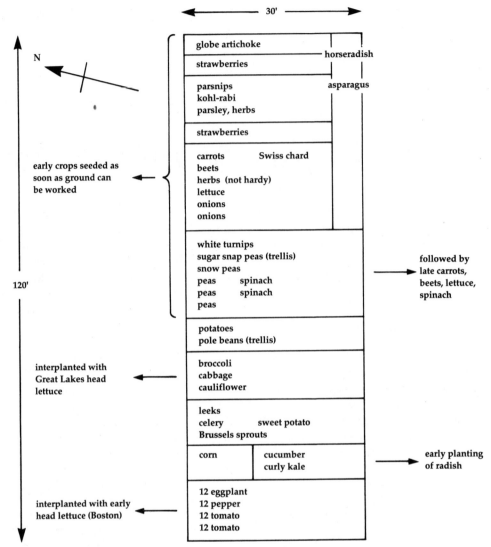

Plan of our vegetable garden for the season during which most of the photos in this book were taken. Our squash, melons, Jerusalem artichokes, rhubarb and raspberries are in another part of the garden.

second plan is our garden. It measures 120 feet by 30 feet, and provides enough vegetables for a family of six for a year. We do not grow a main crop of potatoes, only the early crop.

Raised Beds

This method of vegetable gardening is ideal when space is limited. Each bed can be any-where up to 5 feet wide. A 5 foot bed permits the gardener to work from both sides. Any wider makes it hard to reach into the middle. Raised beds are never walked upon, and be-cause there are no walkways between rows, raised beds increase the productivity of any given area by almost double.

Raised bed gardening is far more inten-sive than row gardening. The crops are planted in blocks and the entire surface of the bed utilized. Other advantages are that the beds warm up earlier in the spring, the drainage is better, and the area to be watered is much smaller than in row gardens.

Intercropping and Interplanting

You can make full use of the entire plot by intercropping. Certain small fast-growing plants such as cress, lettuce, radish and spinach can conveniently be grown in rows between slower-growing larger vegetables such as cabbages, tomatoes or peppers. The fast growing plants will be harvested before the slow growers are ready to occupy the full space allotted to them.

Other methods of intercropping include planting rows of small fast crops like radishes between rows of onions or peas, or planting fast and slow growers alternately in the same row. Whichever method is used, care must be taken not to overcrowd.

Succession Planting

Succession planting is the term used when a second crop is planted to replace an early crop that has been harvested. This is often practised in small gardens where full use is made of the ground all season. With such intensive use, take particular care to ensure that the soil is enriched with humus and provided with sufficient nutrients. An extra application of fertilizer may be required.

An example of succession planting is an early crop of radish, spinach, cress, leaf lettuce, white turnips, multiplier onions, peas, or kohl-rabi, which may be followed by beans, beets, carrots, late cabbage, cauliflower, broccoli, or Chinese cabbage.

It is obvious that in any plot used so intensively it would be hard to maintain a sound

Lettuce planted between cabbages are ready for harvest now. Note space left between plants will allow for cabbages to mature.

Making intensive use of a small garden by intercropping not only between plants but also between rows. The lettuce (in wire cages – a protection against rabbits) planted between the cabbage will be harvested first. The rows of early onions will be harvested in the summer, leaving ample space for the cabbage.

crop-rotation plan. Therefore, take great care to avoid the spread of disease by removing any unhealthy plants from the garden and burning or throwing them in the garbage, never in the compost heap.

The Lazy Man's Garden

Many folks would like to have a vegetable plot, but when faced with the task of preparing an area that may now be meadow or lawn, they have second thoughts. No need! A few hours of light work and you'll be ready to plant.

Select an area that gets plenty of sunshine and is free of roots from large trees and shrubs. Be sure it does not get waterlogged during rain storms. A gentle slope is just fine but avoid too steep a location. Where growth is lush and healthy, the topsoil will be deep and the crops so much the better.

The only additional purchase you have to make in preparing the plot is black plastic, which has the desired property of excluding all light and is sold in various widths. When spread over the ground, it prevents growth under the plastic. To allow for tuck-in, it is convenient to make the width of your plot 6 inches narrower than the width of plastic which you select. As for length, it can be as long as you wish. If you prefer a square area, make two plots with a walk of mowed grass dividing them.

Using stakes and your garden line, measure out two parallel lines 6 inches narrower than the plastic. With a spade, cut into the sod about 3 inches deep all around the lines. Turn the edge of the sod away from the plot. Next, get the garden hose and soak the plot thoroughly. Now you are ready to lay the plastic. Start at one end, tucking the plastic under the sod as you return the sod to its original position. You will end up with a film of plastic stretched tightly over the grass and well secured at the edges. The three inches of plastic buried around the plot prevents the lawn encroaching and keeps the plastic sheet from being undermined by the wind. The

Lazy Man's Garden

1. Mark out proposed site with cord.

2. Lift sod around area.

3. Tuck black plastic under sod.

4. Cut holes out of plastic using bulb planter and lift out earth below.

grass under the plastic will decompose very rapidly, adding nutrients and organic matter to the soil. The sooner this plastic can be put down in the spring, the better.

In our experience, this garden technique is best suited to transplants. Once weather conditions are ready for transplanting, use a bulb-planter or sharp trowel to pierce through the plastic and remove clods of sod at intervals appropriate for the crop. An "x-cut" 2 inches long can be made in the plastic first to allow easier access to the sod below.

You will now have small holes in the sod in which to set the transplants. It is best if the roots of the seedlings have a good quantity of soil around them. You may have to add a little more top soil to fill each hole.

During the season water and apply liquid fertilizer through the holes in which the plants are growing. Take care not to damage the plant roots with too strong a flow from the hose. Push the nozzle under the plastic and slowly soak the area around the plants. Do not waterlog the bed.

In the fall after the crops have been harvested, you may wish to remove the plastic. The ground underneath is easy to dig, and can be prepared as a conventional garden plot for the next spring. The plastic can be salvaged and re-used; it will have the holes already cut for planting. When it is properly laid down, it is not unsightly and can remain in place for several years before deteriorating. The plastic can be covered with mulch to make it more attractive.

Crop Rotation

In several sections of this book, we refer to the importance of crop rotation. There are two purposes in crop rotation: plant nutrition and control of pests and diseases. Related plants, that is, those in the same family, usually prefer similar soil types and remove nutrients from the soil in similar proportions. Planting of related plants such as Brussels sprouts, broccoli, cauliflower or cabbage in the same part of the garden year after year tends to make that soil deficient in the nutrients that the Brassicas have used up. As soon as any one of the essential nutrients is severely deficient, plant growth will be very poor. But if crop rotation is practised so that the same crop family is not planted in the same place for a period of, say, three years, there should

be little or no nutrient deficiencies. That is the nurtitional purpose of crop rotation. As an example of this, while Brassicas require a considerable quantity of nitrogen, they need very little potash; the reverse is true of beets and potatoes. Furthermore, Brassicas do not send their roots down very far into the soil, which means that plant foods deep down are untouched. This plant food is available for deep-rooted crops like parsnips and carrots which may follow on.

Legumes (peas and beans) pack nitrogen into the soil; Brassicas require plenty of nitrogen. Logically , then, Brassicas should follow legumes. This aspect of crop rotation has been neglected in recent years, but with the sharp increases in commercial fertilizer prices, it may again become recognized.

Better Disease Control

Crop rotation helps control pests and diseases that overwinter in the soil. In general, members of each plant family are susceptible to the same ailments. For example, club root (a fungus disease) in Cruciferae (the cabbage family) will not attack any other family, and if the host plant for club root is rotated to a different section of the garden, there will be nothing for the fungus to feed on.

It follows that if you plant the same family year after year in the same location there will be a build up of soil-borne diseases destructive to that family. This is why we stress the importance of knowing to which family each vegetable belongs.

Based on the above, here is a simple example of a crop rotation plan:

potatoes ➤ root crops ➤ legumes ➤ Brassicas

To help you develop your own crop rotation plan, in the section dealing with individual vegetables we have grouped the vegetables in families rather than dealing with them in alphabetical order.

CHAPTER 6

The Naming of Plants

You can grow an excellent garden without knowing the correct names of plants in English, let alone in Latin, but most gardeners run into complicated nomenclatures in pamphlets and seed catalogues. We think, then, that you will find this section informative and helpful.

Since the beginning of time, it has been one of man's characteristics to name things and try to arrange them into an orderly fashion. Even Noah had the members of the animal kingdom named and grouped into orderly pairs for their voyage in the ark.

Animals and plants must have proper names which allow us to distinguish between the two major living kingdoms. Similarly, because of the great number of species involved, a nomenclature is needed which will ensure distinctions within the individual kingdoms.

The system for the naming of plants, which has been developed and improved over the years, is a universally accepted one; it encompasses both identification and classification. By the particular name given to a plant, it is possible to identify the group to which it belongs. This is helpful, as each group possesses unique characteristics which separate it from the many other groups. Similarly, it must be possible to classify plants into a particular level within the kingdom structure. This classification would depend on the similarities in the plants' appearances and their genetic relationships.

When a new plant is developed or discovered, it is given a specific botanical name. This name, which by international agreement is in Latin, immediately classifies and identifies it in such a way that botanists who have not even seen it can visualize its characteristics.

One can only imagine the great difficulty and complexity involved in devising a system of rules for naming all the plants in the world. In the beginning they were arranged into groups by their appearance; the ones with similar features were classed together. This system has developed into a more natural and precise one, using characteristics other than just physical appearance alone. With modern science and technology we can delve into the actual evolution and gene make-up of the plant. This means that when comparing plant to plant, they can be even more closely grouped together.

To help us understand the many levels within the plant kingdom, imagine a large area of land, a country. Most countries are divided into various major states, divisions or provinces. Within the provinces we find distinct regions in which people have more in common among themselves than they do with those in neighbouring territories. And furthermore, groups are formed within the regions, namely cities or even smaller, more individual communities. Obviously, the people living in a town have more in common with those in their community than with the people living throughout the larger territory.

The same idea applies to plants. At the top level it is customary to divide all plants into divisions, or phyla. How they reproduce, how their leaves develop, how they conduct water and food are all important but general factors, which help to separate plants into these divisions. The divisions that concern us most as gardeners are the bacteria and fungus phyla (Thallophyta) which house some of the garden diseases, and the seed-bearing plant phyla (Spermatophyta) which includes our garden vegetables. All divisions end in "phyta" such as Bryophyta, which we know as mosses and liverworts, and Pteridophyta which includes ferns and other related plants. If we look more selectively at the Spermatophyta division (more commonly referred to as the seed-bearing division), we can see how this major phyla is divided into increasingly specific units.

The first two major subdivisions of this phyla are Gymnospermae and Angiospermae. Plants are placed into either of these subdivisions because they have more characteristics in common with the members of that subdivision than with the plants in the other subdivision. Gymnosperms are plants that have unprotected or naked seeds like the ones you find on a cone scale. All of the coniferous trees are in this subdivision. The Angiosperms, or flowering plants, are the ones with seeds that are protected by a structure or ovary such as a green pepper, orange, or apple. In other words, all of our fruit and vegetable crops are in this group.

The flowering plants, in turn, are divided into two classes, which are now beginning to become more scientifically selected as to their common characteristics. For example, if the protected seed, when it begins this development, has one embryonic leaf form, it is classed as a Monocotyledonae (onion, lillies). On the other hand, plants whose seeds form two embryonic leaves (peanut, bean) are called Dicotyledonae. You may have heard these classes referred to by their more common abbreviated names, monocot and dicot.

And so the kingdom continues to be divided, always drawing finer and finer distinctions between plants. Classes divide into subclasses, and in turn into orders, families, genera, species, varieties and cultivars.

For example, cultivars of one variety are much more closely related to each other, genetically and by appearance, than are those members of a whole order.

Gardeners may be forgiven for being confused over the naming of plants in general, as many of them even have several different common names. To be accurate and correct, use the Latin botanical name.

A common practice among commercial growers and seed catalogues is to call a cultivar a "variety". Botanically this is incorrect. Government publications use correct botanical names, but in this book we are occasionally showing both where there might be fear of confusion.

The following family trees of *prairie rose* and *corn* show the "plant kingdom". Don't worry if you can't remember all the names. Since horticulture has a universal language, I believe that this information will be useful to gardeners who wish to broaden their interest and knowledge.

Prairie Rose

Kingdom – Plantae
  Subkingdom – Embryophyta
    Division – Anthophyta
      Class – Dicotyledonae
        Order – Rosales
          Family – Rosaceae
            Genus – *Rosa*
              Species – *Rosa setigera*
              Variety – several

Corn

Kingdom – Plantae
  Subkingdom – Embryophyta
    Division – Anthophyta
      Class – Monocotyledonae
        Order – Graminales
          Family – Gramineae
            Genus – *Zea*
              Species – *Zea mays*
              Variety – several

CHAPTER 7

Hardiness of Plants

There are two main categories of garden vegetables; perennials and annuals. The perennials occupy a permanent position in the garden, while the annuals are started from seed each year. In our climate some perennials such as globe artichokes and certain herbs are treated as annuals. Hardy perennials, for example rhubarb and asparagus, once established in a garden can go on growing for many years. The principal factors restricting their vigorous growth are poor soil conditions, lack of moisture, and damage by wind and sun when newly planted. Also, their growth can be arrested if harvested before they have become thoroughly established. In general, hardy perennials can stand the severe frosts of our winters, although they generally respond better to mulching or heavy snow coverage.

Not all annuals can be seeded directly in the garden in early spring because not all species are equally hardy. Some annuals are tolerant to severe frosts, others to moderate frosts. Some prefer cool growing weather, while others thrive in hot conditions and are unable to withstand even the slightest frost. With these factors in mind, planting vegetables and fruits has to be carefully timed to avoid early season set-backs. The following chart will serve as a guide. Notice that certain plants are seeded directly into the garden, but the transplants that have been raised under controlled climatic conditions during the preceding weeks are set out as young plants. Transplants are plants that are started indoors under lights or in greenhouses to give them a head start on the season. Our first seeding is in March and comprises both hardy and tender crops.

Hardy Perennials	
Asparagus	Sea kale
Raspberries	Strawberries
Currants	Jerusalem artichoke
Rhubarb	Some herbs

All hardy perennials need a permanent place in the garden. When planting, bear in mind that they can remain where planted for many years.

Frost-Hardy Annuals	
Transplants	*Direct Seeding*
Broccoli	Beets
Brussels sprouts	Carrots
Cabbage	Chicory
Cauliflower	Cress
Chinese cabbage	Kale
Kale	Kohl-rabi
Kohl-rabi	Lettuce (leaf)
Lettuce (head)	Mustard
Onions	Onion seed
	Onion sets
	Parsley
	Parsnip
	Peas
	Radish
	Rutabaga
	Spinach
	Turnip
	Some herbs

Hardy vegetable transplants are planted as soon as the ground can be prepared. With us this is the end of April or early May. In our garden we seed small quantities of the early crops such as beets, carrots, and lettuce. We re-seed successive crops to ensure a fresh supply throughout the season. Details are discussed under the description of individual vegetables.

Semi- Hardy Annuals

Transplants	*Direct Seeding*
Celery	Chard
Globe artichoke	Chinese cabbage
Leeks	Endive
Lettuce (head)	Mustard
	Potatoes
	Sweet corn

Semi-hardy vegetables can be planted two to three weeks before the last frost is expected. We start seeding around the second week in May. Often, if the potato or corn shoots are killed to ground level by frost, there will still be enough material left in the tuber or seed for it to send out new growth and quickly regain its vigour. Possible frost damage may be prevented by mulching or protecting with row covers.

Frost-Tender Annuals

Transplants	*Direct Seeding*
Cucumbers	Beans
Eggplant	Cucumbers
Peppers	Muskmelons
Tomatoes	Okra
Garden huckleberry	Pumpkins
Muskmelons	Squash
Watermelons	Watermelons

Frost-tender vegetables should be planted only after all risk of frost is past. We use May 24th as a guide, but use our judgement to determine if the soil has become warm enough to assure no set-back. Although one is anxious to get the garden planted out as soon as possible, we have found that, very often, later seeded vegetables grow more rapidly and have a tendency to mature in less time than the earlier seeded ones. When this latter group is damaged by frost it will not recover and re-seeding will be necessary. The only possible exception is corn.

The preceding classifications may be used to determine the earliest days on which certain vegetables can safely be planted outdoors.

We continue eating the hardy vegetables such as curly kale, broccoli and Brussels sprouts well into the winter. Curly kale is the hardiest and will survive hard frosts and snow and has often provided a green vegetable over the Christmas holiday. Parsnips and Jerusalem artichokes also are extremely hardy and can be eaten fresh as long as the ground can be dug. The clean up of the rest of the garden is well underway.

CHAPTER 8

Purchasing Seeds and Plants

Most experienced gardeners order their vegetable seeds through mail order seed houses. Once you are on a mail order list, the catalogue usually arrives automatically each winter. We receive several catalogues because we order varieties of vegetables that are offered only by certain seed houses. We also like to compare prices and see what new cultivars or varieties are being offered.

Botannically, the terms cultivar and variety have different meanings. But, as the difference is unimportant to the home gardener and most seed catalogues refer to varieties where, in fact, they should refer to cultivars, we are using the terms interchangeably in this book.

What is a Hybrid?

A hybrid is any plant whose parents are distinctly different. A hybrid may show some of the characteristics of each parent, or possibly some of its own. Hybridization is practised by seed growers who specialize in producing new cultivars (varieties) of plants with more vigour, faster growth, disease resistance, and as much as 25% higher yields.

F_1 hybrids (the first generation of a cross) usually produce stronger, better plants and are worth the extra cost. Amateur gardeners will be disappointed if they collect seeds from hybrid plants and expect to obtain identical results the following season. Seedlings will not come true to the hybrid parent. Those interested in learning more about this science should study Mendelian Law and modern books on plant breeding.

Disease-Resistant Seed

When ordering seed, and especially with crops such as peas, we prefer varieties that are "disease resistant" and where the seed is "treated" with a fungicide. The tiny amount of chemical involved often prevents seed decay and damage by soil-borne diseases. Such conditions are more prevalent early in the spring when the ground is still cold and wet. In our short growing season, several weeks of valuable growing time would be lost by poor germination of the first seeding. Organic gardeners will not agree with using a chemical fungicide, but we feel that, as with many chemicals and drugs, they have their place in our society. However, there is little doubt that such additives should be used only with caution and, in any case, untreated seed is available for the purists. The words "disease resistant" marked on the package mean what they say. They do not state that the plants are immune to disease, only that they are less prone to certain diseases.

Choosing Seeds

Seed catalogues make fascinating reading, and for most of us avid gardeners, many enjoyable winter evenings are spent planning the garden and making decisions regarding the varieties of different crops we plan to grow. For instance, there are over one hundred cultivars of tomatoes from which to choose. The growing habits of each are

Germination and Longevity of Seeds			
Crop	Transplant or Direct seeding	Germination Time (days)	Avg. Longevity in Years
Beans	D	6-14	3
Beets	D	8-10	5
Broccoli	T	3-10	5
Cabbage	T	4-10	5
Cantaloupe	T-D	8-10	5
Carrot	D	10-17	4
Cauliflower	T	4-10	5
Celeriac	T	10-21	5
Celery	T	10-21	5
Corn	D	6-10	1
Cress	D	2-4	5
Cucumber	D	6-10	5
Eggplant	T	7-14	5
Garden huckleberry	T	5-15	5
Kale	T	3-9	5
Kohl-rabi	T	3-9	5
Leek	T	8-10	2
Lettuce	D	4-8	5
Muskmelon	T-D	4-8	5
Okra	D	10-15	2
Onion	T	7-12	2
Parsley	D	14-28	2
Parsnip	D	15-25	1
Peas	D	6-15	3
Pepper	T	10-20	4
Pumpkin	D	6-10	5
Radish	D	3-10	5
Spinach	D	6-14	5
Squash (winter)	T-D	6-10	5
Swiss chard	D	7-10	5
Tomato	T	6-14	4
Turnip	D	3-10	5
Zucchini	D	3-12	5

Note: Keep seed in an air-tight container in a cool, dry place. Test for germination before planting. Test old seed well ahead of time by counting out a small quantity of seed, planting in growing medium or rolling up in a damp paper towel, and counting the number that germinate.

Most gardeners do not use all the seed in every package every season. The above chart shows the length of time seed can be kept when properly stored.

clearly described in the catalogue, as are the characteristics of other vegetables.

By having the catalogue at home for leisure reading, there is no need to make hasty decisions. You can take days if you wish. We mention this because we consider it to be a great advantage of mail order seed purchases versus store-bought seed. If a gardener only plans to grow a few salad vegetables, this might not be a consideration. For a garden of a larger size, however, and for those who plan to increase the size of their garden as they gain experience, seed catalogues are invaluable. In addition to information about plants, they contain numerous gardening and cooking tips, as well as a section on garden equipment.

Growing your own vegetables permits you to select varieties of exceptional quality and flavour. The commercial grower is concerned primarily with the durability of the crop during shipping and storage. Avoid varieties recommended as suitable for shipping; they will probably be of a coarser quality.

Another feature to look for in seeds is a variety that will produce a succession of buds and can be harvested over a long period of time. Commercial growers are looking for varieties that will ripen all at the same time to allow for harvesting by mechanical means. Again, these varieties will not have the tender qualities of our home-grown crops, freshly picked for each meal.

Here are some other features to look for in selecting seed:

1. Size of variety when mature;
2. Early or late maturing;
3. Number of days to maturity (after transplanting in garden);
4. Size of fruit;
5. Winter-keeping properties;
6. Resistance to diseases;
7. Untreated seed available for organic gardeners.

I do not intend to give the impression that there is something wrong with seed purchased off racks. Excellent seed is available in garden centres and other stores, but it is important to check that this seed is distributed by reputable seed houses that will guarantee the product. The quality of the seed you plant in your garden will determine, to a certain extent, the quality of the crop you produce. If the seed is of poor quality, no matter how good your cultural standards, the resulting produce will be poor.

Gardeners who want to try unusual crops will find that many Chinese, Italian or other ethnic stores carry packages of vegetables and herb seed unavailable elsewhere, usually of excellent quality. We have visited both Chinese and Italian homes and seen superb gardens thickly planted with vegetables unknown to most North Americans.

Purchasing Transplants

Transplants of tomatoes, peppers, eggplant, leeks, celery, Brassicas, and many other vegetables are available in garden centres and from many market gardeners. The novice gardener should be aware that the variety of each plant should be on the label so that he can determine the ultimate size and shape of the fruit or vegetable. For example, Tiny Tim tomatoes are small plants, suitable for hanging baskets, whereas Sweet 100 grows into a large bush about four feet tall. The fruit on both is the same size.

If you have a seed catalogue, take it along for reference. Otherwise, ask at the nursery for information about the various varieties. Check the plants carefully for signs of stress, disease or insects. If they are not perfectly healthy, do not risk bringing problems into your garden.

Purchasing Plants

Nursery stock of strawberries, raspberries and asparagus is available at garden centres, nursery gardens and through nursery garden catalogues. Always deal with a reputable firm which can guarantee that the stock it is selling you was inspected by a government official during the growing season and certified as disease free. If no appropriate label is attached to the plants, it would be wise to inquire.

When we first moved to the farm we were given different varieties of raspberries by several friends. By accepting these (most gratefully at the time), we introduced a mosaic leaf virus to the garden. The entire raspberry patch had to be dug up and burned, and no raspberries planted in that area for three years. This experience has taught us to be cautious when bringing any new plants into the garden.

*Oh, Adam was a gardener, and
God who made him sees
That half a proper gardener's
work is done upon his knees.*

Rudyard Kipling
1865 - 1936

CHAPTER 9

Starting the Season Indoors

The gardener who makes two blades of grass grow where only one grew before is doing a great job. The gardener who crowds his vegetables is making a great mistake. Vegetable plants even at the seedling stage need space.

Growing Transplants

Transplant is the term applied to certain annual plants which need a longer growing season than prevails in your area. A transplant is started from seed either indoors, in a hot-frame, in a greenhouse, under lights, or in a sunporch or sunny window long before the outdoor temperature has warmed up sufficiently for the young plants to be set-out. By growing transplants we can extend our growing season by one or two months.

Most experienced gardeners grow their own transplants, but we would recommend that a novice purchase ready-grown plants from a reputable nursery. It is better to start experimenting with transplants after you have gained some practical gardening experience.

The economics of growing transplants should be considered. A small garden where only five or six tomato plants are to be grown does not warrant the purchase of seed and growing medium. On the other hand, the pleasure of growing one's own plants from seed may outweigh economic considerations. We enjoy growing transplants and by doing so are able to select varieties of tomatoes, etc., that are unobtainable as transplants at nursery gardens. Certain vegetables such as

globe artichoke may be purchased only as seed through seed catalogues, and therefore growing them yourself is the only way to produce your own crop.

Because we grow our own transplants, we know that from March 15, the date we sow our first seed, until the first week of June, when the last plants are set-out in the garden, we cannot take a holiday. There can be no casual approach to raising these seedlings. A set-back during their early growth may affect the quality of the mature plants. Maybe this is the reason why purchased transplants sometimes perform poorly, and the purchaser has no way of knowing the cause of his poor crop.

The Growing Medium

The growing medium should be sterile and well drained. At no time should the soil be soggy, nor should the seedlings ever be allowed to dry out. A good medium will help avoid these undersirable conditions. Excellent materials are now available through mail order catalogues or at garden centres. These include: vermiculite, Pro Mix, Jiffy Mix, Jiffy-7's, fibre pots (to be filled with a soil mix) and many others.

Many of these mixes have little nutrient value, in which case the gardener knows that he must provide a complete fertilizer, added after the plants have developed true leaves. At this point liquid fertilizer should be given at half strength, and the strength gradually increased as the plants grow and are potted-up.

The better-quality mixes have sufficient nutrients to supply the seedling for a few weeks. The package label will state whether nutrients are present and will suggest when feeding should begin.

Ready made mediums have gained tremendous popularity in recent years. They are labour saving, easy to use and to store, and virtually eliminate the risk of damping-off (see the section on starting seed). Jiffy-7 is the trade name for a compressed, dried peat pellet the size of a checkers pawn. This pellet is enclosed in a nylon mesh and expands about six times when soaked in water, forming a small pot. Jiffy-7's should be left overnight to drain before being seeded.

Experienced gardeners often prefer to make their own growing medium, consisting of:

1 part garden soil (sterilized)
1 part peat moss or leaf mold (sieved)
1 part coarse sand or perlite.

Moisten the peat moss before adding it to the other ingredients.

Sterilizing Soil

Place containers of soil in the oven at 250° to 300° Farenheit (121-149° C) for thirty minutes. Use metal pans and cover the soil with tin foil. Allow to cool before using.

or

Put a bushel of soil in a plastic garbage bag. Sprinkle with a solution of 2½ tablespoons of formaldehyde in one cup of water. Close the bag, shake, and set aside for three or four days, or until the smell has gone.

Starting the Seeds

Seeds require warm temperatures and moisture for good germination, and sunlight for strong early growth. All gardeners growing seedlings for the first time must be aware of a fungus disease called "damping-off", which can wipe out a tray of seedlings virtually

Cauliflower seedlings showing damping-off symptoms.

overnight. This happens as a result of excessive moisture, poor drainage, fluctuating temperatures and inadequate ventilation. The seedlings topple over and a dark, rotted area can be seen at the soil level, even though the rest of the plant appears to be healthy. There is no hope for recovery. Damping-off can also strike before the seedlings emerge through the soil.

Using seed treated with a protectant is helpful for prevention of damping-off, as is sterilizing soil and growing containers. If any seedlings show evidence of damping-off, the entire crop should be treated immediately with an appropriate fungicide.

We plant three seeds in each Jiffy-7, place them in a container, slip the container into a clear plastic bag and set it in a place where it will have a constant temperature of around 75° to 85° F, (24° to 29° C) until the seeds germinate. Little or no watering should be necessary during this period. Many home gardeners find that the top of their refrigerator provides ideal conditions for the germination of seeds. The constant base heat is just what is required.

Light is not important until the seeds germinate. But immediately the seedlings

Seeding Jiffy-7 pellets.

emerge, the plastic bag must be removed and the seedlings placed in full sunlight or under fluorescent lights. The fluorescent tube should be kept at a constant distance of about one or two inches above the tops of the plants.

From now on the seedlings should be grown with day-time temperatures of 70°-75° F (21°-24° C) and a night-time temperature of 60°-65° F (15°-18° C). Twelve hours of light are essential for strong growth. When seedlings do not receive sufficient light, they will become spindly and weak. For another technique, see the section on mini-green-houses.

When the seedlings are about three inches tall and have developed "true" leaves, use scissors to snip away all but the strongest plant in each pot. Pulling out seedlings may damage the tender roots of the remaining plant. Never grow more than one plant in a Jiffy-7.

We prefer Jiffy-7's or peat pots because from the time the seed is planted until the time the plant is set out in the garden, the root system is never disturbed. No "prick-ing-off" is required, so time is saved. (Pricking-off is a term used by horticultural-ists when transplanting seedlings too small to be moved by hand. A penknife or wooden label is used to lift the tiny seedlings from the seed-bed to the flat or pot.)

Some gardeners prefer to sow seeds in small containers either by broadcasting, that is, scattering, or in drills and covering them lightly with soil. The depth of covering depends on the size of seed being sown and should be approximately three times the diameter of the seed. The covering for small seeds should be sieved. After seeding, tamp the soil lightly to ensure that the seed comes in contact with the soil. Then lightly water the container before enclosing it in a clear plastic bag. Once germination has taken place, remove the bag immediately and place the seedlings in good light.

Seedlings grown by this method either in vermiculite or other media must be pricked-off after the first true leaf is formed. Take great care not to damage the root system. Tomatoes, peppers, and eggplant seem to prefer individual 3-inch pots; Brassicas do well spaced in flats. Only early Brassicas need to be started indoors; the main crop can be seeded in a cold frame or garden seed-bed.

Both methods produce satisfactory results. We are sure other old-time gardeners could tell us of many more techniques. Our advice to gardeners is, if your method works for you, stick with it.

Sterilizing Containers

All previously used flats, flower pots and other containers should be sterilized to prevent disease lurking in particles of soil remaining in the containers, which could contaminate the seedlings. It is a tedious job and requires scrubbing the containers, rinsing them with a hose and then dipping them in a disinfectant solution, such as Javex. We prefer to do it outdoors; it is a splashy and messy job.

Miniature Greenhouses

There are a variety of miniature greenhouses on the market today. These vary from simple containers with clear dome-shaped covers, to elaborate models with base electrical heat

Transplants		
Vegetable	*Where to start seeds*	*Approximate growing time in weeks before setting out in garden*
Eggplant Pepper – sweet Pepper – hot Globe artichoke	Indoors	8-10
Tomato Garden huckleberry Ground cherry	Indoors	Depending on variety 5-8
Leeks Onions Celery Celeriac	Hot-frame or Indoors	8-10
Cabbage – early Cauliflower – early Broccoli Brussels sprouts Red cabbage Kohl-rabi Curly kale	Hot-frame or Indoors	6-8
Squash Melons	Indoors, if early crop desired	3-4

and fluorescent lighting. We have never purchased either, and, instead, find our home-made type serves our needs most satisfactorily.

We use a plastic kitty-litter tray or a styro-foam flat lined with plastic; three 2-foot lengths of wire; and a large plastic bag of the type used by drycleaners. These miniature greenhouses are excellent for propagating seed and getting the seedlings established.

Mini-greenhouse for propagation.

Many homes do not have a room with good conditions for plant propagation and free from draughts. The climate inside a mini-greenhouse remains relatively constant and extra light can be given where necessary. It is especially good in very dry houses where the growing medium would be liable to dry out rapidly. When seedlings are well-established, open the bag at one end and allow the air to circulate around the plants. After a few days remove the bag. This will introduce the seedlings to normal household conditions as a step towards facing the outdoor environment.

Frames

Unless seeds are planted directly into the garden, vegetables have to be started under controlled conditions, then subsequently transplanted. Frames are used either to provide controlled conditions for growing seed or as a half-way stage for seedlings between indoors and the garden. Frames can be regarded as a nursery where seedlings are prepared to withstand outdoor conditions in a process generally referred to as "hardening".

Basically, a frame consists of a box, the top of which is made of transparent material such as glass or clear plastic to allow the sun's rays to enter. Seeds or seedlings inside the box can thus be more or less protected from extremes of temperature during their early growth and prior to being planted out when the weather is "set-fair".

"Hot-frames" are so named because some form of heating inside the box raises the temperature day and night. Thus, seeds can be planted directly in a hot-frame in early spring when the garden itself is still much too cold. A "cold-frame" merely provides protection from the weather, like an unheated garage, and is ideal for hardening plants originally grown indoors. It is also useful for forcing some early vegetables such as cress, radishes, lettuce and spring onions.

Garden frames can be purchased, but most people make their own using old storm windows as "lights". These lids, or lights, as they are sometimes called, can be hinged and should fit the base closely enough to prevent cold drafts damaging the plants.

We purchased one of our frames, containing three windows, very cheaply from the local demolition yard. With a few minor adjustments, permitting the windows to lift up, we have a set of frames that can be moved around the garden as needed.

Frames should face south and be exposed to full sunlight. A wall or fence protecting them from north and east winds is desirable. The "light" should slope towards the south or front of the frame and be approximately 6 inches lower at the front than at the rear. This allows more sunlight to reach the plants and also sheds rain water.

The depth of the frame depends on the purpose which it is going to serve. Generally speaking, deeper frames are more flexible than shallow ones. If flats of small seedlings

Homemade hot-frame incorporating old storm windows. The box is filled with fresh horse manure (providing heat) to level A-A, and with soil to level B-B

Hot-frames being filled with fresh, strawy horse manure, topped with a layer of soil. Note in background 45-gallon barrel containing earth is available in early spring before the garden has thawed out.

are set out in a deep frame, they can be placed on raised boards when small, and the boards lowered as the seedlings grow. The seedlings should be within a few inches of the glass.

Cold-frames are heated by the sun, but cool off at night. Therefore, tender plants should not be put out in them until all danger of severe frost is past. The plants can be protected from mild frost at night by covering the "lights" with old rugs, sack or carpeting.

A cold (unheated)-frame can be converted into a hot (heated)-frame by either installing electric cables, or placing the frame on a bed of fresh horse manure. We prefer the latter method. Not only does it produce steady heat (unaffected by any possible electrical failure), but over a period of several months the manure breaks down and can be worked into the garden in the fall, adding humus and enriching the soil.

The manure should be strawy and not more than one month old, in fact, the fresher the better. Nowadays it is not always possible to find a stable that beds their horses in straw, often wood shavings are used instead. Such a mixture is acceptable but not as good. As you make the hot bed, tread each layer down firmly or beat it with a fork. As the breakdown of the manure takes place, the height of the hot bed will be reduced. The manure should be at least 18 inches deep.

Watering the fresh manure makes it heat up very quickly.

If the hot-frame is to be used for direct seeding, cover the manure with 4 to 6 inches of soil, the surface of the soil sloping at the same angle as the "light", with approximately 6 inches between the soil and the "light". When the frame is prepared, replace the "light" but prop it open slightly to allow steam to escape. In five or six days the soil temperature should be 75° to 80° F (23° to 26° C) and the seed may now be sown. A soil thermometer permits accurate temperature reading, and eliminates guesswork for a novice gardener, but we have always relied on our own judgement.

Electric cables purchased from garden centres are an alternative method of heating a hot-frame. They are easy to install if the instructions are carefully followed. The cables should be covered with 6 to 9 inches of soil. Prior to seeding, allow 24 hours for the soil to reach a uniform temperature.

When hot-frames are needed in early spring, the garden plot is still frozen. Therefore, you must plan ahead in the fall by storing sufficient soil in a location where it will remain dry and thaw out early. We prepare this soil on a warm day by sieving it into 45-gallon drums, which we cover over.

Many gardeners now prefer to use an artificial soil mixture as a substitute for soil. It is

These A-Frames make excellent hot beds. One has electric heating cables, the other is heated with horse manure. The work can be done from either side.

costly, but reduces the risk of soil-borne diseases, has good drainage and is free of weeds.

The correct ventilation and watering of frames is most important: the risk of burning seedlings on a sunny day is just as great as the risk of damage by freezing. Ventilation needs care. On cold, sunny days it may be sufficient to open the lights very slightly. On warm, still days the lights may be lifted during the day and replaced at night. During very hot, sunny weather it is often necessary to protect the seedlings from the direct rays of the sun. We use an old bamboo blind, which filters the sunlight perfectly. Newspapers or old sacking are acceptable, but might be blown away by the wind unless firmly anchored.

We place the bamboo on top of the light, then prop the light open with a stick, which allows sufficient ventilation. It does not take long to learn to operate a frame, and my experience has taught me that when we plan to be away all day, we must always place the bamboo on top of the glass before leaving. Dull mornings often turn into hot, sunny afternoons, and if seedlings have a severe setback from overheating, they never fully recover. Naturally, as the plants become stronger, they can be exposed to more direct sunlight. Before seedlings are set out in the garden, the frame should be kept completely open day and night for about a week.

Water in the morning, taking care to ensure that the moisture has reached below the roots of the plants. In very hot, dry weather it may be necessary to water again at midday. Avoid watering at night, as damp night conditions are conducive to fungal infection.

Avoid using icy cold water. We use stored rain water when possible because it is the same temperature as the atmosphere. Tap water with the chill removed is perfectly suitable. Try to avoid using water that has been conditioned by a water softener.

Some local gardeners have successfully grown lettuce in their cold-frames in September for early spring use. The seed germinates and before winter sets in, sturdy young plants have formed. These are protected by the lights during the winter and re-emerge in the spring to produce a very early crop.

The Greenhouse

A greenhouse is a glorified hot-frame and plays no essential role in the home vegetable garden. We have one because gardening is our hobby, and it enables us to enjoy gardening year round and to grow annuals for the flower garden.

The cost of heating our small greenhouse has risen dramatically over the last few years, even though we insulate it with bubble plastic. We would recommend to anyone considering this large captial outlay that they inquire about the latest technological developments in this field. Many improvements such as double glazing have taken place since we purchased ours.

Hot- and cold-frames, a sunny porch or flourescent lights are all that are required to grow vegetable transplants. An unheated sunporch facing south can usually be converted into a greenhouse by mid-March, after the severe cold of the winter is past. Some form of heating is usually required for dull days and cold nights, and a flourescent or Gro-light is of benefit if seedlings are becoming leggy due to lack of sunlight.

Bubble plastic insulation applied to the glass on the inside is a great heat saver and is available from greenhouse suppliers. It is easy to install. First, mist both the glass and the bubble side of the plastic with a mixture of one tablespoon of glycerine and 24 fluid ounces of hot water. Apply the bubble side to the glass and it will adhere. In the spring remove this insulation and store it for use the following winter. When it is left on the glass all summer, it deteriorates rapidly.

A warm, sunny window can provide ideal conditions when only a few seedlings are being grown. Make sure there are no drafts which could injure young plants.

All germinating seedlings benefit from

base heat. Electrically controlled propagating mats are available in various sizes. They take the guesswork out of growing seeds, but most gardeners manage well without them. They are nice to have but not an essential.

After a year or two of experimenting, most home gardeners find a satisfactory way to grow their own transplants. It sounds far more complicated than in fact it is.

Hardening Transplants

Hardening the transplants means gradually introducing the plants to the great outdoors. Start by giving them an hour or two each day, being sure not to set them in a draft. Increase the outdoor time gradually until, weather permitting, the seedlings can remain outdoors day and night. This usually takes one or two weeks.

The ideal method of hardening plants is to set the flats in a cold-frame. This eliminates hauling them in and out of the house. Just

These flats of transplants started indoors have been brought out to be hardened in a cold-frame.

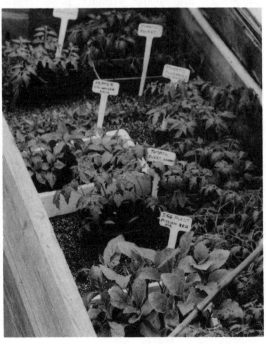

put them in the frame and adjust the lid daily according to the weather conditions. If there is any risk of very cool weather or frost, a cover can be thrown over the lid at night. Another idea is to put the flats in the garden cart; it can be pushed outdoors during the day and brought in under cover at night.

The hardening of plants is very important, but with experience a gardener soon learns to judge when his transplants are ready to be set out permanently. Even though plants may look sturdy and ready for the garden while still in a controlled environment, this transition period is critical in preparing them for both the lower temperature and humidity conditions that prevail outdoors. Without the hardening process a great many transplants could be lost.

Watering must be carefully monitored at this period. When outdoors, flats tend to dry out in the wind and sun. Some days they may even need watering twice. A set-back at this stage in growth may cause poor fruiting later on, even if the plants appear to have recovered perfectly.

Overwatering also has an adverse effect. As much damage is caused by allowing plants to become waterlogged as is caused by drying out; the roots of plants need oxygen. Watering should be done early enough in the day to allow quick drying of the soil surface.

A disadvantage of purchasing transplants, however cheaply from unreliable sources, is that you have no way of telling whether the nursery plants have had any early set-backs. Also, it is often hard to find plants of the variety you may wish to grow. Occasionally, too, mislabelling of seedlings leaves gardeners disappointed to find that the crops they eventually harvest bear little resemblance to what they thought they were buying. Recently in a garden centre, I saw a small child with a handful of labels. She was having a great time replacing them in other containers. A message is here for parents to please keep their children closely supervised.

CHAPTER 10

The Season Outdoors

When spring comes and warmth is in the sun, we have a tremendous urge to start working outdoors. There will still be snow in shaded areas and where drifts have lain, but gradually the ground thaws out, dries and work can commence.

The Spring Clean-up

The first outdoor job that we tackle is a general "clean-up". Although we tidy the grounds in the fall, it is surprising how much debris accumulates during the winter. Our debris is organic, but in city gardens there may be all kinds of litter that has blown in and become hidden under a blanket of snow. As well as being good for the garden, this early spring clean-up is cosmetic.

Although you may be anxious to get started on the job, it is very important not to walk on or start work on lawns and grass paths while the frost is still coming out of the ground. Lawns can be severely damaged at this stage, requiring a great deal of unnecessary work to get them back into shape. Wait until they are dry, and your footsteps leave no depression.

Rake the lawn with a grass rake. This removes the dead grass which has often formed a thick mat, and any leaves or debris that may have been missed in the fall. If the growing points of the grass do not receive air and light, they will suffocate and die, leaving bare patches. If winter-kill has caused damage to the lawn, now is the time to re-seed.

Hedges also need to have leaves and grass removed from the base of the bushes. This allows air to circulate and the growth of the hedge to remain thick at ground level. Straggly hedges are badly maintained hedges. Spring hedge care is very important; it is in the spring that all plants make their strongest growth.

Removing Mulch

All plants that have been mulched in the fall for winter protection should have the mulch gradually removed, exposing the growing points of the plants to light and air. The mulch can be spread on the ground around the plants to control weeds. If, subsequently, a heavy frost is anticipated, the mulch can be replaced temporarily. It is late frost that is the most usual cause of damage to strawberry blossoms. In home berry patches we can usually protect against this.

Preparing the Garden Plot

The vegetable garden plot takes much longer than the lawns to reach a workable condition. Do not walk on it if you "sink in". Test the soil by picking up a handful, rolling it into a ball and then "flicking" it with your finger. If the soil disintegrates like breadcrumbs, it is ready to work. If it breaks in small lumps, it is still too wet.

Clay soil takes longer to dry out in the spring and should not be handled while still sticky or gummy.

Another way to judge if the soil is ready to work is whether or not it sticks to the fork,

The garden in spring after the planting has started. In the foreground fibre pots cover the sea-kale. The supports for peas and beans are in place and floating row covers are protecting the newly planted Brassicas. The drip irrigation system along each row is ready to switch on when needed.

spade or blades of the rotary tiller. If it does, you're too early.

Never work a garden plot until the soil is ready. Ground worked too early in the spring will remain lumpy all season, and the resulting crops will be of poor quality. In most gardens some sections dry out much earlier than others. (Our first seeding of hardy annuals is planted in these areas.) Some years when a late spring is encountered, it is hard to maintain good crop rotation practices, but as long as the previous year's crops were healthy this is not too serious a problem. However, if any diseases were encountered, refrain from growing any member of that particular plant family in that location.

If no manure or compost was available to spread on the garden plot in the fall, now is the time to do it. We sometimes also apply a complete fertilizer in granular form and till the two into the ground together. I will not suggest the amount and ratio of fertilizer to use, as the specific needs of every garden will differ. The only way to ascertain the exact re-quirements of your garden is to make a soil test. We do not consider this essential every year. If the crops were excellent the previous season there may be no need for either a soil test or additional fertilizer, but if the crops were poor, an accurate and complete soil test should be made. The growing crops will always let you know if the soil conditions do not meet their requirements.

Small garden plots can be dug by hand. Some gardeners use a spade; others, like my-self, prefer a fork. The finished results are very similar. The soil should be "friable" or "in good tilth", which means its texture should be like breadcrumbs. This is the type of soil every gardener desires, aims at maintaining or, in gardens with poor conditions, tries to develop over the years.

When the ground is being worked, take

care to remove any quack grass, dandelion or other noxious perennial weeds. Annual weeds may be turned under, where they will decay, adding humus to the soil. Destroy quack grass roots. A simple method is to let them dry out and die in the sun. They will create havoc in the compost if there is any life left in them.

Seeding

You are now ready to make a seed bed. The soil will be loose in texture. Rake it with the garden rake to level and pulverize the top

Seeding in a drill.

Covering seeded drill with board.

Removing board as seedlings germinate.

inch or so, which will aid germination. Seed can remain dormant a considerable time if buried among clods or put into ground that has been hardened by too much tramping or a heavy rainfall.

Before sowing the seed, use the garden line to keep the rows straight and evenly spaced. The space between rows depends on the crops being sown. To open up a drill or shallow trench for the seed, use either the handle of a rake or one corner of the blade of a draw hoe. The depth of the drill will vary with the type of seed being sown. After the seed has been sown it must be covered. Use the garden rake to draw soil over the seed, then, with the prongs flat on the ground, tamp until the soil is in close contact with the seed. This prevents the soil from drying out too rapidly, and the emerging plants being deprived of essential moisture and nutrients.

Sow seed in accordance with the directions given on each packet. Small seeds can be trickled out of the seed package; larger ones can be spaced out one by one.

Novice gardeners are inclined to plant seed far too thickly, and most of the seedlings have to be pulled up and thrown away. With the ever-increasing cost of garden seed it would be a saving of both money and labour to sow the seeds at the distance recommended. In gardens where space is limited, more intensive planting can take place. In this case it is best to intercrop, seeding rows of fast-maturing vegetables between the rows of slower growing main crops, or between main crop plants. Crops grown in such crowded conditions must be thinned and weeded carefully, and given extra fertilizer.

Labelling

Label each row after you plant the seed. A common practice is to push a stick into the ground at each end of the row and use the empty seed packet as the marker. This is fine unless the wind blows it away, or rain washes out the print. We prefer to use zinc labels and write on them with a grease pencil. One year I used the wrong marking pencil on plastic labels, and all the writing was washed off in the first rain!

We like to mark each label with the date of seeding, name of variety and the seed house. This way I can keep a record of the performance of different varieties.

Covering the Seeds

To prevent soil drying out, perhaps in anticipation of a hot, rainless spell, cover the seeded rows with an old board or something equivalent until the seed shows signs of germination. This technique is especially good every season for slow germinating crops like parsnips and parsley.

Old boards placed between the rows of vegetables are handy for the gardener to step on when the soil is wet. This prevents footsteps compressing the soil and saves shoes from getting muddy.

Plant Support

Crops such as peas and pole beans should have the necessary support erected at seeding time. Plant supports are discussed later in detail under the individual vegetables. It is important to ensure that plants do not get blown over and lie on the ground. Adequate support keeps plants upright, allows air to circulate and sunshine to penetrate. This, in turn, helps prevent disease.

Setting Out Transplants

The early broccoli, cauliflower and cabbage plants that were started indoors should be hardened by now and ready to set out in the garden. The day before planting out, thoroughly moisten the soil in the flats. The best weather for planting out is a cool, rainy day. If you must plant out in hot weather, wait until the cool of the evening. In addition, give the young plants some protection from the sun and wind for a few days. Artificial shade can be provided in many ways.

Preparing to plant young seedlings outdoors. You need a trowel, a roll of plaster-board sealing tape (or equivalent paper), a broad-bladed knife to separate the soil into "cubes" and the flats of hardened transplants.

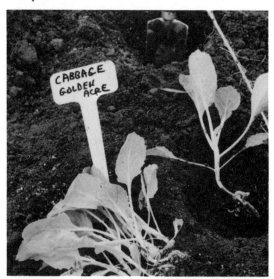

Before planting, mark your bed with a garden line.

Wrap paper collar around the stem of the plant. Plant the seedling, ensuring that the collar is partly buried and partly above soil level.

Plant supports are neatly erected to accommodate seedlings already beginning to show up. Note the martin house in the background. The martins will, we hope, keep the garden area mosquito-free during the season.

Seedlings emerging, but well marked by plastic labels. Hoeing keeps weeds down until we mulch between the rows.

Examples are inverted fibre flower pots or cedar shingles stuck firmly in the ground at an angle.

Some transplants are grown in individual pots, like peat pots or Jiffy-7's, while others are grown in flats. Before removing plants from a flat, divide them by slicing sections with a knife as you would a pan of brownies. Using a trowel, lift each plant out singly with as much soil around the root system as possible. The less the roots are disturbed the better. Plant each seedling in a trowel-made hole, the lowest leaves flush with the soil, and the soil made firm above the roots. Paper collars can be used to prevent damage by cutworms. Water each plant as you set it out.

Hoeing

The early garden will now be under way, and it will not be long before signs of life spring up all over the ground. Unfortunately, the annual weeds are usually the first to emerge. All gardens with good soil also grow excellent weeds. These must be hoed as soon as possible.

When the weeds are still only an inch or so tall, it is time to hoe them. This is best done when the top of the soil is dry and the weather hot and sunny. In these conditions the weeds, when disturbed, will shrivel and die, whereas in moist, cool conditions they might re-establish themselves. The importance of having straight, well-marked rows is appreciated when doing the first hoeing. Weeds germinate faster than vegetables. If you are unable to identify the vegetable seedlings, you can always stretch a line between the row markers and then hoe safely between rows. Hoeing at this stage is very light work and saves hours of labour in the long run. Unless the ground is mulched it will be necessary to hoe frequently, but the work will be easy and quick each time if the weed seedlings are still tiny.

Thinning

It is very seldom that home gardeners sow seed so correctly spaced that no thinning is necessary. Most of us sow seed far too thickly and as a result must thin the rows. Vegetables need space, within reason, to produce high-quality crops and avoid disease.

If seed is planted too densely the seedlings will be weak and spindly, and the need for more space will become greater with subsequent growth. Thinning will be necessary and must be done according to each plant's requirements. Pull out surplus seedlings complete with their roots, causing as little disturbance as possible to adjacent plants. This is easiest to do when the soil is moist, and the remaining plants can be easily made firm again in the ground.

The thinnings need not always be wasted; beets, carrots, and onions, for instance, can be used in the kitchen. Thinning should not take place in one operation, but in stages over a period of time, providing the house with a regular supply of early crops. We find these young vegetables far more tasty than their mature brothers (or sisters!).

Weeds and Weeding

There are hundreds of weeds that thrive in our gardens in spite of our cold winters. These are, for all general purposes, divided into two categories: annuals and perennials.

The annual weeds do not pose a serious

A row of Brassica seedlings are hidden by this jungle of annual weeds. The pigweed shown here harbours mosaic disease, and aphids carry this to other plants. The problems next year for this garden's owner will be dreadful.

problem if the emerging seedlings are hoed down before they go to seed. Purslane, for example, which has minute seeds, can produce over 190,000 seeds per plant each season. These seeds can remain viable for many years when plowed under the soil. The same can be said for many other weeds. For this reason, and because they harbour pests and diseases, I stress the importance of hoeing down emerging weed seedlings and maintaining as weed-free a garden as possible.

The perennial weeds can be a far greater problem to eradicate. There are some with vigorous, fast growing, underground root stocks, which are able to send up new shoots at many places throughout their length. If these are cut up and tilled into the ground, each segment will grow and potential plants are distributed all over the garden plot. Quack grass (an unsolicited import from Europe) is the most common member of this group. There are also perennial weeds with deep taproots. If the entire root is not removed, any remaining sections left in the soil are sufficient to grow new plants: witness the notorious dandelion.

Perennial weeds should be burned. If you want to throw them on the compost heap, leave them in the sun first to wither and die. Be certain they are dead. Quack grass roots growing in a compost heap give the gardener many unnecessary hours of hard labour when they are returned to the garden plot.

In the spring and early summer we like to weed the garden in the rain or just after a rainfall. To weed when the ground is wet, place a board between rows to stand on so that the ground does not become compacted. We know that removing weeds from between the seedlings during a soft rainfall will do little or no damage to the tender young roots of the crop, whereas weeding the rows in dry weather can cause considerable damage.

Later on, when the crops are so advanced that working between the rows would cause me to brush against the plants, we wait until the foliage is dry to prevent the possible spread of disease.

The golden rule concerning weeds in the garden plot is to hoe emerging annuals and to remove and destroy all perennials. Do not put them on the compost until they are truly dead.

It is self evident that all weeds compete with crops for available nutrients in the soil. We wage an unending battle against weeds and have found that mulching is a tremendous help.

Mulch

What is a mulch? In its simplest terms it is the gardener's version of what has been happening on the floor of our forests over many decades. Trees collect around them an accumulation of leaves, twigs, branches, and dead plant materials that have decayed through a natural process and created top soil.

In our gardens we attempt to reproduce nature's work with what we call a mulch. This consists of any material that can be applied to the soil surface without causing injury to the plants. Such a covering not only prevents growth of weeds between cultivated plants, but also reduces soil moisture evaporation.

Types of Mulches Recommended	
Hay (spoiled):	Sometimes available free from farmers after being damaged by rain. An excellent mulch, but may introduce annual weeds.
Lawn clippings:	We repeatedly apply thin layers on top of newspaper. If applied too thickly, they may heat excessively.
Leaf mold:	Made by composting leaves raked in the fall.
Manure:	Obtained from farms or stables. Excellent mulch containing nutrients. If too fresh, may burn plants. Should be well-rotted.
Mushroom compost:	Available from commercial mushroom growers. Good nutrient value.
Peat moss:	Purchased from garden supply stores. A fine texture and good appearance, but has a tendency to dry out and become impervious to water. Best used as a soil conditioner rather than a mulch.
Black plastic:	Purchased from garden supply stores. Practical for large gardens, but unattractive and liable to be blown about in windstorms if not securely anchored. Does not break down into soil as do organic mulches.
Landscape fabric:	A strong permeable material for setting between rows. It prevents weeds from germinating. Can be re-used for several years.
Sawdust:	Usually obtained free from sawmills and lumber yards. A good general mulch. May cause a nitrogen deficiency which can be corrected by fertilizing. Should not be worked into the soil.
Straw:	Obtained from farms. Coarser and more durable than most kinds of hay. A good mulch.
Newspaper:	This should be laid flat on the soil several layers deep and weighted down with other organic materials such as grass clippings to prevent it being blown away. Do not get distracted by reading the old news which somehow always acquires renewed interest when it is lying on the ground!

Grass clippings laid over newspaper makes an excellent mulch. The clippings are spread thinly to prevent overheating and added to as more become available.

Wood shavings covering landscape fabric are being used around a tomato plant. The shavings protect the fabric from deteriorating. It will be reused for several years. The shavings will be added to the compost during the fall cleanup.

While mulching does create some extra labour initially, in the long run it is a great saver of time and effort, and it almost certainly produces better crops. A real advantage to mulching is that the labour it saves comes at a time when I am busy processing the produce. Without this mulch I would be devoting time to watering or weeding.

For several years we have been experimenting with different types of mulches. Basically, we use whatever is easily available to us, provided that it is aesthetically suitable for the different areas of the garden. For example, we use sawdust for the raspberries; plastic film for the melons; compost, well-rotted manure, hay, straw, and grass clippings for the vegetable garden. We do not apply fresh garden and household refuse directly as a mulch. We prefer to compost it first and spread it after one or two years. Our method allows us to have a much neater garden than the ones where all refuse is used directly in the garden as a mulch.

Because we prefer to roto-till the entire garden in the spring and fall, we apply only sufficient mulch during the season to conserve moisture and control weeds. We incorporate the mulch when we roto-till. In warmer areas some people apply a very deep mulch and never cultivate their gardens. In the spring they rake away enough mulch to plant their crops. This is the method advocated by Ruth Stout, author of several organic gardening books, which I have read and enjoyed thoroughly. We were also fortunate enough to have visited her in her garden shortly before she died. I have utilized her methods wherever possible in my garden; however, I cannot overcome my preference for a neat, nice looking plot. Her garden had a wild look well suited to the rugged countryside in which she lived.

Ruth Stout made the added claim that deep mulching also controlled cut worms, slugs, root maggots, and in fact virtually every underground pest. While I can confirm that her soil was in excellent condition and produced beautiful crops, I am unable to verify her stand on pests. She may well be right, but for us, leaving a deep mulch on our garden would prevent the soil warming up early in the spring, a most important factor in short season areas.

When planning to incorporate the mulch in the soil each year, consider the types of mulches that can be used. For example, if heavy layers of newspaper are used, they would not decompose sufficiently to be easily incorporated into the soil. Similarly, too much sawdust might cause a lack of nitrogen. We attempt to rotate the mulches as we do the crops. I am sure most home gardens have a variety of mulches just as we do. Where the richest nutrients are applied one year, that is where the heaviest feeding crop will be planted the next.

We test the soil from several locations in the garden most years, but this is not really necessary. If the ground is not producing excellent crops, the plants will tell you that the soil is not right, and you must take appropriate steps to correct the nutrient deficiencies.

Care of the Surroundings

If lawns or grass paths surround a vegetable garden, they need to be kept trim. Not only does this give the garden a more pleasing appearance, but it discourages mosquitoes and blackflies, which prefer damp, thick vegetation; two sufficient reasons to make most gardeners groom their property. But the most important aspect is in the eradication of host plants for the pests, or "bad-guys," with whom we wage a constant battle.

Many weeds belong to the same plant families as our vegetable crops. If we allow these weeds to grow wild around the vegetable plots, we are providing protection and food for the pests, hence diseases, which we are trying to eliminate from our gardens.

In large gardens where a farm tractor is used for cultivation and no cut lawns surround the vegetable plot, the surrounding area should either be tilled and kept black, or grass and weeds cut low.

A string trimmer makes light work of keeping the garden looking neat and tidy.

Our vegetable garden plot is surrounded by cut grass paths. In order to prevent the grass encroaching on the plot it is necessary to keep the edges straight and trimmed. This is a tedious job, but so greatly improves the visual aspect that we consider it time well spent. This job needs to be repeated several times during the season.

It is our experience that the things that are wrong or untidy in a garden are far more likely to attract the eye of the beholder than those that are in good order. We prefer our garden to be remembered for its good features rather than its bad ones. Straight rows of vegetables and straight grass edges may sound unimportant, but they tell the difference between well and poorly kept gardens.

Summer Work

Summer work in a garden is continuous. The frost-tender main crops must be seeded and frost-tender transplants set out in their final locations. The hoe is busy controlling weeds and any available mulch should be spread between the rows. This stage of gardening is tremendously rewarding. The growth of all plants is very rapid, and harvesting of early crops will be well under way. As the ground is emptied it should be dug and enriched for successive plantings.

In late May or early June the seeds of late Brassica crops should be sown in a cold-frame or a seed-bed in the garden. These seedlings will be ready for transplanting into the garden by early or mid-July. The culture is the same as for early crops.

Inspecting for Ailments

When crops are growing actively, it is wise to take time each day to wander through the garden inspecting the crops for any signs of distress. If wilted plants or leaves, chewed leaves, gun-shot damage to leaves, blossom drop or any other unusual symptoms are noticed, the plant should be closely examined, the cause of the problem determined and the necessary steps taken to prevent further damage.

The arrival of white butterflies indicates that their eggs will soon be laid on the undersides of Brassica leaves. These eggs hatch out as caterpillars that chew cabbage, cauliflower, broccoli, and Brussels sprouts. We now protect our Brassicas with Floating Row Covers. These covers should be put on as soon as the plants are set out in the garden, and held down with stones or soil around the edges. The covers should be loose enough to permit the plants to grow freely. The environment created under the cover is superb for growing all the Brassicas.

An old-timers' method of controlling caterpillars in cabbages is to sprinkle pickling salt down in among the leaves, making three or four applications during the growing season. At my home we used to spray the cabbages with a solution of a handful of salt to a bucket of water. To the best of my recollection, it worked remarkably well.

It is interesting also that the use of soaps was popular fifty years ago as a method of pest control. This remedy is coming back into favour because of its property of killing specific pests while not affecting the "good guys" such as bees, lady bugs or parasitic wasps.

Watering

For optimum growth, plants must always have an adequate supply of moisture at root level. Ascertain the depth of moisture in the soil by actually checking with a garden fork. If watering is needed, make sure each watering is sufficient to reach below root level. If watering is done from overhead, do this early enough in the day to allow the foliage to dry off before nightfall. Seepage watering can be done at any time, day or night.

Do not move among the plants when the

We set out the drip irrigation system before planting the garden. In the foreground floating covers are protecting the Brassicas. Next to them the tomatoes are growing in cages.

foliage is wet, either from dew, sprinkling or rain, because this can cause spread of disease such as rust spots on beans.

Harvesting

As the season progresses, crops ripen and harvesting becomes a daily routine along with garden maintenance.

Most perishable crops must be harvested when still in prime condition. Sugar or snow peas left on the vine only one day too long will be coarse and stringy, as will overripe kohl-rabi. Many people are turned against certain vegetables because, on their first encounter, those vegetables were of inferior quality or poorly cooked.

Putting the Garden to Bed

By mid-August many of the main crops will have been harvested, leaving empty spaces in the garden. In areas where frost is not expected until late September, these spaces can be reseeded with fall crops of lettuce, Chinese cabbage and spinach. Once you know your garden and its climatic variations, you will be able to judge how many crops you can grow successfully. In northern areas re-seeding in mid-August is out of the question, with the exception of Pepper cress and Arugula.

Frost-tender annual herbs should be harvested and dried before there is any risk of frost. Hardy perennial herbs may be cut back and the prunings dried if needed. Cutting back shapes the plants and prevents them from becoming straggly.

Chives can be cut back, potted-up and brought into the house for winter garnishes. They will shoot up again in no time. Parsley can also be potted-up and brought indoors. We like to leave the rest of the parsley row in the garden as, being a biennial, it will usually grow again in the spring to provide the house with an early crop before finally going to seed. Other frost-tender perennial herbs such as rosemary and bay should be brought indoors in good time. We like to keep ours permanently potted, setting the pots out in the garden during the summer.

As soon as the various vegetable crops are over, the debris should be cleaned up and taken to the compost heap. Any annual weeds still in the ground should be hoed, and the

Left: Harvesting Blue Lake pole beans that have grown well over the top of the 6-foot trellis. They provide a heavy crop which is harvested over an extended period. *Below:* Compost and peat moss being spread in the areas no longer occupied by plants. This helps maintain the tilth of the soil.

perennial ones removed and destroyed. Now is the time to start transferring the well-rotted compost to the garden and spreading it in the vacant areas. If manure is available, all the better. This process continues throughout the fall while the late crops are gradually harvested. Root crops can remain in the ground until October; a light frost is said to improve the flavour of some.

Broccoli, Brussels sprouts, cabbage, celery, Swiss chard, curly kale, leeks, and spinach can withstand quite a lot of frost. We like to leave these crops in the garden as long as possible. We usually continue eating freshly picked produce well into November.

The hardiest of these are Brussels sprouts and curly kale. They stay in the ground all winter for the simple reason that the ground has frozen over before I have finished harvesting them. The other vegetables should be dug up before the ground freezes and brought into the cool room, or root cellar. We can usually eat our own fresh vegetables until Christmas.

Parsnips can remain in the ground all winter, ready to be dug as soon as the ground thaws in spring. We always bring enough into the cool room to supply us during the winter months. We have never been successful overwintering carrots and leeks in the garden. We are sure this is because our garden is too wet in the spring, and it is at this stage that these vegetables rot. However, I know people who do overwinter these crops in this way, and I believe it is because their gardens dry out quickly in the spring.

Some gardeners leave tilling the ground until spring. We prefer to do it in the fall as well. We are convinced we get better results. We know we save time in the spring when so much has to be done all at once. This end-of-season digging or tilling, incorporating mulch into the soil, should be completed when the ground is dry, before freeze-up.

Cultivating wet soil leaves it in hard clods.

The surface should be left rough or in ridges so that the frost may penetrate more of the ground. Freezing breaks up soil into small particles, leaving it more porous. It also helps to kill the eggs of many insects by exposing them to sun, wind and birds.

Once the ground has frozen, mulch can be applied to plants that need protection. Asparagus, sea-kale, strawberries, raspberries, rhubarb, globe and Jerusalem artichokes all benefit, as well as many herbs. Rhubarb benefits most from a heavy application of well-rotted manure. It is a rich feeder.

Rodents can do severe damage to the garden in winter. We protect young trees with either plastic tree guards or by painting the bark with a bitter-tasting repellant. In the raspberry patch, we set out pop cans, partially filled with mouse poison. This technique eliminates any fear of birds picking up the "seed" but deals most satisfactorily with mice.

After all the leaves have fallen they should be collected and, unless needed for leaf mold or winter mulch, added to the compost heap. Leaf mold is an excellent substitute for peat moss and is also weed free.

When all the organic waste available has been added and the compost heap is complete, it should be finished off with a final layer of soil and a sprinkling of high nitrogen fertilizer. There will be plenty of internal heat in it in the spring; an ideal location for growing canteloupe.

If the crops in your garden have not been satisfactory and you have never had the soil analyzed, now is the time to do it. When we first started developing our present garden we sent soil away for a full analysis. This enabled us to apply nutrients in the correct proportions. Now we test only when the crops tell us their nutrient needs are not being fully met.

CHAPTER 11

Diseases and Pests

In the preceeding part of this book we have attempted to describe the practical aspects of vegetable gardening with particular reference to methods which seem to suit us best.

The next part of the book deals with diseases and pests. Sooner or later we all run into gardening problems arising from plants clearly sending out distress signals. We believe that at that time you will find it useful to compare such problems with those described or illustrated here. In this way the cause of the problem can be identified and remedied. Because prevention is better than cure we have summarized many of the control measures needed to deal with gardening problems before they arise.

Readers will already be familiar with our views on the use of chemicals. In our home gardens where we are only dealing with small quantities of each crop there is no need to use toxic chemicals. Healthy soil and healthy crops have a far greater resistance to disease. Good garden hygiene will prevent the spread of many problems. However, when problems do occur steps should be taken right away to correct them. We control most insects with applications of Diatomaceous earth, Rotenone and insecticidal soap (or just soapy water or even just a little detergent).

It should also be noted that the scientific knowledge of plants is undergoing rapid change. Plants are being genetically engineered so as to resist certain pests and diseases. As a result, we now appreciate that plant life is not as simple as it was once thought to be. From the gardeners' point of view, it is important to know something of the way plants grow, because this has a direct bearing on how plants become the victims of disease.

Plant Diseases

Plant diseases can be roughly divided into three categories: physiological diseases due to improper nutrition, which we have already discussed; infectious diseases caused by micro-organisms; and diseases caused by pests like insects, slugs and nematodes, which bite or bore their way into the plant. This section is concerned with infections, although all types of disease are interrelated. A weak plant suffering from a trace element deficiency is more likely to succumb to a fungus attack than a healthy one, and insect pests often introduce viruses during their ravagings.

Diseases are naturally spread by wind or rain drops carrying infectious particles from one plant to another. Birds and animals also aid dissemination by carrying plant material and soil with them as they move about. Insects, as we shall see, play a major role in spreading virus infections, and even the gardener, tramping between the rows of plants, may cause bruising and so increase the risk of infection.

The incidence of disease is greatly affected by the weather, and conditions of temperature and humidity which favour one disease may discourage another. All we can be sure of is that no two years will be the same.

A pathogen is an agent which causes disease. It is usually a microscopic organism, and plants are susceptible to attack by three main kinds of pathogens: fungi, bacteria and viruses.

Most infectious diseases in plants are caused by fungi, microscopic cousins of the familiar mushrooms and toadstools. To begin with, we will take a general look at what happens when a fungus invades a plant. When a spore lands on a plant, it germinates, producing very fine branching threads called hyphae. These hyphae penetrate by boring through the outer epidermis of the plant, or growing through the breathing pores (stomata), or through a wound. Once inside, they branch and grow, excreting substances which dissolve the cell walls so that they can feed on the plant tissues.

Cross section of a leaf showing infection by a fungus.
A: Fungus spore producing hypha, which is
   penetrating leaf through pore (stomata).
B: Leaf epidermal cells.
C: Leaf cells with green chloroplasts.

After the infection is well developed, some of the hyphae near the surface of the plant will organize themselves to produce millions of tiny new spores which are easily borne away by the wind to start new infections on neighbouring plants. Late in the season the fungi stop their attack and develop tough resting structures, or special spores, in the dead tissues of the plants they have killed, or in niches under the bark of trees or perhaps in the soil. In this condition they wait out the winter. The following spring new hyphae develop which produce a new crop of spores to start the cycle of infection over again, if the weather conditions are favourable. In this way there are often two stages to the spread of disease in the garden. First, the arrival of unwanted spores, perhaps only a few of which may land on a single plant; this is followed by secondary spread throughout the growing season to other plants of the same family growing nearby. Not all fungi attack the aerial parts of the plant. Some live on dead organic matter in the soil and, when they come in contact with a susceptible root, they will invade it and spread through the whole root system and up the stem.

It is very important to understand that many, but not all, of the fungi which cause plant diseases are able to live on dead plant material when there is no suitable living plant around to attack. This is the reason for the crop rotation and garden hygiene we have talked about. It would be foolish to plant new young plants in a part of the garden where a pathogen is suspected to be lurking in the soil; we know it is there because the plants of the same family which grew there last year were diseased. To repeat the planting would lead to a build-up of infection in the soil that might take years to eradicate.

All this sounds as if a plant is doomed to certain death when attacked by a fungus. Not so. It can fight back and is able to produce antibiotic substances with which it tries to stop the fungal advance. If it is successful it is called a resistant variety. It can also develop thickened, corky layers in the cells surrounding the advancing infection, and so wall off the area and starve the invader.

Fungal Diseases

These diseases are grouped mainly according to the symptoms exhibited by the plants, although identical symptoms may result from infections by quite different fungi. For example, if the root system is extensively damaged or the water-conducting tissue of the stem affected, the main symptom will be general wilting, with no indication of which fungus is causing the trouble. On the other hand, some diseases are so characteristic, such as potato blight or corn smut, that they are immediately recognizable.

Let us now take a brief look at some of the types of diseases commonly seen in the garden.

Leaf spots and anthracnoses: As the name implies, these fungi are characteristically confined to the local areas of the plant where the infections take place. The fungi do not usually penetrate deeply, and the host plant is able to build a barrier around the site, leaving necrotic (dead) patches. If too many of these necrotic spots occur on a leaf it may die, and if too many leaves die the plant becomes defoliated and dies too. This is rare, however, and most plants continue to grow, although with impaired vigour. Anthracnoses are not confined to the leaves and cause blackened, burned-looking irregular spots on any part of the plant. These infections may be severe, especially on peas and beans, where the fungus

Leaf spot on parsnips.

also may invade the pods and so infect the seeds. If these seeds are kept for planting the next year, disaster will follow; the young plants will be systemically infected, and those that survive will not produce a crop worth harvesting.

Wilt diseases: Fungi which are not confined to the superficial tissues of the plant but penetrate deeply may interfere with the water supply of the shoots and thus induce wilting. This may be partly due to the physical blocking of the xylem by the fungal hyphae, but it is mainly a result of chemical reactions of substances released by the growing hyphae which interfere with the mechanisms for water transport in the plant. If the fungus invades at a point on the stem, only the shoot above that point will wilt, but when the roots or stems at soil level are attacked (root and collar rots) the result is wilting and collapse of the entire plant.

Blight diseases: This term is used to describe infections which progress rapidly so that shoots, or even whole plants, which appear to be healthy one day may be dead within forty-eight hours. Late blight of potatoes is the classic example. The coincidence of a cloud of wind-borne spores with a period of humid weather spells trouble for the potato patch. Potato blight is one of the few fungal diseases able to cause extensive epidemics and was the reason for the infamous Irish potato famines of the nineteenth century.

Mildews: These diseases are exceedingly common on a great variety of plants and are recognized by the white powdery effect which they produce on the leaves, stems, and sometimes flowers of the host plants. They are different from the fungi we have talked about so far, in that they are "obligate parasites," that is, they are unable to grow on dead plant remains and only attack living hosts. They usually make their appearance when the plants are reaching maturity, and

Above: Eggplant severely infected with Verticillium
wilt compared with healthy specimen.
Right: Late blight on two outer petioles of celery.
Central petiole is healthy.
Below: Late blight on tomato leaf.

do not kill but cause discolouration and weakening.

Rusts and smuts: These descriptive names embrace a group of highly specialized and destructive pathogens. Fortunately, only two of them appear to plague us in the vegetable garden: corn and onion smut. Both rusts and smuts produce their spores gathered in large masses in pustules or galls situated below the epidermis of the host. This finally breaks open to reveal the orange-red rust spores or sooty-black smut balls. Smuts infect only the actively growing tips of the host plant, the fungal hyphae keeping pace with its growth and frequently dying out in the older parts of the plant. Often there is no indication that the plant is infected until the galls form and break open.

Rusts do not pose a problem in the vegetable garden, except for infections on gooseberry and currant bushes. The infections may not be severe in themselves, but the bushes serve as alternate hosts for the white pine blister rust which has killed so many beautiful white pine trees. They present a hazard we should not countenance in our gardens. We must keep a sharp eye for signs of rust. If it appears, eradicate the bushes.

Botrytis grey mold and miscellaneous rots: This category is not really concerned with diseases so much as with nuisances. Botrytis is an ever-present fungus which isn't much of a pathogen itself, but is very quick to enter a wound or attack weakened plants, especially when they are crowded and ventilation around them is poor. It grows rapidly, reducing plant tissues to a soft mush covered with a grey fuzz.

Some fungi will cause rots in the root storage organs, as well as attack the aerial parts of the plants, but these types of rot are more often of bacterial origin. Another nuisance which should be mentioned is potato scab (not actually caused by a fungus) which spoils the appearance of the tubers though not their eating quality.

"Damping-off" of seedlings is a soil-borne infection which occurs in humid conditions when seedlings are planted too closely together. The fungus weakens the young stems at soil level, causing the seedlings to fall over and die. This is a greenhouse infection and rarely troubles seeds sown in the open.

Bacterial Diseases

So far we have considered only fungal pathogens, which are the cause of the most troublesome infections in our gardens. Bacterial diseases play a relatively minor role. This is quite the reverse of the situation in the animal kingdom in which bacterial diseases cause severe and widespread illnesses, and fungal infections are superficial or rare.

Bacteria are tiny single-celled organisms, so much smaller than the fungi that they can barely be seen under the light microscope. They grow by dividing into two daughter cells that rapidly regain the size of the original cell and divide again. Their numbers multiply much faster than the fungi, and one bacillus may become several million within a few hours. With a few exceptions bacterial pathogens live in the soil, feeding on nutrients released during the breakdown of organic matter. They do not produce airborne spores and so do not spread readily from garden to garden, but generally gain entry into the plant through natural pores, or through wounds or holes caused by boring insects. They often follow, and complicate, infections initially caused by fungi. Many species of bacteria are able to invade a wide range of host plants and do not have to confine their attentions to a single plant family, so there are few characteristic bacterial diseases to describe, happily for us.

Bacterial soft rots: These affect the underground storage organs of many vegetables such as turnips, carrots, and onions, as well as the succulent parts of cabbages, broccoli and celery, etc. Infection always takes place through a wound, caused perhaps by careless hoeing or by slugs. While the growing leaves may not at first show signs of what is happening below the ground, they will wilt and die as the rot progresses. We are all familiar with the sight of the occasional carrot whose inside has rotted to a pasty white mush that has washed away in the rain, leaving only the resistant rind to show what might have been.

Crown galls: Galls are a plant's response to invasion by fungi, bacteria or insects. The plant cells at the site of invasion are stimulated to start dividing in a somewhat haphazard fashion and the result is the production of irregular, tumour-like growths, sometimes of enormous size. Crown galls, as the name suggests, are produced on the crown of the plant just at or below soil level. The bacteria which cause them differ from the soft rotting organisms in that they are unable to produce the substances which dissolve the plant cells and so rot the tissues. Instead, they excrete substances which stimulate the plant cells around them to divide in an uncontrolled manner. Crown galls are not a great source of economic loss and are mainly seen on raspberry canes and fruit trees.

Viruses

Viruses can, and do, infect all animals and plants, even the very same fungal and bacterial pathogens that we have just been describing. They are very tiny infectious agents, so small that they cannot be seen under the light microscope, and they are different because they are not really "alive" in the usual sense of the word. Unlike other micro-organisms, they cannot grow and divide by themselves. A virus particle consists of a central core of nucleic acid, which is the material responsible for the genetic code, surrounded by a protein coat. It does not have any of the organized structures necessary for the life of a true cell, and so the term particle

Mild mosaic symptoms on two outer leaves. Centre leaf is healthy.

(or virion) describes it very well.

If viruses are so small and inert, how do they get about and cause diseases? In the case of plants they are mostly carried by leaf-sucking insects such as aphids. When an aphid feeds it sucks up sap from the plant; it then wanders around and tries a fresh area, usually near the growing buds and young leaves. When the insect pierces the epidermal cells, it dribbles in a little saliva before it starts to feed and, if it has been previously taking sap from an infected cell, some of the virus particles it has imbibed from that cell will be dribbled into the new cell with the saliva. Once inside the host the virion sheds its coat, the nucleic acid is then exposed, and it is able to influence the genetic code of the host cell and instruct it to make new virus particles. If the virus is a very forceful one, it can order the host cell to stop its normal activities and direct all its energies to making virus particles, until it bursts and dies, releasing the millions of new virions it has made. At the other extreme, the virus may cause little or no disruption in the host cell's activities, ensuring only that a few new virions are made which lie dormant in the cell.

The interactions between the host and the virus determine what symptoms appear on the infected plant. Most viruses can only multiply within a single susceptible species, or family of plants, because the cells of unrelated plants are able to resist instructions given by the viral genetic code. A virus which can cause severe symptoms on a potato plant may not cause any signs when inoculated into a tomato plant, although the host cells will then replicate, that is, reproduce identical virus particles. We then have the confusing situation of apparently healthy "carrier plants" harbouring a potentially virulent virus without showing any symptoms, while providing a reservoir from which travelling insects can spread infection. These carriers are just as likely to be weeds as other related garden plants.

To add to the confusion, no exact criterion exists for the diagnosis of a plant virus disease. None of the symptoms is exclusive, but the commonest is probably the mottling of leaves in different shades of green and yellow, which is described as "mosaic". This symptom is unfortunately also found in various deficiency diseases. Sometimes there is a yellowing, or chlorosis, which may become generalized over the whole leaf or may be restricted to chlorotic areas arranged in concentric circles called "ring spots". Some virus infections produce dark-green bands bounding the veins, while in others the veins appear translucent. Various types of leaf curl and crinkle are also characteristic of virus infections, as is the appearance of necrotic spots. Viruses may prevent the elongation of the stem so that all the leaves grow in one place, producing symptoms known as "bunchy-top" and "rosette". Other infections result in a proliferation of shoots described as "fern leaf" and "witches broom". The best advice is to pull up and burn plants showing any abnormal growth patterns and mottled leaves; they may be sources of virus infection in your garden.

Another condition attributable to viral infection is the so-called degeneration of plant stock. This occurs in plants such as raspberries, strawberries and potatoes, in which next year's plants are propagated from the roots or stems of the old plants. When the stock becomes infected by a mild or slow virus, as it almost inevitably will, a progressive deterioration in the condition of the plants will be seen in subsequent years. A similar type of transmission of virus from one generation to another may take place during grafting if either root stock or scion is infected.

In recent years some of the plant "yellows" infections previously attributed to viruses have proved to be yet another diverse group of pathogens called spiroplasmas. This is the only mention we will make of them, since they are insect-transmitted, and as far as the home vegetable garden is concerned, they behave like viruses.

Pests

This is only a general guide to common garden pests; later sections on individual vegetables include a greater variety of them, along with advice on their control.

Aphids: These are a continual menace in the garden. They attack virtually every plant and weed, sucking the juices from stems, leaves, flowers and roots. They not only spread disease, but also secrete honeydew which attracts ants and provides suitable conditions for the growth of sooty mold.

There are many different types of aphids which vary in size and colour. These insects have a complicated life cycle and produce many generations in one season. The eggs overwinter in the soil and hatch in the spring.

It is essential to control these pests, a relatively easy task. Douse with a strong jet from

Aphid

the garden hose or bucket of soapy water, or dust with rotenone. Also, the defenceless aphids have many natural predators, the most important being the lady beetle.

Earwigs: The European earwig is now a pest in many parts of the country. It attacks fruits, ornamentals and many vegetables including raspberries, beans, carrots, celery, corn, lettuce and potatoes. The adults are about three-quarters of an inch long and reddish-brown in colour. The males have a large pair of curved pincers at the rear end which are, in fact, harmless. The female lays eggs in the soil, and when the young are about one-quarter of an inch long they leave the nest and search for food. Nocturnal, they hide during the day in crevices and on plants with closely packed leaves. A second batch of eggs may hatch in July. In seasons when the insect is very numerous, the earwigs can become a nuisance in the house as well as in the garden. As adults they overwinter in the soils.

Flea beetles: These pests derive their name from the fact that they jump like fleas when disturbed. There are many types of flea beetles; all attack the foliage of plants. They can carry with them virus diseases, and the holes they chew in leaves are open invitations to fungal and bacterial infections. The adults overwinter in garden refuse and in spring eggs are laid in the soil, the larvae emerging at planting time to feed on germinating seeds. They are a particular problem during a long, cool spring when germination is delayed. The fall garden clean-up is most important, as is the control of insects during the growing season.

Leafhoppers: There are many species of this pest that attack most of the common garden vegetables. Leafhoppers are usually pale green to yellow in colour, are wedge-shaped and measure half an inch in length. When plants are disturbed, the winged adults can be seen hopping around while the wingless nymphs scurry under the leaves. Damage is caused by the hoppers sucking the juices from the plants, transmitting diseases and laying scores of eggs on leaves and stems. Several generations occur each season, and therefore regular insect control is essential.

Tarnished plant bug: Most of our vegetable and fruit crops, as well as many ornamental plants can be damaged by this bug which injects a poison into the plant causing various injuries. A blackening of the leaf tips on the various plants is the first important signal of their presence.

The adult bug is tarnish-coloured, flat, oval shaped and measures a quarter of an inch in length. The distinguishing feature is a clear, yellow triangle containing a black dot on the lower part of each side of the bug.

Treat with rotenone or Diatomaceous earth immediately the blackened leaf tips or the bug itself is noticed.

Earwig   Flea beetle   Leafhopper   Tarnished plant bug   White grub

Whitefly: Whiteflies are rarely a serious problem outdoors, but in the house or greenhouse they can cause considerable damage if not controlled. These pests are seldom noticed until the plant is dusturbed at which time they fly out in a cloud.

They are sucking insects that feed on the sap of the plants, leaving a sticky secretion called honeydew, which is an ideal breeding ground for sooty mold. This mold or fungus can easily be detected with the naked eye, and the gardener, alerted to the fact that whiteflies are probably the cause, can be on the lookout.

It is not easy to control whiteflies in the garden. Spraying the undersides of leaves with a strong jet of water may help. If the infestation is severe and causing distress to the plants early in the season, it would be advisable to consult your local agricultural representative.

Whiteflies found outdoors late in the season are unlikely to damage the crop. Indoors, they must be controlled by repeated spraying with a recommended insecticide or soap.

White grubs: These are the larvae of the June bug (sometimes called May beetle). The life cycle is complex and provides the grub two summers in which to feed on the roots or tubers of plants. During the first season the June bug lays eggs in grassy areas. They hatch in about two weeks' time. The grubs spend the first summer a few inches below the soil surface, feeding on roots and burrowing quite deeply to overwinter. As the second season begins, they again come to within a few inches of the surface, where they remain, feeding on available material. They burrow again in the fall to spend a second winter underground. The third season they pupate in early summer and remain in the soil as an adult for the third winter. The fourth season they emerge as June bugs, and the life cycle starts all over again. White grubs are most often found in gardens that are being newly developed from lawn or sodded areas. After a garden has been worked for a year or two, white grubs are not a problem.

"Good Guys"

The good guys in our gardens are the predators and parasites which feed on harmful insects. Among the predators are the ground beetle and the lady bug or beetle.

Ground beetles: These insects are large, black, fast-moving beetles, whose long pointed jaws are ideal for grasping other insects. Both adults and larvae feed on several garden pests.

Lady beetles: Lady beetles are small, orange, hemispherical beetles with a varying number of black spots, but the norm is twelve. This welcome visitor to the garden dines constantly on aphids and mealybugs. Be aware that lady beetles can be mistaken for Mexican bean beetles and squash beetles, which have eight and seven dark spots, respectively, on each front wing.

Praying mantises, snakes, toads, and aleochara are also among the many fairweather friends in our gardens. Biological control of insects is a relatively new field that is developing rapidly. Readers who are interested in investigating further should obtain the most up-to-date information available.

Ground beetle   **Lady beetle**

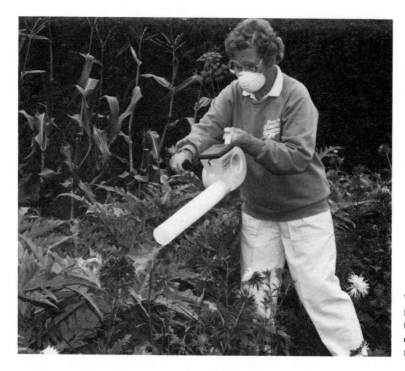

When dusting plants with a fungicide or insecticide follow the instructions on the label carefully and always wear a face mask.

Controling Pests

Gardeners use many different techniques to achieve the same ends. The method we have found the most effective and safest to use is the Floating Row Cover. Not only does it keep the flying insects out, it also creates a beneficial climate around the plants. This climate provides for more rapid growth in the early spring and hence, earlier crops. Row covers are made of a very light spun-bonded material under which the plants grow. The covers need to be anchored to the ground on either side with stones or with soil piled along the edges. Enough space must be left under the covers to permit the plants to grow. Also, crops that are insect pollinated, such as tomatoes and peppers should not be covered.

When row covers cannot be used or are not available, it may become necessary to either spray or dust. We prefer to dust as it is much faster. We keep the garden duster in the tool shed filled and ready to use. Destructive insects should be controlled as soon as they are noticed and not allowed to multiply and spread through the garden.

Diatomaceous earth is a non-toxic control of soft-bodied insects. Rotenone, although poisonous to fish, is relatively safe for use around animals. It should be used with caution. When dusting, always work up-wind and apply the dust when the leaves are wet from either rain or early morning dew. It is important to protect yourself against the risk of inhaling the dust. Wear a mask and protective clothing. Read the label before using any product.

Some gardeners prefer to spray. In a small garden a ready-to-use spray mixture may be all that is needed. Insecticidal soap is effective against some pests. We have also found detergent helpful. It should be washed off shortly after using to prevent leaf burn.

We like to use products that are biodegradable and leave no residual effects. Rodale's book, "Pest and Disease Control in the Home Garden," is the most up to date comprehensive publication available for home gardeners.

Disease and Pest Control in the Garden

The foregoing plant problems that may occur in your garden can be controlled to a major extent. The following summary of controls will also remind the reader of some of the gardening practices recommended in earlier parts of this book.

Spring

1. When raising seedlings indoors, use sterilized soil (or medium) and containers.
2. Use only top quality virus-resistant seed treated against fungus infection, if available.
3. Plant only fruit canes, bushes, or plants carrying disease-free government certification.
4. Plant only seed potatoes that are government certified disease-free.
5. Space crops and rows to allow for good ventilation and avoid overcrowding as plants grow.
6. Practice crop rotation.
7. When rotating crops, make sure that the new plants are not susceptible to the same diseases as the ones they replace.
8. Use paper (or other) collars on transplants to avoid cutworm damage.
9. Use only well-rotted manure or compost.
10. Use fertilizers and lime with caution. A soil analysis is recommended.
11. Certain controls must be used early to be effective (for example to fight the cucumber beetle).

Summer

1. Practice the best possible garden sanitation. Pull up and destroy (do not compost) diseased plants as soon as noticed.
2. Control weeds in and around the vegetable plot. They can harbour fungi and virus-carrying insects.
3. Water only as needed. Drip irrigation is preferable to sprinkling.
4. Maintain adequate moisture level in ground at all times. When watering, soak the ground thoroughly. Never apply light sprinklings.
5. Do not walk around rows of plants, brushing against them when they are wet.
6. Keep plants and particularly fruit off the ground by staking or other means.
7. Do not overfertilize, particularly with nitrogen.
8. Watch raspberries for signs of cane borers. Prune 6 inches below tell-tale entrance holes, or until pith is no longer discoloured.
9. Pull pea vines as soon as main crop is harvested.
10. Compost all post-harvest litter unless infected.
11. Prune fruit to minimize crowding of foliage in centre of bush, thereby allowing sunlight to enter and air to circulate.
12. Check Brassicas regularly, particularly when white cabbage butterfly is seen. Also check potatoes for blight or beetles. Treat if necessary.

Fall

1. Remove and burn old raspberry canes as well as weak, spindly new growth.
2. After crops are harvested, remove remaining debris to the compost heap. Burn any diseased materials.
3. Spread well-rotted manure or compost on vacant areas. Cultivate.
4. When harvesting crops for winter stoage:
   a) take care not to damage produce
   b) dry roots and tubers outdoors in sun shine before storing
   c) store at recommended temperatures.

PART TWO

Vegetables, Fruits and Herbs

"The cure for this ill is not to sit still,
Or frowst with a book by the fire
But to take a large hoe and a shovel also
And dig till you gently perspire."

Rudyard Kipling
1865-1930

CHAPTER 12

Vegetable Families

The vegetables in this book are grouped by families. The reason why is explained in the section on "Crop Rotation". Although, in a small garden plot, crop rotation principles are not always workable, it should be practiced as much as possible.

AMARYLLIDACEAE: The Onion Family
Includes Garlic, Leeks, Onions and Chives

These members of the Onion family vary widely in flavour and play a very important role in cooking. Without onions, chefs would be hard-put to produce their many delectable dishes.

Garlic: *Allium sativum*

Garlic is an herb native to southern Europe and was transported to many other parts of the world at a very early period in history. The ancient Egyptians held it in great esteem, while the Israelites in the wilderness lamented to Moses about the lack of it. The Romans fed garlic to their labourers to strengthen them, and to their armies because of its health-giving properties. It was probably the Romans who introduced garlic to the rest of Europe. In North America we consider garlic to be a culinary herb of some importance. The juice of a small clove greatly enhances the flavour of many dishes.

Garlic is easy to grow if it is planted either in the fall or as early in the spring as the ground can be worked. Cool temperatures for early growth are essential. However, at the late stage of growth garlic can tolerate hot weather, and for this reason it can be planted in the main garden where it will get full sunshine. In too shady a location bulbs will be poorly formed. A mature garlic bulb consists of a number of bulblets, or cloves, each of which can be planted. One such bulb will produce enough cloves for the average home gardener to plant. Because few seed catalogues include garlic, many gardeners use bulbs purchased at the supermarket for propagation.

These cloves should be planted with the fat end down, one or two inches deep and four to six inches apart. The soil should be well-drained but with a high organic content. An area that was well manured the previous year is perfect. As the bulbs reach maturity, withhold fertilizer and water. The plants will look like onions and will be about one foot high.

During the summer the leaves can be cut and added to salads or used in cooking. The main harvest will take place after the tops have died down. The bulbs should be pulled up and left lying on the ground until the tops are completely dry, then brought into a shed and cured like onions. Some people like to braid the stalks and hang them up. Others prefer to cut the tops off and keep the bulbs in an airy container.

Garlic is subject to most of the same ailments as onions, but seems to be more disease-resistant.

Leeks: *Allium porrum*

The leek is a plant native to southern Europe and the Near East. Records indicate it was revered by the early Egyptians who grew it among the vegetables under general cultivation. The Romans are believed to have introduced leeks to Britain, and Saxon writings record them as being considered valuable food. To this day, leeks are very popular in Europe and the British Isles, and should be seen far more often in North American kitchen gardens.

The leek that grows wild in eastern North American forests has a very pungent odour and is in no way similar to our garden variety.

The cultivated leek is the aristocrat of the onion tribe, being both mild and delicate in flavour. Many novice gardeners find leeks hard to grow, and the instructions given on most seed packages are not sufficient to produce a good crop.

Leeks need a long growing season to mature. To assure a good crop, the seed must be started eight to ten weeks before planting-out time. Leeks can tolerate light frost and can be set out in the garden about two weeks before the last frost-free date. For people who do not have a hot-frame, start the seed indoors in the same manner as other transplants. We use a hot-frame and sow the seed quite thickly in drills. Because germination is often irregular and poor, it is easier to thin the rows

1. Leek seedling removed from seed bed.
2. Seedling with top and root trimmed prior to transplanting.
3. Leeks planted in trench. Good soil should be placed on top of well-rotted manure or compost.
4. Fill trench as plant grows.
5. Hill leeks as necessary to ensure blanching.
6. Dig carefully, removing soil first, to avoid damaging mature plants. Leeks develop a strong root system.

if necessary than to have insufficient plants. The seedlings remain in the frame until they reach the size of a thin pencil and are ready to be planted out in the garden.

The best results are obtained by planting leeks in a trench dug with a spade. Dig a trench 8-10 inches deep and the width of the spade. Pile the soil on either side of the trench or spread it over the bed. If the topsoil in the garden is shallow, do not make the trench so deep. Well-rotted manure or compost should be forked into the bottom of the

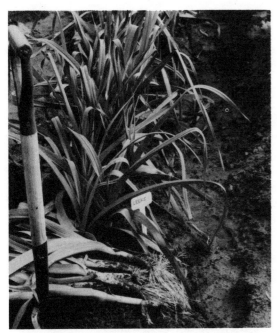

The first harvest. Remaining crop continues growing. Leeks are harvested August through October.

trench and some good soil placed on top of it. Use a small pointed stick or pencil to make holes for planting. Trim the tops and roots of the seedlings before planting. Keep well watered. Fertilize the plants every two weeks with weak liquid manure or fertilizer (5:10:5). As the plants grow, gradually fill in the trench with the soil from either side, or peat moss, leaving the green fan-like growth exposed. If the trench is not deep, hill the plants to blanch them. Unblanched leeks are tough and lack good flavour.

Some harvesting may be done as soon as the plants are large enough. Leeks can withstand quite a hard frost when mature, and should be kept in the ground as long as possible. Dig only as needed for immediate use. I dig all our plants before freeze-up, and put a four-week supply in the crisper; the rest go in the freezer. Gardeners whose land dries out early in the spring can leave a crop in the ground over winter, and have freshly dug leeks the following spring.

Leeks do not require processing before being put in the freezer. All they need is careful washing to remove any sand particles from between the leaves. The thick, white stems should be cut into 2-inch lengths, bagged and frozen. The more tender of the green tops can be thinly chopped and frozen for later use in soups.

It is the long white stems of the leek that we eat. These can be sliced finely and used as a substitute for onions in salads, or cooked.

BOILED LEEKS IN CREAM SAUCE
Cut the leeks into whatever lengths you desire. I prefer them about 6-inches long. Steam or boil until tender, using as little water as possible. Strain and keep this water. Make a cream sauce using the water and a dash of sherry and serve hot.

Leftover leeks and mashed potatoes can be combined, creamed in the blender and diluted with chicken stock and/or milk to make a delicious soup that can be served either hot or cold. A garnish of chives or parsley completes the dish.

Onions: *Allium cepa*

Of all the vegetables, the onion is the most widely used in cooking. It may be eaten raw, cooked as a vegetable on its own, or as an important addition to many thousands of recipes. Onions are believed to have originated in southwest Asia, although various members of the onion family are known to be native in many other parts of the world. The Greek historian, Herodotus, has recorded that in the Great Pyramid of Cheops there is an inscription which states that 1,600 talents of silver were paid to supply the workers with onions, garlic and radishes. The Egyptians held the onion in exceedingly high esteem and worshipped it as a deity, believing the layers of the bulb represented the various spheres of the earth, heaven and hell. They were aware of the rich food value of the onion and gave the workers a daily ration.

The onion belongs to the Amaryllis family and is closely related to garlic, leeks and chives. Nowadays we have a wide range of varieties to choose from, but before selecting seed, consider the method of cultivation to be adopted. There are three methods commonly used in growing onions: by sets, by seed and by seedling plants.

Onion sets: The simplest and most dependable method of growing onions for the novice gardener is the onion set. These are small onion bulbs that have been grown under controlled conditions from seed the previous year. The sets should not exceed a 3/4-inch diameter; 1/2-inch is the ideal. Large sets are likely to "bolt", that is, mature too rapidly, and go to seed. The onion, a biennial, has a tendency to form seed in the second year of growth.

Sets are planted in drills deep enough to cover the bulbs. I plant two drills about 6 inches apart. Some people prefer drills 12 to 18 inches apart to allow for cultivation between rows. If the sets are to be grown as the main crop for winter storage, allow 3 to 4 inches between bulbs. If you want small, early green onions, plant them more densely, harvesting as desired.

For winter storage we grow main crop onion sets. There are now many varieties on the market offering such differing characteristics as colour, shape, size and keeping quality. Some new hybrids can be stored for as long as eighteen months.

If any of the plants go to seed, break off the seed blossom, and use these onions quickly for they will not store well.

Multiplier sets will produce very early spring onions. These sets each have several cloves or bulblets that can be divided and

A forest of healthy, growing onions. They were seeded in rows 18 inches apart directly in the garden in late April.

Drying onions in the garden prior to bringing them into a shed. Those in the foreground were planted as "sets". Some have gone to seed and will not keep long in storage.

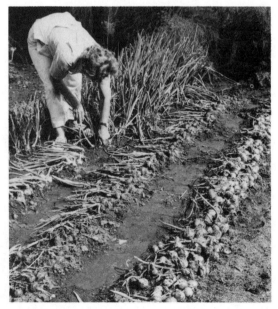

planted individually. Each set or bulblet will send up a cluster of very tasty young shoots ready to harvest in three to four weeks. Successive planting should be made for about six weeks or as long as the bulblets remain firm.

Seed: Onion seed can be sown directly in the garden as soon as the ground can be worked. If the seed is sown thickly, thin the seedlings when very young and use the thinnings as scallions or green onions. If the plants are left growing in crowded conditions, the bulbs will be very small. With certain varieties these small bulbs, when cured, can be used the following year as sets. If the plants are thinned to a space of 4 to 6 inches, they will form large bulbs, suitable for storage and winter use.

Onion seedling plants: These should be started indoors in February or March. When large enough to handle, transplant the seedlings into flats and harden before transplanting into the garden when danger of severe frost is past. These seedlings should be the size of a pencil and be spaced 6 inches apart in the rows. Very large onions can be grown this way, but they require a great deal more time and effort.

It is important to prepare the ground thoroughly before planting any onions. The soil should be fertile and high in organic matter. Work in well-rotted manure, compost and wood ash if available. A sprinkling of 5:10:5 or 5:10:10 fertilizer also helps. If clay conditions prevail in the garden, make a raised bed to ensure good drainage. Onions are very sensitive to wet, soggy ground. Onions are one of the few crops that you can grow in the same bed several years running; it is therefore well worth putting extra work into the preparation of the bed, especially important in gardens with poor soil conditions.

Onions are heavy feeders and benefit from additional fertilizing. A balanced fertilizer or weak liquid manure can be given after the plants are growing strongly, but not when the

Onions drying in a shed. Curing takes two to three weeks.

bulbs have started to form. For their early growth onions prefer cool weather conditions and plenty of moisture (but not sogginess), during which time they make strong leafy growth. Then in July and August, during hot, dry conditions, they form a large bulb.

Green onions and scallions can be grown in partial shade but the bulbs must have full sun. Onions are sensitive to day length, and should attain maximum top growth before the days become shorter.

As the onion bed is rich, fertile and moist, it is also an ideal place for weeds. Weeding the rows by hand, when the weeds are small, is a relatively simple job. If the weeds are allowed to grow sufficiently large that the root system will interfere with the onion, damage will occur when weeding. Hoe between the rows.

In late summer or early fall the onion tops will start to die down naturally, so there is no need to bend them over. If you decide to give them a little help, be careful not to bruise the necks, this will shorten storage life. When the tops have died down, pull the bulbs out of the ground, place them in rows and leave them to dry in the sun for several days. Next, bring them into the garage or tool shed, spread them out and leave to cure for several weeks. If you intend to "braid" them before hanging them, leave the tops on; otherwise, cut them off one inch above the bulb.

Before there is any risk of freezing temperatures, bring the bulbs indoors and store in a cool, well-ventilated and dry area. Only certain varieties are recommended for winter storage.

We ran into an unexpected problem during the curing stage. A family of squirrels discovered our onions in the garage and made off with a large part of the crop before we noticed. Fortunately, we found their cache in a box in the rafters above.

Problems and Controls

Onion maggots: The most serious problem usually encountered with the onion family is the onion maggot. The first sign of something amiss is when the plant begins to wilt. Experienced gardeners detect maggot damage very quickly and take immediate steps to remedy the situation.

Onion bulb infested with maggots.

Onion maggots are the larvae of a small fly, which lays its eggs on the soil surface around the onions. The maggots are about 1/3 inch long and burrow into onion bulbs, killing the young plants. Our method of controlling maggots is to use floating row covers. If I notice any wilting plants, I remove and destroy the damaged bulbs. There are other products on the market for controlling maggots and new developments are reported in government pamphlets.

Thrips: Small, yellowish sucking insects called thrips may attack the leaves of the onion family. If the leaves have a mottled appearance, look for thrips. They can be controlled satisfactorily by dusting or spraying with a recommended pesticide.

Onion smut: This fungus can live in the soil for years. It attacks only young seedlings (not sets), usually in cool, damp seasons. Onion smut is not often encountered in home gardens. If it should occur, make sure you do not plant onion seed or seedlings in the same soil for several years following. In fact, it would be safer not to plant onion seeds at all for a few years. The fungus can be identified by a blackening of the small seedling and can be avoided by planting disease-resistant sets.

Downy mildew: This fungus disease occurs during cool, wet weather. It is a light-coloured, downy coating that will cause the leaves to yellow and die. It can be easily controlled by several applications of a recommended fungicide. As soon as the mildew is noticed, begin treatment.

Thick neck: While harvesting, you may notice that some of your onions have not died down properly and will have quite a thick neck. These onions will not cure, and should be eaten first as they will not last in storage. The term "thick neck" describes this condition.

CHENOPODIACEAE: The Beet Family
Includes Beet, Chard, and Spinach

Beets: *Beta vulgaris*

Beets, or beetroot as it is known in England, is native to southern Europe. It is a coastal plant, and although it does best in a sandy loam, it will thrive in any good soil. Beets do well in full sun but can tolerate partial shade. As with all root crops, the soil should be worked to a depth of at least 8 inches and be free of clods and stones. Well-rotted manure dug into the soil enriches it, allowing better germination and rapid growth of the plants. The more rapid the growth, the better the quality of the beets. Each beet seed will produce a cluster of three or four plants. Plant about ten seeds per foot of row at a depth of half an inch. Cover and tamp firmly. Allow 12 to 15 inches between rows. Germination takes eight to ten days. If the weather is dry and hot, we cover the row with a board, removing it at the first sign of germination. This prevents the seed and soil from drying out at the critical stage. When the seedlings are four to six inches high, thin them, using the thinnings as greens. Subsequent thinning should be done as the roots mature and become crowded in the row.

Beets are at their prime when they are young. Harvest them when they reach about two inches in diameter. Also, the tops may be eaten either in salads or cooked like spinach. Make successive plantings every two weeks until mid-July.

Beets benefit from a light application of salt worked into the ground before seeding, not more than an ounce per square yard. We also give our plants one more treat when they are four to six inches tall: one tablespoon of salt to one gallon of water. We give the plants a good soaking. This should be applied only when the plants are actively growing and the soil is moist. Never allow beets to dry out or they will become "woody".

There is now a golden beet on the market. This variety is especially valuable as a dual-purpose vegetable. While the root is still growing, the leaves may be picked and used like spinach. The root does not "bleed" and will not discolour other ingredients in a salad. Beets are now available in various shapes and sizes, with maturing times ranging from 40 to 80 days.

I would recommend that the novice gardener study a seed catalogue before purchasing any seed, and avoid novelty varieties in the first year.

Beets do not have many problems. Our worst enemy is a very pretty goldfinch who pecks holes in the leaves.

In overlimed gardens black spots, dry rot and scab may occur on the roots because boron is less available to the plants in sweet soil. A soil test will determine the pH level, which should read between 6.0 and 6.8.

Beets taste better when freshly harvested, so pull only enough for immediate use. However, when the main crop is ready, the

Rinsing newly harvested beets in a rainwater barrel.

beets should be harvested and frozen, pickled or stored in the cool room for winter use.

To freeze, cook thoroughly, cool before dicing and put in plastic bags or containers in the freezer. For the cool room, either pack in boxes of sand or in ventilated plastic bags. I prefer the latter method and find the beets remain firm for several months.

Chard: *Beta vulgaris cicla*

Chard, also called Swiss chard, is a close relative of the beet, and also native to southern Europe. For best results the soil should be rich in organic content and have good drainage. The seeds should be sown 3/4-inch deep and thinned to a distance of 8 to 12 inches. Allow 2 feet between rows. Chard can tolerate partial shade, and prefers cool temperatures.

In our garden we grow four plants, which are ample for our needs. Chard is rather like rhubarb in appearance, having a long thick stalk and a large leaf. Both the stalk and the leaf are eaten. The stalk is cooked like celery and the leaf used in the same manner as spinach, either cooked or in salads. Chard

will grow to a height of 2 to 2½ feet, and will produce well into the fall as only the outer leaves are cut or pulled, leaving the rest of the plant in the ground to continue growing.

There are several varieties available. Some have green or white stalks, while the colourful rhubard chard with its bright crimson stalks and crumply leaves is very appealing to the eye, and may be grown in flower beds.

Chard is relatively free from troubles. Aphids and leaf miners are sometimes a problem, but can be controlled by covering plants with floating row covers.

Spinach: *Spinacia oleracea*

Spinach is one of the earliest vegetables known to man. A most important green vegetable, it is very rich in vitamin A, iron and calcium, high in ascorbic acid, and riboflavin, and also has some thiamine.

Spinach is a fast-growing, cool-weather crop that must be seeded directly in the garden as soon as the ground is prepared. Spinach requires rich, moisture retentive soil. The seed bed should be enriched by digging in well-rotted manure or compost. The

Left: Chard in late season. *Below:* A healthy row of spinach ready for harvesting in early June.

ground cannot be too rich for this crop. A light soil and short drought will cause the plants to bolt.

I like to grow spinach in small plots, three rows wide, with the rows 6 inches apart and the plots 18 inches wide. Some gardeners prefer to grow spinach in single rows 12 inches apart. Another method is to broadcast the seed in a prepared seed bed, then rake it in and tamp it down. Successive plantings may be made during early spring, but not during the summer because of the plants' tendency to bolt quickly during hot weather. Plants must be kept well watered, and the addition of a high nitrogen fertilizer to the soil before planting is helpful.

When watering the growing plants, use liquid manure or a high nitrogen liquid fertilizer. Wait until early August before planting seed for fall crops; light frost will not hurt spinach.

Spinach can tolerate partial shade, but we have found that when grown in full sun, growth is more rapid and the quality of the crop much better. We start harvesting the leaves about six weeks after seeding, or when they are sufficiently mature. This will vary from season to season. We pick only the outer leaves and allow the plants to continue growing until they show signs of going to seed. The entire crop is then harvested by cutting the stems at ground level, usually about ten weeks after seeding. This is the crop that I process for the freezer.

Poached eggs and spinach make a delicious breakfast dish, and is quick and easy to prepare. Early season salads can be prepared using only spinach. We prefer the crinkly leafed savoy varieties for this purpose. A freshly picked spinach salad is hard to beat.

New Zealand Spinach: *Tetragonia expansa*

This is not, in fact, a member of the beet family, but belongs to the Aizoaceae, the carpet-weed family. It is included here because, for culinary purposes, it is treated like spinach.

Unlike ordinary spinach, this plant thrives in hot weather and produces throughout the summer. It is called a perennial spinach in the seed catalogues, but I have found that hard frost will kill it. Many home gardeners grow New Zealand spinach and enjoy it; it is not, however, a favourite in our house. This is simply a matter of taste, probably because there are so many other more luscious vegetables which thrive in the hot weather and mature at the same time as the New Zealand spinach. Two or three plants would be sufficient for the average family, as this variety of spinach becomes a small prostrate bush spreading about 2 feet in all directions. For use, pick the tender young leaves at the tips of the branches and cook in the same manner as ordinary spinach. When eaten raw in salads, it may leave a dry taste in the mouth.

Problems and Controls

Leaf miner: This pest is common to both beets and chard. It is a small, white maggot that burrows into the tissue of the leaves, causing considerable distress to the plants. The main vein of the leaf will show discolouration, and the leaves will be misshapen and wilted. The leaf miner can be controlled by the use of floating row covers.

Web worm: These larvae attack the undersides of the leaves. The insects are not generally considered serious problems and can be controlled by spraying or dusting.

Spinach yellows: This virus disease is spread by aphids. You can recognize it by a mottling and yellowing of the leaves and stunted growth of the entire plant. The best control is to purchase disease-resistant seed, and if aphids are seen, dust or spray the plants. Any diseased plants should be burned. Generally speaking, beets, chard and spinach are easy crops to grow and are not normally disease prone.

COMPOSITAE: The Sunflower or Thistle Family
Includes Globe Artichoke, Jerusalem Artichoke, Endive, Escarole, Witloof Chicory and Lettuce

Globe Artichoke: *Cynara scolymus*

The globe artichoke is a gourmet vegetable only recommended for the garden where space is not a concern and the gardener enjoys experimenting. We have grown artichokes for a number of years. Usually we have a most successful crop; occasionally, a failure.

The globe artichoke is a perennial plant native to the Mediterranean region and the Canary Islands. Therefore, it must be grown in full sunlight. It closely resembles a thistle and attains a height of two to three feet. The flower buds are the edible portion of the plant. In our climate it is treated as an annual, but in milder areas globe artichokes may survive the winter if heavily mulched after freeze-up. Globe artichokes must be started indoors in early March using the same method as for other transplants. If the transplants become too large for the Jiffy-7's or flats, it may be necessary to pot them up individually. Don't grow too many. Ten plants in the garden should be ample for the average household.

Set the transplant outdoors the third week in May if the weather is warm. Allow three feet between plants, as well as between rows. Artichokes need rich soil and plenty of water. Feed regularly with a balanced fertilizer or manure tea. The first or main bud should be ready to harvest by early August, after which side shoots will produce smaller buds that are just as tasty as the original.

The only problem we have encountered is a small black fly that attacks the buds. Watch for it and control by spraying or dusting.

Harvest buds when the petals are still tight by cutting the stem two to three inches below the bud. This stem is also edible. Wash thoroughly and soak in cold, salted water for

Globe artichoke ready for harvest. Notice the secondary bud which will be left for a later harvest. The leaves show signs of damage by the flea beetle; however, the buds themselves are free of injury.

thirty minutes before cooking.

Cook in boiling water until the stalk-end is tender when prodded with a skewer. Drain upside down. Serve hot with melted butter, or cold with a salad dressing or Hollandaise sauce. If the buds open and are no longer edible, these flowers can be air dried and used in flower arrangements.

Jerusalem Artichokes: *Helianthus tuberosus*

A tuberous perennial plant native to eastern North America and the Pacific coast, the Jerusalem artichoke grows in moist, peaty soils.

Nobody seems to know why it is called "artichoke"; it is in no way similar to the globe artichoke. It is, however, a member of the sunflower family. Nor does it have any connection with the Holy Land. The name "Jerusalem" is probably derived from the Italian word "girasol" (turning to the sun), so called by the Italian sailors who reputedly brought the tubers back to Europe after being introduced to them by the North American natives.

The Jerusalem artichoke is far better known in Europe and the British Isles than it is in its native North America, and deserves far more attention in the home garden when space is available. It is exceedingly easy to grow and seems to have no enemies. The only disadvantage of this vegetable is that unless allotted a large separate area of the garden, it can take over the whole plot and become very hard to eradicate. These sun-loving members of the sunflower family will send up a strong upright stem and grow to a height of eight to ten feet.

For these reasons I plant it in a 10 by 10 foot plot, treat it as a perennial and do not rotate. Instead, I ensure that sufficient nutrients are provided through manure and fertilizing. The tubers are the edible part and are planted like potatoes, 12 inches apart in rows with 1½ to 2 feet between rows. They do well in any soil, but best in a light, sandy loam enriched with well-rotted manure. After planting, we water the bed thoroughly if it is dry, then apply a mulch. The mulch controls the weeds and retains the moisture so that very little care is needed before harvesting in the fall. Frost improves the flavour and quality of the tubers. Dig only the amount required for immediate use and continue harvesting all through the winter if conditions permit. We often dig tubers at Christmas when it is necessary to clear the snow and mulch away before getting to the tubers.

In the spring, continue harvesting until the tubers begin to sprout. Then, dig up the entire bed, removing the tubers; dig in more manure or compost; add a complete fertilizer (a few handfuls sprinkled lightly over the area) and re-plant in rows. You are sure to have plenty of tubers left over; keep these in plastic bags in the cool room or refrigerator until used. The artichokes you keep to eat should be the size of medium potatoes. The tubers are nobbly, and for this reason smaller ones are very tedious to prepare for the table. They are best kept for seed.

Left: When we are ready to "do" the artichoke patch, I bring the garden cart and a spade. First, I pile the old mulch along the edge of the bed. Then I dig systematically, throwing the tubers, which will have begun to "shoot", into the cart. *Below:* The new planting, fertilized and watered, soon begins to "take off". No more attention is needed until the fall, except for the occasional watering in very hot, dry weather.

Above: After the first frost the tall, sunflower-like plants are cut down to about one foot and covered in mulch. (The old mulch will probably have "broken down".) Thereafter, I dig tubers as I need them until Christmas. The tops are carted away and can be composted. *Right:* Harvesting Jerusalem artichoke tubers.

ARTICHOKES IN CREAM SAUCE
To prevent discolouring, peel thinly under water to which is added one teaspoonful of lemon juice or white vinegar; add one teaspoon of lemon juice or white vinegar to cooking water; simmer until tender; strain; serve in white sauce.

JERUSALEM ARTICHOKE SOUP
Prepare artichokes as in previous recipe; use stock for cooking; when tender puree in blender; thicken with flour, cornflour or arrowroot (blended with milk); season to taste. Mashed potato added to the puree gives a better consistency.

JERUSALEM ARTICHOKE SALAD
Slice thinly or grate artichokes; sprinkle with lemon juice and add to salads.

BOILED ARTICHOKES
Wash thoroughly; place in a saucepan; cover with boiling water; simmer until tender when prodded with a skewer (about twenty minutes). Serve the same as potatoes.

Endive and Escarole: *Chicorium endivia*

Endive is believed to have orginated in East India, spreading throughout Europe and the Orient at a very early date in history. The ancient Egyptians used it as a vegetable and the Greeks as a salad and pot herb.

The endive we know today differs little from its ancestor, and is used mostly in salads. There are two major varieties: "green curled", which has very curly, serrated leaves, and the "broad leafed Bavarian" which has large, closely packed, upright leaves and is usually marketed under the name escarole.

The general culture of these two varieties is similar to that of lettuce. Endive does best in well-drained soil enriched with plenty of well-rotted manure or compost. Never use fresh manure as this would cause the flavour of the endive to be rank and the growth too lush. Endive is a cool-weather crop which can tolerate partial shade and requires about three months to mature. The seed should be sown as soon as the ground has been worked in the spring. Sow only a small amount at one time, but make subsequent seedings every two weeks or so, as with lettuce. Thin the plants to one foot apart after they have developed sufficiently. Endive can be sown in a seed-bed and the seedlings transplanted to the main garden. Both methods are equally satisfactory.

The flavour of endive is rather bitter unless the plants are blanched three weeks prior to harvesting. When plants are nearing maturity, cover them with an inverted flower pot or with a box or boards. Usually three large flower pots or boxes are all the home gardener requires; this gives a succession of plants being blanched. One large head of endive supplies the average family with ample salads for a week. Endives can also be served cooked or steamed in the same way as spinach. Plants ready for harvesting should be cut before going to seed.

For winter use the roots of Endive can be dug up, repotted into a deep pot and brought indoors to a cool dry, dark location. Shoots will emerge and these should be blanched in a similar manner to outdoors.

As endive is a cool-weather crop, it is best grown early in the season and again as a salad crop for late fall use. Sow the last seeds towards the end of July or early in August. Endive can tolerate fall rain and early frost, since the late crop is protected from frost by blanching. If a severe frost is anticipated, apply extra protection.

Endive is easy to grow and can extend the home-garden salad season well into the fall after other crops are over. Slugs are its main enemy, and in unfavourable weather conditions stem-rot may occur.

French Endive, or Witloof Chicory: *Cichorium intybus*

French endive, or chicory, is a biennial plant native to Europe and the Orient. It is extremely popular in France and other European countries and ranks high in the gourmet class of vegetables. The shoots can be eaten either raw in salads or cooked. For the ultimate in flavour and tenderness, blanching is desirable.

The cultural requirements are similar to those of lettuce, endive and escarole but, since it is a biennial, the roots can remain in the ground all winter to send up shoots in the spring to provide an early vegetable for the household. These shoots should be blanched too. The plant is normally more vigorous in the second year than the first.

At my home in Ireland, French endive roots were brought into a shed in the fall after the first season, packed closely together in boxes of soil and "forced" for winter use. I have tried this method in our basement here, but found the work involved did not give an adequate return. It was a constant battle with the cat who decided that my indoor boxes of soil were there for her convenience, and the job of carrying soil up and down the basement stairs seemed like too much hard work. We grew enough for several delicious dishes, but not sufficient to justify repeating the experiment.

The roots of French endive (chicory) can be roasted and used as a substitute for coffee. Essence of chicory is sold in liquid form and is more popular in Europe than in North America.

COOKING FRENCH ENDIVE
Cook endive shoots slowly until tender. Steaming is the best method, but if this is not possible use a minimum amount of water. Strain, set in an open casserole, cover with cheese sauce and place under the broiler until brown. Cooking time is about twenty minutes.

Lettuce: *Lactuca sativa*

It is said, that the effect of eating too Much Lettuce is 'soporific'. I have never felt sleepy after eating Lettuces; but then, I am not a rabbit. They certainly had a very soporific effect upon the Flopsy Bunnies!

Beatrix Potter

There is no doubt that lettuce is the most

popular salad plant. Rabbits seem to like it too! Ask anyone whose garden has been visited by that unwanted guest!

Lettuce is among the earliest of recorded vegetables, popular with the Persians and Romans as early as 500 B.C. It is a cool-season crop, and it is likely to "bolt" to seed if grown in the heat of the summer. There are a great many varieties listed in our seed catalogues, and they have only slight differences in their characteristics, namely: number of days to maturity; size of head; texture of leaf; resistance to disease or drought.

For practical purposes the varieties can be divided into four groups: loose-leaf lettuce; crisp heading lettuce; cos or romaine lettuce; and butterhead, or Boston, lettuce.

Loose-leaf lettuce: This is the most popular variety with home gardeners because it is so easy to grow. It does best in a light fertile soil and can tolerate full sun in the spring and fall. Lettuce will, however, bolt in the heat of the summer. Therefore, the summer crop can be grown in partial shade. The first seeding is made early in the season, the end of April or the beginning of May, and successive seedings are made every two weeks until July. You should only sow as much as your household can use in a two-week period, usually about 4 feet of row. Allow 18 to 24 inches between rows; cover seeds lightly and thin seedlings (using these in salads) to 6 inches apart. If any difficulty is encountered with seed germination, particularly during hot weather, try refrigerating the seeds for a couple of days prior to planting. Normal germination time for all lettuce is four to eight days.

Crisp heading: Crisp heading lettuce has dark green outer leaves and a light or blanched heart. When fully grown it can measure 12 or 15 inches across. Plant seed indoors or in the hot-frame in April for very early plants. Plant seed in the cold-frame or seed-bed in May for successive crops. Transplant to the garden when small sturdy plants have formed, allowing 12 inches between plants in rows 18 to 24 inches apart.

In our garden we do not give head lettuce a separate row. Instead, we plant a seedling between each of the cabbage, cauliflower and

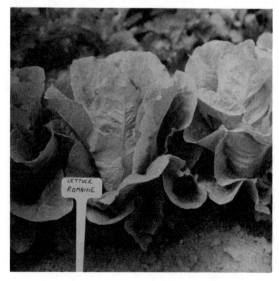

Left: Butterhead lettuce ready to harvest between young pepper plants. Note heavy straw mulch.
Below: Cos or romaine lettuce.

broccoli plants. The lettuce will have matured before the Brassicas need the space, and as the Brassicas grow they give the lettuce some shade which is most beneficial. We do not even attempt to grow head lettuce during the summer heat.

Cos or romaine lettuce: This tall, upright lettuce appears to have a somewhat coarse texture, but, in fact, its long slender heart leaves are sweet and tender. It will also stand up to intense summer heat much better than other lettuce types. Culture is the same as for crisp heading lettuce.

Butterhead or Boston lettuce: This variety has a very tender texture to the leaves and may be either seeded directly or grown as a transplant. It is very popular in the home garden but will not stand up well to intense summer heat. Freshly picked butterhead lettuce is hard to beat!

All lettuce must be kept well watered, and regular application of liquid manure or high-nitrogen fertilizer aids rapid growth. This is essential for top grade lettuce. Never permit the lettuce plants to dry out; the quality of the crop will be permanently damaged. For fall use, plant seed at the end of July or early August and treat in the same manner as the spring crop.

The most usual way to eat lettuce is raw or in salads. But you will often find that you have more than you can use before it goes to seed, so why not treat it like spinach. Your spinach crop will be over by the time lettuce is ready to "bolt". In France, lettuce is frequently served braised as a hot vegetable.

BRAISED LETTUCE

Remove the coarse outer leaves; cut the head into quarters; place in saucepan, adding a very small quantity of hot stock or thickened gravy; simmer for about eight minutes or until tender; add seasoning and serve.

Problems and Controls

Slugs: Lettuce has few insect enemies; the most common is the slug. To control, use slug bait or, better still, flat dishes of stale beer set in the ground with some kind of cover to keep out the rain. Slugs love beer and drown (happily, no doubt) in it. Another control for slugs is the use of salty water. Dissolve a small handful of pickling salt in a 2 gallon watering can. Water the area where the slugs are hiding.

Slug

Fungi: There are many soil-borne diseases which attack lettuce. The most common of these are three fungi, all of which cause rotting of the lower leaves and stem.

To avoid fungi, purchase disease-resistant seed and rotate your crops. Allow good circulation of air around and under the plants. Remove and destroy any diseased plants. Remember to remove all old plant refuse. Maintain dry soil around plants with shallow cultivation.

Water the plants early in the day in order to allow the foliage and soil surface to dry out before night.

CONVOLVULACEAE: The Morning Glory Family
Includes Sweet Potatoes

Sweet Potatoes: *Ipomoea batatas*

The sweet potato is native to the tropics of America. It should not be confused with the yam, which comes from Africa and is not generally considered edible by modern man but rather an animal fodder. Many supermarkets sell"yams", but these are incorrectly named since they are, if fact, sweet potatoes.

Sweet potatoes require a very long, hot growing season. We grow only one or two hills in our garden, just for the fun of it. The tubers do not have time to ripen sufficiently for winter storage. In areas with a long frost free season, they can be grown to maturity quite easily, or they can be grown in containers, where they become a very attractive trailing plant.

Growing sweet potatoes is an excellent way to involve children in gardening. In February or March, look in the supermarket for a tuber whose"eyes" look alive or, better still, have already started to sprout. Store-bought tubers have been treated with a gas to inhibit sprouting, but there are always a few in each shipment that remain viable. Each tuber will have as many as 50 eyes.

Place the tuber in a glass of water in such a way that only its bottom half is immersed in the water. The top half, where it was joined to the plant, is exposed to the air. The bottom will develop roots and the top, shoots. These shoots can be cut from the "mother" and rooted in water or moist peat moss. After hardening, plant them out in the garden or in a large container. The mother tuber can be left to grow as a house plant or vine. Sweet potatoes are very frost-tender, so don't be in a hurry to plant them outdoors; the first week in June is time enough in our garden. Be sure that all danger of frost is past and that the soil has warmed up.

Unlike most garden vegetables, sweet potatoes prefer a slightly acid, sandy loam. A sunny area in the garden where other vegetables have not done well will often suit them fine. As with all root crops, work the ground deeply before planting the sprouts. A handful of complete fertilizer is beneficial too.

The sweet potato is a vine with trailing and rooting stems. One hill of three plants will occupy an area of 3 to 4 square feet. Some varieties need more space than others, but with a store-bought tuber, it is impossible to know which you are growing. If the season is good, tubers will form wherever the stems put down roots.

Mulching after the ground is really warm conserves heat and controls weeds.

The leaves can be eaten in salads and the tubers harvested after the tops have been killed by the first frost. Unless the tubers are fully mature, dig only as many as you need for immediate use. Our experience is that they will keep better in the ground than in the refrigerator. The entire crop should be used within a few weeks after the foliage has been killed; otherwise, the tubers will rot. Mature tubers can be stored in the cool room in boxes of sand.

Sweet potatoes are not a guaranteed crop in northern climates and should be given a very low priority in gardens where space is limited. If grown in a container, bring indoors before there is any risk of frost and allow the tubers to continue growing until mature.

Problems and Controls

There are various diseases and pests to which sweet potatoes are susceptible. However, when growing only a few plants, these will not be a problem to home gardeners in temperate zones. Any insects noticed can be controlled by dusting or spraying and diseased plants removed from the garden and destroyed.

CRUCIFERAE: The Mustard or Cabbage Family
Includes Broccoli, Brussels Sprouts, Cabbage, Cauliflower, Chinese Cabbage, Kale, Kohl-rabi, Rutabaga, Summer Turnip, Cress, Radishes, and Sea-kale

The cabbage-like members of this family are known by most people to be related crops. However, I have found many gardeners do not realize that turnips, radishes, cress and sea-kale also belong to this category. Cabbages and most of the other vegetables in this family are members of the Brassica genus and have much in common with regard to cultivation and susceptibility to pests and diseases. The cultivation of cress, turnips, radishes and seakale, is different from the other Cruciferae and is treated under their separate headings.

The Brassicas

For the novice gardener a little information on the background of this group will help to understand their culture. The cultivars we grow in our gardens today are mostly horticultural hybrids whose common ancestors were native to Europe and the Mediterranean region.

All the Brassicas are sun-loving, cool-weather crops and will vary in quality according to the season. When purchasing seed, decide whether early, mid-season or late varieties are required. Early crops must be started indoors as transplants. Late crops can be seeded directly in the garden and either thinned or transplanted.

Brassicas will grow in a wide range of soils, but do best when the pH level is around 6.5. If the soil is acidic, it should be limed. The ground should be fertile, high in humus and with good drainage. The organic matter should be worked into the ground during the fall, prior to planting. We try to locate the Brassicas in the area occupied previously by legumes, (peas and beans), because they need the nitrogen that the legumes pack into the soil. During the growing season it is very important never to permit the ground to dry out; a lack of moisture, even for a relatively short period of time, will cause a serious setback, especially to the cauliflower. Sudden heavy rain or watering after a dry spell will cause cabbages to grow rapidly and split. If there is sufficient humus in the soil and the soil is kept moist, these problems are less likely to occur.

In highly fertile soils additional fertilizing at planting time is unnecessary. In poor soils an application of 10:10:10 at the rate of up to 4 pounds per 100 square feet is beneficial. After three or four weeks, when the plants are growing well, they benefit from a side dressing of a high nitrogen fertilizer or a watering with liquid manure.

Our experiences have shown that mulching is a definite help in conserving moisture and controlling weeds. Brassicas should never be allotted the same location in the plot in successive years, nor for two croppings in the same season. When possible allow three years to elapse before replanting Brassicas in any one section of the garden. This helps prevent a recurrence of any disease which might remain dormant in the soil. We have found it is convenient to group all the Brassicas together in the garden; by doing so, the pest control program for Brassicas is confined to one area. For blemish-free crops, pest control is essential.

Broccoli: *Brassica oleracea italica*

As the botanical name suggests, broccoli was introduced to us from Italy and has only been a popular vegetable in North America since the 1920's. Broccoli is easy to grow, and plants will remain productive for three to four months, or as long as the gardener keeps harvesting the young shoots. Broccoli transplants can be set out in the garden as soon as the ground has been worked. When the plants are hardened, they will not be damaged by light frost. Protection against cutworms and root maggots should be provided.

There are several varieties on the market. We grow the sprouting broccoli, starting the plants early indoors. This one planting keeps us supplied throughout the season.

Sprouting broccoli is a green vegetable that produces a large central flower head. This head must be cut when still compact, leaving the rest of the plant in the ground to branch and produce a constant supply of secondary shoots. With subsequent cutting these shoots become smaller, but are just as tasty as the main shoot.

Broccoli is an excellent vegetable for the small garden, much easier to grow than cauliflower, and it provides a very long harvest season. Broccoli can be eaten raw in salads or with dips, cooked, or processed for the freezer. It is a most delicious vegetable, very rich in vitamins, especially the leaves.

A common complaint of broccoli growers is the little green caterpillar that so quickly turns people against eating this vegetable. If the controls that are mentioned later are observed, this should not be a problem.

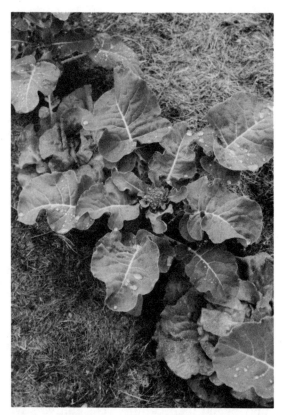

Above: Broccoli interplanted with lettuce.
Below: The large, central flower head of broccoli ready to be harvested. Smaller secondary heads will grow on side branches if the plant is left in the garden.

Broccoli seedling. Note the strong root growth which should be disturbed as little as possible.

Brussels Sprouts: *Brassica oleracea gemmifera*

Brussels sprouts derived their name from the Belgian city of Brussels where they have been grown since approximately the fourteenth century. They are not currently popular in North American gardens, possibly because World War II veterans stationed in England were served an abundance of this vegetable. Sprouts deserve more recognition, and should provide the family with a fresh green vegetable well after the main crops have been harvested, and right up until severe freezing occurs. In fact, the flavour is improved by a frost.

Brussels sprouts is an erect plant with a single stalk that grows about three feet high and develops sprouts in the axils of the leaves. The sprouts are like miniature cabbages, measuring one to two inches in diameter. Because the sprouts develop first on the lower portion of the stalk, break off the adjoining leaves, thus allowing the sprouts more room to mature. Harvest when they are still tightly closed by breaking the sprout away from the stalk with a sideways jerk, or by cutting with a knife. The plant will continue to push out new leaves at the top, and a new sprout will form in the axil of each leaf.

In areas like ours, where the growing season ends in early November, I find it is best to pinch out the growing point of the plant in mid-September to force the remaining sprouts to mature. In milder areas this growth should be left untouched.

Brussels sprouts can be stored for four to six weeks at a temperature slightly above freezing. To do this, the entire plant must be dug up and hung upside down in the storage cellar.

Brussels sprouts have a distinctive flavour. They are rich in vitamins, as well as iron and calcium.

Cabbage and Red Cabbage: *Brassica oleracea capitata*

There are literally hundreds of varieties of cabbage, which vary in colour, size, shape,

Brussels sprouts ready for harvesting. The lower sprouts should be broken off now to allow the upper ones to develop. Note that the upper leaves have been slightly damaged by caterpillars, but the sprouts are perfectly healthy.

texture, days to maturity and resistance to various diseases. The experienced home gardener knows that at the same time as his early cabbages are maturing, there is also an abundance of other vegetables. So it is wise not to plant too many early cabbages; six green and six red are enough for most families. Plant more of the late winter storage types, the kind that will keep in the cool room until well into the New Year.

If early cabbages are grown and the space is not required for another crop, harvest by cutting off the head with a sharp knife, leaving the stalk and root still growing. Cut a cross on top of the stalk with the knife, and in October four small cabbages will have formed, providing a second crop from one plant. It is important to continue your pest control program on these second crop plants.

With so many varieties available, it is hard to decide which to grow. Our favourite is

Savoy, both early and late. I consider it to be the "King of the Cabbages". We also grow red cabbage which we eat raw in salads, cook in the German style, and pickle for winter use.

New cultivars are constantly appearing on the market, mainly available through seed catalogues. Some advantages of new hybrids are improved flavour and the ability to remain mature in the garden for a couple of months without splitting.

RED CABBAGE – GERMAN STYLE

Shred finely one medium cabbage. Soak in salted water for about half an hour. Melt bacon fat or butter in a large saucepan. Add one medium onion, chopped. Cook until transparent. Lift the cabbage out of the water and put into the saucepan. Cook slowly for one hour with the lid on. Add two apples, cored and thinly sliced. Continue cooking for another hour. Stir occasionally. There should be enough juice to prevent sticking, but if the cabbage is drying out, add a little water. It is more usual for there to be too much juice, in which case remove the cover and allow the moisture to evaporate. Dissolve 2 tablespoons of flour and 4 tablespoons of brown sugar in 4 tablespoons of vinegar. Add this to the cabbage and simmer for another ten minutes or until thick. This recipe freezes well.

Cauliflower: *Brassica oleracea botrytis*

Cauliflower is the least dependable of the Brassicas for the home gardener to grow. They are always treated as transplants. The early crop must be started indoors or in a hot-frame in March or April and hardened before being set out in the garden. Late spring frost will not damage the hardened plants. Cauliflower is a cool-weather crop, and the quality of the early plants will to a great extent depend on the season. The earlier they are set out in the garden, the better. At no time should the plants be allowed to dry out, because this checks the growth of the heads, causing them to become runted and button-like.

The late crop can be seeded in an outdoor seed-bed in May and transplanted into the garden during the summer. We like to transplant these seedlings at intervals as they mature. This provides an extended harvest of cauliflower during the fall. They should be transplanted on cool, rainy days and shaded from the sun until re-established.

Most people prefer pure white cauliflower. To obtain this purity, it is necessary to blanch the head (or curds). Shortly after the button-like head appears, bring the outer leaves up and over it and hold them together with a rubber band or length of twine. The curds will continue to grow, and will remain white

A healthy, mature ball-head cabbage showing no sign of pest damage.

A healthy, mature Savoy cabbage. In this variety the leaves are crinkly.

because the light has been excluded. Cauliflower heads must be harvested before the curds begin to "rice" and discolour. It is very easy to remove the rubber band to check, and essential to cut the heads when they are ready. After harvesting, remove the remainder of the plant from the garden, and if free from disease, put on the compost heap. Some gardeners, including myself, prefer to burn the stalks; they take too long to break down.

There are new self-blanching varieties on the market, as well as a green-curded one, but neither of these has proven too popular to date. As with cabbages, new varieties are constantly being introduced. Again, the seed catalogues are the best source of information.

Chinese Cabbage: *Brassica chinensis*

This cabbage originates in China and is a cool-weather crop. If exposed to summer heat and long days it will quickly go to seed.

For the best results plant seed directly in the garden in late July or early August. Thin the seedlings to ten inches apart and keep them well-watered. From seeding time to harvest will be between 60 and 80 days.

Chinese cabbage is usually served as a salad, but can also be cooked. The flavour is milder than regular cabbage.

Kale: *Brassica oleracea acephala*

Kale is also known as borecole, collard, cow or green cabbage, German greens, or curly kale. It has been under cultivation for many centuries and is probably the ancestor of the various Brassicas grown today.

Kale is definitely not a hot-weather crop and should be grown for late fall harvesting. It is the most hardy of all the Brassicas and can usually be harvested throughout November in our area. Three or four kale plants warrant a place in the garden to provide the family with fresh late garden greens. Kale is very high in nutritive value; rich in vitamin A, thiamine, and ascorbic acid.

Plant seed directly in the garden in late May or early June, preferably in a sunny location. We find it best to thin the seedlings several times over a period of weeks, ending up with the four strongest plants about 18 inches apart. The plants will become sturdy bushes about three feet tall. The leaves are picked as required, leaving the plant to continue growing.

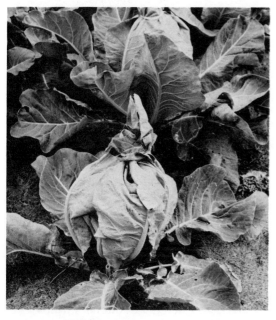

Above: Cauliflowers with their outside leaves gathered together by rubber bands. This helps the flower to blanch and prevents unwelcome visits from the cabbage butterfly. *Below:* A fine example of a white cauliflower curd ready to be harvested.

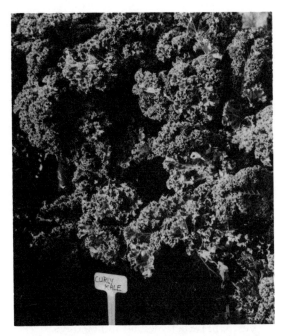

Curly kale ready to be harvested. The growth can be noted from the plastic marker which is about 9 inches above ground.

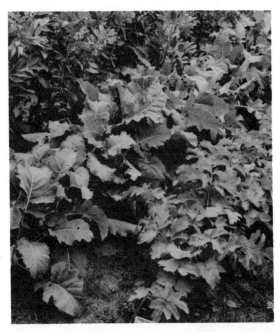

A row of kohl-rabi between broad beans (left) and parsnips (right). This area was well-mulched.

Kale has no serious enemies. If holes are noticed in the leaves, a light dusting with Diatomaceous earth will control the chewing insects.

In some parts of England, boiled potatoes and cooked kale or cabbage, when fried together are known as "Bubble and Squeak". It is a remarkably tasty way of eating leftovers, and a little chopped onion gives added flavour.

To cook kale, wash the leaves, chop them and cook in a covered saucepan until tender. With young leaves this takes about ten minutes.

Kohl–rabi: *Brassica caulorapa*

This unusual vegetable is often referred to as a "Turnip-Cabbage". It is very easy to grow and gives a good return for the space it occupies. Kohl-rabi is a Brassica with a turnip-like swelling of the stem above ground level. The swollen part should be eaten while it is still young, juicy and tender. Most kohl-rabi sold in supermarkets are well past their prime and are stringy and coarse. We enjoy eating kohl-rabi raw with a dip or with salads. When cooked, they can replace summer turnips.

Kohl-rabi is one of the easiest Brassicas to grow. Plant the seed directly in the garden as soon as the ground is worked. Thin the seedlings to four to eight inches apart. Harvest in about two months, before the swelling reaches the size of a tennis ball. Keep the plants free from weeds. Never permit the ground to dry out as this will cause even small kohl-rabi to become woody.

To ensure a good quality crop, make successive small plantings every couple of weeks until the weather gets hot. Kohl-rabi grows best in cool seasons and can tolerate partial shade and light frost. Whether kohl-rabi is grown as an early or late crop, it is important to maintain rapid growth.

The pests are the same as with the rest of the cabbage family. Because kohl-rabi is a fast maturing crop, its space can be replanted with fall crops such as carrots, beets, late spinach, Chinese cabbage or lettuce.

DIP FOR KOHL-RABI
Add one packet of dried onion soup to 2 cups of sour cream or plain yogurt. Add fresh herbs in season as desired. Thin if necessary with milk or cream. Allow to stand for several hours before serving. This gives the dried soup time to swell and thicken the dip. Cut the kohl-rabi into sticks.

Rutabaga (Swede Turnip or Winter Turnip): *Brassica napa napobrassica*

The turnip is a root vegetable known to have been grown by the Romans. Probably it was introduced to other parts of Europe and the British Isles during the Roman occupation. The first mention of turnips in North America was in 1540 when Cartier, on his third voyage, sowed turnip seed in Canada.

Rutabagas have a protruding neck and a mass of roots that grow from the base of the vegetable. Their smooth, hairless leaves are covered with a bloom that gives a bluish appearance, and the flesh is a yellow-golden colour. A most important feature for home gardeners to know is that rutabaga are slow-maturing roots for winter storage.

Rutabagas do best in a well-limed soil. The seed should be sown directly in the garden in the spring at the same time as semi-hardy annuals. They prefer full sun. Allow 20 to 24 inches between rows, and thin the seedlings 4 to 6 inches apart. Further thinning will be needed as the plants grow. The seed should be planted half an inch deep. Light frost will not damage rutabagas; in fact, many people claim fall frost improves the flavour of the mature roots. Turnips are vulnerable to the same diseases and pests as the other members of the mustard family.

Unlike parsnips, rutabagas cannot be left in the ground over winter, but should be dug on a warm, sunny fall day and left on the ground for a couple of hours until the roots are dry before being brought into the cool room. This also allows any wounds that may have occurred during harvesting to heal over, thus protecting the roots from possible infection. Some people enjoy the young green leaves as a spring vegetable, but I find the flavour rather strong.

MASHED RUTABAGAS
The flavour of mashed rutabaga is greatly enhanced by adding a pinch or two of curry powder. Cooked rutabaga can be frozen if cool-room space is not available.

Summer Turnip: *Brassica rapa*

The leaves and stems of summer turnips are hairy and coarse, and the flesh is usually white. They are a cool-weather crop and should be sown directly in the garden as soon as the ground has been worked. Like rutabaga, they dislike an acid soil and should, if possible, be grown in an area that has recently been limed. Early culture is the same as for rutabaga, but white turnips mature rapidly and should be harvested when about three to four inches in diameter. If allowed to grow larger, they will be coarse and stringy. Seed can be sown again in late July for a fall harvest. Do not try growing summer turnip in the heat of the season; the resulting crop is seldom worth the trouble. Turnips taste better if they come to maturity quickly. Therefore take care not to let the soil around them dry out.

Most, but not all, summer turnips are white fleshed. Seed catalogues give clear descriptions of varieties. The most common problem we have encountered with both rutabagas and turnips is the root maggot. To guard against this, protect the young plants with floating row covers. As members of the cabbage family, they are subject to the same ailments and to the came crop rotation program.

WHITE TURNIP IN CREAM SAUCE
Trim, peel and dice the turnips. Cook until tender in an equal quantity of milk and water, seasoned with a bay leaf and a blade of mace. Drain in a sieve. Put in a casserole. Make sufficient white sauce to cover. Add salt, pepper and nutmeg to taste. Stir in finely chopped parsley. Pour over the turnip. Reheat in oven or microwave.

Cress: *Lepidium sativum*

Cress, or pepper grass, is very simple to grow. Sow a short row of seed outdoors as early as possible in the spring. Sprinkle the seed thickly in the row, cover lightly and tamp with the back of a rake. Germination is rapid, usually two to four days, depending on the temperature. The plants will be ready for cutting in three to four weeks or when about four inches tall. Make successive plantings throughout the summer. Keep the soil moist, otherwise the plants will go to seed very quickly. Cress can be grown in full sun or partial shade.

It is delicious in salads and sandwiches.

Radishes: *Raphanus sativus*

Radishes are very easy to grow in the early spring; they do best in cool weather, and the first seeding should be made as soon as the ground can be worked. Radishes can tolerate light frost and partial shade. Successive plantings can be made at two-week intervals until mid-June. Seed thinly to eliminate the need for constant thinning later. The plants will be ready to harvest in three to four weeks. They prefer a well-worked, well-drained, not too rich soil. The plants should never be allowed to dry out, or they will become woody. Daily watering is necessary in dry weather. Radishes taste better when they are brought to maturity rapidly. Thinning is most important; overcrowding prevents their roots from swelling into juicy, crisp vegeta-

bles. We do not bother growing radishes in July and August because they dislike hot, dry weather. Unless the summer is cool, radishes will be inferior and woody.

The tastiest radishes are grown in the hot-frame in early spring. The flavour is not as sharp as those grown outdoors and the texture much finer.

Because the radish germinates so quickly, it is often planted with slow-germinating seeds to mark the row. The radishes will be harvested before the other crop requires the space to grow. When used as a row marker, the seed should be sown sparsely.

Radishes are not prone to many pests and diseases. The most common pest is the cabbage root maggot, which can be controlled by the use of floating row covers. If aphids attack the leaves, dust with rotenone.

Freshly picked radishes are very high in vitamin C. We treat them as one of the main ingredients of salads, rather than as a garnish.

SORE THROAT REMEDY
Thinly slice radishes onto a saucer. Sprinkle with sugar and let stand for a few hours. Drain off the juice. Take a teaspoonful as required to relieve a sore throat or cold.

Sea–kale: *Crambe maritima*

This perennial plant is native to the sea coasts of western Europe and Asia Minor. It was always considered an important vegetable at my home in Ireland. The fleshy, celery-like shoots provide a most succulent dish early in the spring before the asparagus comes in. We have been growing it with great success ever since we moved to Evergreen Farm. It is a hardy perennial, and should be given a permanent site in the same manner as asparagus and rhubarb.

Sea-kale is not an economic plant for a small garden, but gives excellent returns for many years when a sunny location and rich soil can be spared in the larger home garden.

We grew our stock from seed, as no root cuttings were available. Raising plants from seed is a slow business, but has proven most rewarding.

Sow the seed outdoors as soon as the ground can be worked. Scatter thinly in drills one inch deep; cover and tamp. Seed takes about 20 days to germinate. Before the seedlings become congested, thin them out to six inches apart. A year from sowing, the seedlings are fit to plant in their permanent positions.

In some areas it may be possible to purchase sea-kale roots, which are available in the spring. The roots will be four to eight inches long. They should be planted two feet apart, upright in the ground, and the tops covered with about one inch of soil. Only one bud should be allowed to remain at each root-top; the others should be removed with a knife. The object is to keep each plant single.

It is extrememly important to know which is the top and bottom of root cuttings. The common practice is to cut the tops square, and the lower end slanted. When propagating your own stock always follow this practice. Sea-kale is extremely easy to propagate from root cuttings. Pencil-thin cuttings will take a year to establish themselves and produce a crop. They are very hardy.

As the sea-kale will remain in its permanent postion for many years, the ground should be prepared thoroughly. Sea-kale in its wild form is a coastal plant and accustomed to salty conditions. Seaweed is to its liking, and anyone close enough to the coast to obtain this superb fertilizer should use it. Growers not able to find seaweed can purchase kelp and its extracts at most garden centres or through mail-order houses.

A sprinkling of pickling salt is beneficial too.

The area designated for sea-kale should be enriched with well-rotted manure or compost. The soil must be well-drained; heavy clay ground should be well-worked and have sand, rubble or ashes added to ensure good drainage. If necessary the bed can be slightly

Above: Tops of mature sea-kale roots in very early spring after mulch cover has been removed. Roots can be divided at this stage. *Below:* Flower pot removed to allow harvesting of young shoots.

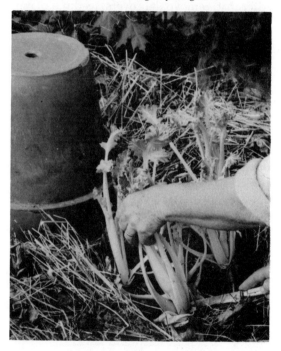

raised. I find a heavy mulch of straw or hay is most beneficial. Leave it on all year round.

The shoots and leaf stalks require blanching outdoors (see Glossary) before eating, to prevent them from tasting coarse and strong. The blanching covers can be placed over the plants in the late fall or early spring. I use old flower pots or boxes; anything that will exclude all light.

Development of sea-kale in early spring. When the shoots appear, they should be blanched with a mulch (as shown here) or a box or flower pot to exclude light.

As the shoots develop in the spring, check the plants regularly and harvest the shoots by cutting with a sharp knife. Harvesting can continue over a period of four to six weeks. After that, remove the covers, feed the plants with a complete fertilizer, and allow them to grow freely.

Sea-kale suffers from very few problems. The most common is slugs. These can usually be attracted by slug-bait or dishes of stale beer, or controlled by sprinkling salt around the plants. A little salt is most beneficial to the plants. If drainage is poor, the roots may rot.

Sea-kale can be served hot like asparagus, or raw in salads, like celery. In Europe it is considered a gourmet dish. This little known and seldom grown vegetable deserves more attention, especially in the home garden.

BOILED OR STEAMED SEA–KALE
Trim off the root end of the sea-kale and wash it thoroughly. Tiny slugs can hide between the leaves. Cook until tender and serve with melted butter or cream sauce.

Water Cress: *Nasturtium officinale*

A European water plant which has become naturalized in the cold, shallow streams of northeastern United States and eastern Canada, water cress is extremely hard to grow unless a cool, permanently flowing stream is at hand. Once established, this perennial plant will last for many, many years.

Water cress must not be confused with the common garden nasturtium that belongs to a completely different family.

Water cress is not a plant for the average home vegetable garden.

Problems and Controls for Brassicas

Cutworms: Newly transplanted Brassicas are extremely vulnerable to attack by the cutworm. These dull-grey grubs come out of the soil at night or on cloudy days and chew the stems of the plants at ground level. To the uninitiated it might appear that the stem has been broken by a cat or dog, but on close inspection you will see it is not actually a break. Sometimes the cutworm will chew only part way through the stem. These plants seldom survive. After feeding, cutworms rest during the day in the cool soil below the plant. I always dig down, find the culprit and destroy it, preventing the same cutworm from doing further damage.

Paper collars are the simplest protection against the cutworm. These collars should be fitted around the stem to give protection both above and below soil level.

Cabbage root maggot: Damage to the roots of Brassicas, turnips and radishes is caused by the larvae of a fly that lays her eggs in the soil beside the plants. These small, white maggots feed on the developing roots, and the first indication of their presence will be a wilting of the entire plant. With experience a gardener will soon learn to identify this particular wilt. When damaged plants are pulled and the roots inspected, the maggots will be visible. The whole plant should be destroyed.

The cabbage root maggot can be controlled by covering the newly set out plants with floating covers. Another control is to lay a thick mat of paper around the base of the plant, which prevents the fly from depositing eggs close to the plant. A little napthaline sprinkled on the mat will help ward off the fly.

Above: Cutworm having Brassica dinner.
Right: Wilted cauliflower leaves indicate root maggot infestation.

Cabbage caterpillars: When we first notice white butterflies fluttering around the garden, we know that unless we take the necessary precautions immediately, it will not be long before the caterpillars are chewing the Brassicas. This butterfly lays her eggs on the undersides of the leaves and, unless deterred, the resulting caterpillars will make the crop unsightly and unappetizing.

Cabbage caterpillars and loopers (see below) can be prevented from damaging the plants by:
a) covering the plants early in the season with floating row covers.
b) dusting with Diatomaceous Earth.
c) dusting with Rotenone if the insects persist.
d) spraying with Insecticidal Soap or with detergent to which a little salt has been added. If using the latter, spray the plants with clear water half an hour or so later.

Cabbage looper: This pest feeds on all Brassicas, as well as lettuce, turnips, tomatoes, radishes, peas and potatoes. This pale-green 1½ inch long caterpillar alternately loops and stretches its body as it moves along, hence its name. It overwinters in the pupal stage on the leaves of its favourite plants, including many weeds. For this reason the fall clean-up in the garden is extremely important and can help keep the succeeding crop looper-free. However, if cabbage loopers do appear, the easiest control

is to knock them off into a bucket of salty water. Other methods are the same as for the cabbage caterpillar.

Cabbage looper

Black rot: This disease is caused by a seed-borne bacteria that causes rot of the stems and veins of the leaves. This problem can be avoided by using disease-free seed and resistant varieties.

Black leg: A soil-borne fungus, Black Leg attacks seeds and seedlings. It can be recognized by a blackening of the stems at the surface of the soil. The best control is to use sterilized soil in the seed bed, and by observing a crop rotation system.

Cabbage yellows: Cabbage yellows is a soil-borne fungus which results in the plant becoming a lifeless yellowish-green a few weeks after transplanting. Control is to purchase yellows-resistant varieties and to practice crop rotation.

Club root: This soil-borne fungus produces gall-like swellings on the roots of Brassicas as well as stunting of the entire plant. This disease thrives in acid soils and once established in a garden is hard to eradicate. Prevention consists of maintaining a soil pH of 6.8 to 7 and following crop rotation procedures.

CUCURBITACEAE: The Gourd Family
Includes Squash, Pumpkins, Cucumbers, Muskmelons, Honeydew, Cantaloupe, Watermelons, and Zucchini

Squash, cucumbers, pumpkins and melons all belong to the same family, generally referred to as "cucurbits". They all need the same cultural treatment and fall prey to the same pests and diseases.

Cucurbits prefer full sunshine and a slightly acid soil. I have never worried too much about soil acidity with regard to cucurbits, because I always grow my squash on the old compost pile where they thrive. For gardeners who do not have a compost heap and grow their cucurbits in the main garden, they require a soil that is high in humus content, fertile, and well-drained.

Cucurbits are heavy feeders and benefit from additional feeding during the growing season. I use liquid manure when available, but otherwise a complete fertilizer.

The soil should be kept moist at all times, since drying out will cause the fruits to be stunted. Preferably soak the soil rather than sprinkle from above. Mulching conserves moisture and controls weeds.

Outdoor Seeding

Here is a method you can try as a headstart for growing members of the gourd family. In our area, we use old car tires to give protection to melons and cucumbers seeded directly in the garden. A week or so before seeding time, place the car tire in the garden, fill the rim with water and cover with clear plastic securely anchored to the ground. The sun's rays will heat the water and the mini-greenhouse will remain warm day at night. If frost is anticipated, an additional cover such as a sack will give the necessary protection. This method allows us to start melons, etc. outdoors several weeks before it would otherwise be possible.

Squash and Pumpkins: *Cucurbita species*

Generally speaking, squash are divided into two groups.

Summer Squash: These are harvested when the fruit is still immature and tender.
Included in this category are:
zucchini
summer scallop squash
straightneck
crookneck
vegetable marrow (immature)

Winter Squash: Winter storage squash should be ripened on the vine until the skin is hard. Exposure to frost damages keeping quality.
Included in this category are:
butternut
buttercup
pepper squash
hubbard
pumpkins
spaghetti squash
vegetable marrow (mature)

There are also many novelty varieties.

Squash and pumpkins are grown in either bush or vine form. Summer squash usually occupy less space than their winter counterparts, but the culture of both types is the same.

Being native to tropical Central America and Mexico, they are very frost-tender. The seed should not be planted until all danger of frost is past. In northern areas it may be necessary to start plants indoors. In our part of the St. Lawrence Valley, direct garden seeding around May 24th has always proven successful.

For small garden plots bush squash are the

most suitable. Even these will spread three feet in all directions. Do not overcrowd. Plant about ten seeds to each "hill". After true leaves have developed, thin out the plants by snipping with scissors, leaving only the strongest three. Vine squash require a great deal of space as the vines often ramble 20 or 30 feet. Allow 8 to 10 feet between rows, and four to six feet between hills. The distance between the squash depends on the variety grown.

The area allotted to squash can be used early in the season to produce the fast-maturing, early cool-weather crops such as spinach, radishes, lettuce or cress. These crops will be harvested before the squash need the space. The squash will remain in the garden until the leaves are touched by frost. Vines can be trained to climb on a trellis or fence. After a number of fruits have set, the vines should be pruned and kept under control. The fruit may need support if larger fruiting varieties like Hubbard are grown.

Squash grow best in rich, fertile soil and need plenty of moisture, sunshine and heat.

Most gardens have a compost pile, and it is here that we recommend growing squash. Last year's compost pile is ideal; there is still plenty of heat being generated, which the squash love, and the unsightly heap will rapidly be covered by the vines and hidden from view.

Prepare the seed-beds by making indentations in the compost and filling these with four to six inches of garden soil before planting the seed. Allow four to six feet between hills.

Take care to select varieties of squash that are suited to the individual garden. It is usual for home gardeners to grow several varieties of both squash and cucumbers. Insects and bees pollinate the gourd family, and those who save their own seeds should realize that with cucurbitaceae the next year's plants might not produce the type of fruits they had hoped for. There is always a strong chance that cross-pollination has taken place, and consequently the seed grown the following year may not come true to the parent. Any amateur gardener interested in keeping

A compost heap consisting of household scrap, farm yard manure, garden debris and leaves makes a good base on which to grow squash. As seeds in each hill germinate, squash vines sprout and begin to run.

The entire compost heap is covered with green growth as the squash vines spread out. We watch carefully for any sign of pests; fortunately, there were none.

Left: The male gourd flower is supported by a thin stem on which no fruit will grow. *Right:* The female flower is supported by a bulbous neck of butternut squash. As the fruit grows and matures, the blossom will shrivel and fall.

seed should study this subject in more depth before experimenting.

It is a common myth that cantaloupe and cucumber cross-pollinate, producing a mongrel fruit during the current season. It is the seed from any cross-pollinated fruit that will produce the mongrel the following year. When seed is purchased from a reliable seed house, you can be reasonably certain of the results.

Many novice gardeners are disappointed that so many of the blossoms on their squash plants never develop into fruit. If they look more closely at the plants, they will notice that some blossoms are borne on long stems, others on short stems. The former are male flowers, the latter female. Only the female flowers develop fruit. There will be ten or twenty male flowers to every female.

Squash seed can be kept for about five years if stored in a dry, dark, cool place.

Pumpkins and squash fall heir to the same ailments as do other members of the gourd family. To help prevent disease, keep weeds under control or, better still, mulch the ground. Burn the old vines in the fall. Do not add them to the compost pile. Do not grow members of the gourd family in the same place the following season.

Cucumbers: *Cucumis sativus*

The cucumber originates in Asia and is a very frost-tender annual vegetable. There are dozens of varieties to choose from. The vines of some cucumber crawl on the ground or can be trained to climb; other types are compact bushes suitable for a small garden or a patio planter. The fruits vary in size and texture; some are for eating fresh, others for pickling.

As with all gourds there will be ten to twenty male flowers to every female. Only the female flowers produce fruits.

In northern climates the seed may be started indoors, but we have not found this necessary in our area. We achieve the best results by direct garden seeding using the car tire method.

Cucumbers need rich, well-drained soil, plenty of moisture, sunshine and heat. Additional feeding with 5:10:10 when the young plants are established promotes rapid growth.

Cucumbers can be planted in "hills" or rows. Do not overcrowd; allow plenty of space for the vines to run.

Cucumbers are subject to the same ailments as the rest of the cucurbits. The plants

Climbing cucumber hanging from chicken-wire netting.

Above: Cantaloupe seed has been planted in hills on the compost heap. A tire is placed on each hill and the rim filled with water.

Above: Tires covered with light plastic to create a warm, humid atmosphere. *Below:* Canteloupe seedlings emerge, and plastic cover is removed during the day.

should be checked daily when young, and if any signs of insect attack or disease are noticed, immediate action must be taken. Left unchecked, the vines can be damaged beyond recovery in a matter of days.

Muskmelon, Honeydew Melon and Cantaloupe: *Cucumis melo*

The muskmelon is native to Persia (Iran) and neighbouring areas. Muskmelons are known to have been cultivated as far back as 2400 B.C. Over the years cultivation of melons gradually spread westward around the Mediterranean. Melons became a common fruit in Spain by the fifteenth century, and Columbus brought muskmelon seeds with him, on his second voyage to the New World.

Today melons and cantaloupe are an important crop in the United States. They are not often grown commercially in Canada, but should be included in home gardens wherever three frost-free months are enjoyed.

There are a number of varieties to choose from, but remember, the dates listed in the seed catalogues are from transplanting time to harvest. Although melons are usually grown as transplants, we find it easier to plant the seed directly in the place the vines are to grow, using the car tire method as described earlier. This is done either on a compost heap that is still generating heat, or a hot bed made from fresh horse manure and located in the garden plot.

First, dig a hole the width of a car tire and about one foot deep. Fill it with some fresh horse manure; replace about 4 inches of soil; place the tire on top; fill the rim with rain water; wait a few days and then plant the seeds inside and cover with clear plastic. Thin to the three strongest plants.

The mini-greenhouse shown in the photo can be started in early May, and the protection removed on hot sunny days after all risk of frost is past. The plants will grow rapidly and not have to suffer a set-back from transplanting. We have also found mulching beneficial. Allow a four by four foot area around

The harvest of cantaloupes is exemplified by this picture – a most satisfactory and heavy crop of healthy fruit. It may become necessary to protect the fruit from frost damage. We protect our cantaloupe bed against early frost, thereby extending the season for ripening.

A zucchini hill consisting of three plants gives the appearance of a large, single bush.

each hill.

Prior to planting, apply a complete fertilizer (5:10:10) and work it into the soil. Feed again with liquid fertilizer when vines start to run, and give a final feeding when the fruits have started to form. The fruits should be ripening in mid-August. Test by lifting the melon and seeing if it breaks away freely from its stem.

Vine ripened fruit are the most tasty, but to avoid frost damage it may become necessary to cut and harvest earlier. We protect our cantaloupe bed against early frost, thereby extending the season for ripening.

Muskmelons are very nutritious and a strong source of vitamin C; the deeper the colour, the higher the vitamin A content.

Melons are susceptible to the same problems as the rest of the gourd family. Check the plants daily for any signs of insect damage or disease.

Watermelons: *Citrullus lanatus*

The watermelon is probably native to Africa, and has been grown in the southern United States since the latter part of the seventeenth century. Varieties have now been developed which are suited to our colder climate. The would-be watermelon grower should check which varieties grow best in his area.

Watermelons are very frost-tender. The cultural requirements and ailments are similar to those of muskmelons.

Zucchini: *Cucurbita pepo 'zucchini'*

Zucchini has become a very popular vegetable in the home garden. It is easy to grow and, if kept harvested, will produce fruit until the first frost. The most suitable type

Several zucchini fruit growing behind female flowers. Zucchini is grown as summer squash and harvested when very young.

for the home garden is a bush variety. The seed can be planted directly in the garden, and we have found the car-tire method very satisfactory. This gives us about a two-week start over seed that has no protection.

Plant about ten seeds inside the ring, and after they are well-established, thin, leaving only the three strongest plants. Remove the car tire when all danger of frost is past. The plants will become good-sized bushes, with large leaves on long stems. Allow a four by four foot square for each clump. Harvest the fruits when they are very young and tender, and not more than six inches long. Zucchini grow very rapidly and need to be harvested every day.

Soil and cultural requirements are the same as for other squash. One hill of zucchini provides the average family with an ample supply commencing six to eight weeks after seeding.

Problems and Controls

During the early stages of growth, cucurbits are particularly vulnerable to attack by insects and the resulting spread of certain diseases. The plants should be checked daily and if any signs of distress or insects are noticed, immediate steps must be taken to prevent further damage.

Squash vine borer: The squash vine borer tunnels into the stem of the plant causing the leaves to wilt. It can easily be detected by a small pile of sawdust-like material surrounding the entry hole. The stem should be slit lengthwise, and the borer removed and destroyed. The vine stem can then be hilled up with soil so that it can re-root.

The mature state of the squash vine borer is a day-flying moth that resembles a wasp.

It lays its eggs on the stems in which the larvae make holes. It is interesting to note that butternut squash is resistant to this pest, while acorn and green Hubbard are quite susceptible. Dusting or spraying will keep the borer under control.

Squash bugs: These hard-shelled pests are black and brown on top and yellow on the underside. They are about half an inch long. The adults overwinter in garden refuse and emerge in the spring just in time to attack young plants, and for the females to lay their eggs on the undersides of the leaves.

The red-brown eggs can be seen in clusters, and the leaves containing the eggs should be removed and destroyed.

Striped cucumber beetle: This yellowish beetle with three black stripes, overwinters in garden debris, and becomes active in early spring. The female lays her eggs in the soil, and the larvae feed on the roots and stems of plants. When mature, the new adults feed on the upper growth of the plants. The cucumber beetle is responsible for the spread of bacterial wilt and cucumber mosaic. These beetles can cause serious damage very rapidly and must be controlled by spraying or dusting as soon as they are seen.

All cucurbits are susceptible to viruses, fungi and bacterial diseases. Control consists of purchasing disease-resistant varieties, practicing crop rotation, controlling weeds and insects, practicing good garden hygiene, and by spraying or dusting with the appropriate pesticide if required.

Squash vine borer

Squash bug

Striped cucumber beetle

GRAMINAE: The Grass Family
Includes Sweet Corn

Corn: *Zea mays rugosa*

> *"Oh the corn is as high*
> *As an elephant's eye"*
>   Oklahoma: Rodgers and Hammerstein

Although sweet corn is the only member of the grass family we grow for food in our gardens, many other members such as wheat, oats, barley, rye and rice form part of our daily diet.

Corn is very popular in the home garden even though it occupies a large amount of space for the quantity of food produced. North Americans know well the delicious flavour of freshly picked ears.

The earliest records of corn came from Guatemala, where the Indians are known to have grown it during the eighth century. Columbus saw it in Cuba in November 1492, and recorded "a kind of grain called 'maiz' of which was made a very well-tasted flour". In 1498 corn was brought by Columbus to Venezuela, and also recorded later in Chile and Peru. It is believed to be native to tropical America. In 1535, when Cartier visited Hochelaga, now Montreal, he recorded "that town was situated in the midst of extensive cornfields". Corn seems to have been grown all over the American continent by the Indians. The first mention of corn in gardening books was in the 1830's.

Sweet corn is grown on all types of soil. A well-drained, fertile, sandy loam is preferred. The richer the ground, the sweeter and more tasty the crop. Corn has a deep, strong root system, and it is therefore very important to prepare the land thoroughly before planting. In addition to humus, work in 6 to 8 pounds of 5:10:10 fertilizer per 100 feet of row. If no humus is available, increase the fertilizer by 2 to 3 pounds. Additional feeding during the

I planted two rows of corn 3 feet apart and thinned them by snipping seedlings with scissors, leaving them 6 to 8 inches apart.

Growing seedlings of corn mulched with grass clippings. The variety "Peaches and Cream" is excellent for the home garden.

growing season is beneficial.

Corn is a sun-loving, warm weather crop, which, if seeded too early, can be damaged by frost after germination. Germination will also be poor if the soil is wet and cold, so it is best to delay planting until the conditions are suitable. Sweet corn can be planted either in drills (rows) or hills. In drills, the thinned seedlings should be spaced 6 to 8 inches apart. In hills, allow three plants to each, with 18 to 24 inches between hills. I prefer rows. However, in either case, keep the rows 3 feet apart.

In our vegetable garden corn is the only vegetable we grow where pollination is done by the wind. Planting corn in a block of short rows, rather than one long row, allows better circulation of pollen around the plants. Without complete pollination, the cobs will have gaps without kernels. If several varieties (for example, early, mid-season and late) are grown, each variety should be in a block.

Corn grows to a height of about 6 feet, depending on the variety. It should be given a location in the garden where it will not shade other plants. It is not a good crop to grow in very small gardens because it does not give a large enough return for the space it occupies. However, in an intensively planted garden, the area where the corn is grown can be occupied early in the season by crops such as spinach, lettuce, radish and cress. I have also visited gardens where the squash has been grown successfully in the corn patch. The disadvantages of this kind of intensive planting is in controlling pests and diseases. We prefer to grow the corn by itself.

Corn is a heavy feeder and benefits from additional fertilizer during the growing season. Apply a balanced fertilizer either in liquid form or as a side dressing. Signs of distress such as yellowing leaves or stunted growth often mean lack of the necessary plant nutrients. If these symptoms should appear, apply a fertilizer and water the crop if the weather is dry.

The plants should never lack moisture, because if they do, the quality of the crop will suffer. The healthier the growth of the plants, the more succulent the flavour of the cobs.

To extend the harvest season, plant early, mid-season and late varieties. These can be planted simultaneously, but will mature in succession.

Here the rows of corn have begun to mature. First the pollen-producing tassels appear on the plant. Three to four days later, silks begin to show on the corn ear shoots. Usually we harvest after the silks have turned brown, two or three weeks after they first appear.

A friend and I make light work of harvesting.

The advantage of home-grown corn is that it can be harvested while the kernels are still plump and the juice is milky. Pick when the silks have turned brown, and the ear is firm and full. You can have the pot boiling before picking the cobs and have them eaten before the sugar in the kernels has had time to turn to starch. The change is very rapid. An hour can make a noticeable difference in flavour. If you've never eaten freshly picked corn, you're in for a treat.

Problems and Controls

European corn borer: Corn borers can be very destructive, attacking the stalks and ears of corn. Its presence is indicated by castings outside tiny holes, broken tassels and wilting stalks.

The flesh-coloured, inch-long worms overwinter in old stalks, pupate in the spring, and emerge as moths to lay eggs during the summer. Control the incidence of borers by planting resistant varieties, and by pulling up and destroying infested corn stalks after harvest. Do not put the healthy stalks on the compost unless they have been shredded as they are slow to decompose.

Corn earworms: These stocky, striped worms are about 2 inches long. They do not usually overwinter in northern climates; the adult moths migrate with warming temperatures. The females lay their eggs on the silks, and the emerging larvae enter the ears and feed on the kernels.

Earworms can be controlled by applying a few drops of mineral oil to the tip of each ear as the silks are first appearing.

Corn smut: This unpleasant looking fungal disease produces large, grey-black boils on the ears. These boils contain a mass of spores that are spread by the wind if the boils are allowed to break open. They should be removed and burned immediately they are noticed to prevent them from infecting the rest of your corn, as well as your neighbour's. If these boils are allowed to burst, the spores can remain viable for up to seven years! Unfortunately, fungicides are not an effective control. The best control is to plant resistant varieties, rotate crops and clean up the garden thoroughly in the fall.

Birds sometimes eat newly planted corn, but using a treated seed usually prevents this. Scarecrows and glitters help to frighten birds away from mature cobs.

Raccoons can be distracted by music from a radio placed in the corn patch overnight, by the presence of a good dog, or by an electric fence placed only a few inches above the ground.

Above: European corn borer. *Below:* Corn smut.

LEGUMINOSAE: The Pea Family
Includes Peas and Beans

Bush Snap Beans: *Phaseolus vulgaris*

The most common bean grown in the garden plot is the bush snap bean, a native of Mexico and Central America. It may be green or golden in colour. If picked frequently, the bushes will continue to produce over a long period of time. There are a great many varieties of bush beans, both green and wax (yellow), available through the seed catalogues. It is often a help to the novice to inquire from a knowledgeable local gardener as to the varieties found to be most satisfactory in his or her area.

Beans grow well in full sun in most gardens as long as the ground is well drained. Too rich a soil will produce lots of leaves but few beans. Snap and pole bean seed should not be planted until all danger of frost is past, and the ground has warmed up. A 60° F (15° C) soil temperature is required for good germination. Bush beans will become a thick 2 foot high hedge when mature. Allow 3 feet between rows. Make a drill one inch deep and space the seed 2 to 4 inches apart. Cover with soil and firm down with the back of the rake. We always plant treated seed, but if untreated seed is used, it should be planted more closely and then, if necessary, the seedlings thinned. With untreated seed, emergence is not always as reliable.

We often hear people complaining that they have so many beans they don't know what to do with them. Our suggestion is to plant half the quantity in the first seeding and the rest two or three weeks later, thereby staggering the harvest. A 25 foot row will yield 15 to 18 pounds of beans.

Beans are easy to grow. The safest way to avoid problems is to purchase seed of disease-resistant varieties; never grow beans in the same location two years running; burn all plants that have any sign of disease; and never work among the plants when the leaves are wet.

Pole Snap Beans

These beans are similar in appearance and flavour to their bush counterpart. However, you can harvest a larger quantity of pole beans from the same space. We also find pole beans are much less tiring to harvest. The culture is the same as for bush beans, but, as their name denotes, they are climbers and must be given a trellis or poles to climb, installed before the beans are planted. Be sure to place them where they will not cast a shadow on the rest of the garden. Pole beans take slightly longer to mature than bush beans, but when picked regularly, continue producing until frost. We

Harvesting bush beans. One row is of the green and the other of the wax variety. The crop is usually prolific, but picking requires constant bending down – a disadvantage for most folks.

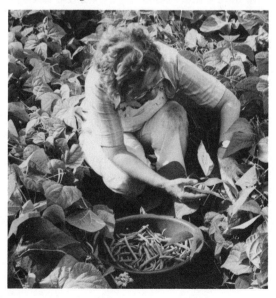

have found the variety "Blue Lake" is very rewarding in our area.

Scarlet Runners: *Phaseolus coccineus*

Scarlet runners are a visually attractive addition to the garden, often planted around a porch or arbour in the flower garden or against a fence as a screen. The 8- to 10-foot vines produce brilliant scarlet flowers, which become 6- to 10-inch long, flat pods. These must be harvested when tender, before the beans mature.

Scarlet runners are best served frenched, or thinly sliced, and are excellent when cooked. The culture is the same as for pole beans.

Bush or Pole Lima Beans: *Phaseolus lunatus* (also known as butter beans)

Limas are usually grown for the beans (rather than the pods) which can be eaten fresh, or allowed to remain on the vine until mature, then harvested, dried and kept for winter use. They can also be picked when immature and cooked in the same manner as snap beans.

The culture is the same as for other bush and pole beans. The important difference is the planting date. Lima beans require a really warm soil for good germination: a minimum soil temperature of 65° F (18° C). Do not sow limas until mid-June. The pole limas are of better quality than the bush, but in areas with a short frost-free season, it is better to grow the bush. Bush limas take 60 to 75 days to mature; pole limas 85 days.

Shelling or Navy Beans: *Phaseolus vulgaris*

These are grown for winter use as dried beans. Unless there is plenty of space available, the shelling bean is not an economical home-garden crop. Culture is the same as for bush beans.

Shelled beans provided the early settlers with a highly nutritious winter food. However, we find that the labour expended in produc-

We grew two pole bean varieties at the same time. The Blue Lake occupied the two sections in the distance and Scarlet Runners the nearest section in the foreground. We found the Blue Lake much more bountiful. Harvesting from a trellis is very simple as the beans are easily seen. Note the Scarlet Runners in the foreground are still in flower, while the Blue Lake are already producing.

ing and drying this crop is not economical. (It should be noted that the beans already discussed are also suitable for drying.)

If there are still plenty of pods on the main crop of pole or snap beans, these can be left to mature, then harvested and dried.

Broad or Fava Beans: *Vicia faba*

Broad beans were introduced into England by the Romans. They became part of the staple diet of the working man, being particularly rich in protein and salts, and sustaining for a hard day's work.

The broad bean is not a reliable crop in our part of the country. A hot spell early in the season makes blooms abort. We plant a row each year because we enjoy the unusual flavour. Some seasons the results are excellent, and we have plenty for the freezer; other times we harvest only a few basketsful.

Unlike snap beans, the broad bean thrives

A row of broad beans in early spring. Note mulch of hay and grass clippings.

Peas: *Pisum sativum*

Pease porridge hot
Pease porridge cold
Pease porridge in the pot
Nine days old.

Some like it hot
Some like it cold
I like it in the pot
Nine days old

Anonymous

History records that peas were highly valued as part of the staple diet of early peoples. The findings of a recent expedition at "Spirit Cave" near the Burmese border of Thailand have carbon dated the seeds of peas and beans at roughly 9750 B.C.

Peas were also found in Egyptian tombs and are known to have been grown by the early Greeks and Romans. It was the pea that Mendel used for his experiments in hybridization, and there are many recorded illustrations of the popularity of peas in both continental Europe and the British Isles.

Peas were used in dried form until the seventeenth century, when they were made into soup or peasmeal pudding. Later, they became fashionable as a fresh vegetable, and still retain their immense popularity today.

Vast strides in plant breeding have made available to us the many varieties offered through the seed catalogues. Peas are very high in food value and rich in vitamin A and the B group, as well as vitamin C. They are always more tasty when freshly picked, and well worth a place in the home garden. Study the different varieties offered in your catalogue and note the following variations:

Height: dwarf or tall (staking)
Maturity: early, mid-season, late
Number and size of peas in pod
Treated or untreated seed
Edible pods

Our preference is for a tall variety, which occupies less room in the garden than the

only in cool conditions. They can be started indoors in 4 inch pots and treated as transplants or seeded outdoors as soon as the ground can be worked. Space the seed 8 inches apart and 3 inches deep, allowing 3 feet between rows. If untreated seed is used, double the quantity of beans in the row, then thin the seedlings to 8 inches apart.

Broad beans are upright 3-foot plants. The thick pods are 6 to 8 inches long and contain up to eight large beans. Most people eat the mature beans, but when young and tender, the entire pod can be cooked and eaten. Broad beans are only recommended for gardens where space is plentiful. Some support may be necessary in windy locations.

The worst enemies of the broad beans are small black flies, or black aphids. These can be readily controlled by regular dustings with rotenone or Diatomaceous earth. When the pods are formed and the plants about 3 feet high, pinch out the growing points. This allows all the strength to go into the beans, and also removes the part of the plant most desirable to the insects. Broad beans take 80 to 90 days to mature. Late spinach or lettuce can be planted as a second crop after the beans are harvested.

dwarf types to produce the equivalent crop. Staked peas are much easier to pick; there is no bending down. We grow an early and a late variety, both of which are planted at the same time but mature ten days apart.

Since peas are a cool-weather crop, it is essential to plant the seed as early as possible in the spring, that is, as soon as the ground can be worked. Later plantings only succeed during a cool spring season. Light frost does not damage pea seedlings.

Over the years we have tested a number of the different varieties of peas listed in seed catalogues. Some had small, very tasty peas, which I found most tedious to shell; others were large, but rather dry and uninteresting. The differing qualities are innumerable and quite distinct. As a result of out tests we prefer "Green Arrow" and "Tall Telephone" for our main crop. These pods are easy to pick and shell, and the peas are of superb quality and flavour for both table and freezer. The catalogue describes them as growing 2½ feet tall, but we have found they always attain a height of at least 4 feet.

Most seed offered in catalogues has been treated with a fungicide. This treatment helps combat damping-off and other destructive organisms which attack both seed and seedling, especially those planted before the ground has had time to warm up.

We always plant treated seed, but purely organic gardeners may prefer their seed untreated. In doing so, however, they run the risk of poor germination or damage to the emerging seedling, a chance we are not prepared to take in our short growing season.

Peas grow best in a good loam that has been enriched in the fall with well-rotted manure or compost. When working the ground in the spring, incorporate a few handfuls of 5:10:10 to each row.

Our method of planting is to dig a trench about 4 inches deep and the width of the spade. We then broadcast the seed in the trench, cover it with one or 2 inches of soil and tamp. As the plants grow, we add more soil. For the tall varieties allow 4 feet between

The shelling peas planted in trenches have germinated. I am driving in metal posts; then I attach poultry netting upon which the vines will climb.

In the foreground poultry netting will support the vines. Behind them is the trellis for taller growing sugar peas.

rows and for dwarf plants, 2 feet. Some gardeners sow their peas in single lines with equal success, but a smaller harvest.

The tall varieties should be staked right away. Use whatever staking materials are available to you: prunings from trees or shrubs, chicken wire, nylon netting, string stretched between rails, old snow-fence or trellis. Even dwarf peas do better if they have some support.

Edible Podded or Snow Peas: *Pisum sativum macrocarpon*

Snow peas are available in both dwarf and tall varieties. Their cultivation is the same as for ordinary peas, but daily harvesting becomes essential. The pods must be picked before the peas form and while they are still flat and stringless. The more regular the harvesting, the longer the plants will continue to produce.

Snow peas are very popular in Chinese dishes. They may be eaten raw in salads, or steamed until tender but still "crisp". They freeze well too!

Sugar Snap Peas

The sugar snap pea is a relatively new cultivar (variety) which combines the best qualities of both snow peas and shelling peas. They are delicious, tender and crisp, especially when eaten raw.

Climbing sugar snap peas develop vigorous 6- to 10- foot vines which must be supported, and the pods must be harvested regularly to promote continuing development of seed pods. Dwarf sugar snap peas also need some support.

Cultural requirements are the same as for ordinary peas. Because you eat both the pea and the pod, sugar snaps provide twice as much food as shelling peas and give you half the work in preparing them for the table. They are a vegetable well worth growing.

There are seldom many problems with peas, adverse weather conditions being the most likely one. For any insect infestations

Above: Two rows of peas in foreground climb poultry netting. In background climbing snow peas in flower have reached the top of the 6 foot trellis. Both varieties were planted on the same day in late April. *Below:* Shelling peas will soon be ready to harvest.

Picking sugar peas which have grown well above the height of the trellis.

we apply Diatomaceous earth or rotenone powder. As mildew has attacked only the sugar peas late in the season after many weeks of harvest, we pull up the plants and burn them. This is the best way to prevent the fungus from spreading.

Peanuts: *Arachis hypogaea*

Although peanuts are listed in seed catalogues, they are grown only as a novelty plant in home vegetable gardens. The hot growing season in more northerly regions is not nearly long enough for peanuts to ripen. We have several friends who have grown them with moderate success, but for northern gardeners whose space is limited, there is no economic value from growing this plant. The greatest value will be as an experiment for children.

The peanut is a member of the pea family, but its growing habits are very different to ordinary garden peas. The nuts should be planted outdoors in May. The plants will grow 12 to 18 inches tall and, after the flowers have been pollinated, the stalks will become elongated, bend down and root themselves in the soil. The peanuts develop in clusters under the ground. Peanuts prefer the poor,

slightly acid, sandy soil that sweet potatoes like.

Harvest before the first frost by digging up the entire vine and hanging it in the garage or open shed to cure. Peanuts are relatively trouble free.

Supports for Beans and Peas

Many vegetables need some kind of support to prevent them from being blown over by the wind or collapsing under their own weight. Climbing vegetables such as sugar snap peas, snow peas and pole beans can reach heights of 8 feet or more and definitely need support. Supports are usually constructed from whatever materials are at hand and according to the whims and skills of the gardener.

If brushwood is available locally (brushwood is the thinnings from shrubberies or woods), it makes an excellent inexpensive support. To stand firm in high winds, the brush must be pushed into the ground with some force.

Teepees, made from tall poles are excellent for pole beans, especially the scarlet runners. They also make delightful play houses for children. Make sure you secure the poles firmly at the top.

For our shelling peas, which grow to about 4 feet, we use metal fence posts to support the chicken wire. The vines grow up the wire hooking on to it with their tentacles. The posts and wire last for many years and should be stored under cover for the winter.

Hopson trellis: We are indebted to Anne Hopson of Carsonby, Ontario for introducing us to a trellis designed by her engineer husband, and tested with success over many years. Basically, the Hopson trellis, illustrated here, consists of a series of A-frames which incorporate open-ended boxes at top and bottom; the frames are connected by a ridge pole at the top and one at each side at the bottom. The upper ridge poles have 1½-inch galvanized nails set every 4 inches along the top, while the lower poles have similar nails along

The Hopson Trellis
1. Ridge poles
2. A-frame elevation (front)
3. A-frame elevation (side)
4. Trellis assembled and extended

the outer sides. The ridge poles slide into and are pinned firmly to the open-ended boxes by means of 5 inch nails. The entire trellis is itself secured to the ground by 2 by 2 inch stakes, 18 inches long. These are driven through a small box fixed to the lowest cross pieces on each A-frame. Once the trellis is in position, lace binder twine securely between the upper ridge pole and the base, using the galvanized nails to keep the twine correctly spaced. These trellises withstand high winds, even when loaded down with heavy vines. In exposed areas, however, extra support may be needed. A metal fence post or strong stake can be driven into the ground and secured to the trellis.

The wood used for our trellis is 1 by 3 inch treated cedar. Such trellises can be made to any size, but ours are 6 feet high and 3 feet wide. The ridge poles are all 9 feet long. There are numerous pictures of these trellises in this book, and I think you will agree that they are practical and look attractive. Unless you make them yourself, they are not cheap. However, they should last a good many years, if well treated.

Planting bean seeds at the base of a Hopson trellis.

Pole beans starting to climb the Hopson trellis. Note mulch of grass clippings.

Above: Trellis using 2-inch by 2-inch cedar posts.
Below: Trellis used by the Central Experimental Farm in Ottawa consists of stout cedar poles supporting open nylon netting.

An alternate method of staking peas is the use of brushwood or prunings from trees and shrubs.

overwinter in piles of leaves and emerge in the spring at about the same time as the beans are germinating. After a week or two the females lay eggs on the undersides of leaves which hatch within fifteen days. The larvae and adults then feed on the undersides of leaves, chewing holes right through and giving the leaves a lacy appearance. They will also attack the stems and pods when a garden plot is badly infested. It is important when spraying or dusting to reach the undersides of the leaves.

Mexican bean beetle

Problems and Controls

Mexican bean beetles: Mexican bean beetles can easily be mistaken for lady beetles, but they are slightly larger and always have sixteen spots. Lady beetles can have as many as twelve spots and as few as two. These pests

Leafhoppers: These are small pale green insects that move rapidly when the plant is touched. They are often hard to see. They damage the plants by sucking the sap from the undersides of the leaves causing stunted growth and crinkling of the leaves. Treatment is the same as for Mexican bean beetle.

Bean weevils: Dry beans in storage may be infested by small, white grubs called bean weevils. To prevent this happening, bake the beans for thirty minutes on a cooking sheet with the oven temperature set at 130° F (54° C).

Anthracnose: A seed-borne fungal disease, Anthracnose attacks stems, leaves and pods of beans, causing reddish-brown, elongated sunken areas to appear. Prevention consists of planting Western-grown seed, and not working among the plants when the leaves are wet. The fungus can survive in the remains of diseased plants. Diseased plants should be burnt or put in the garbage; never in the compost heap.

Bacterial blight: In beans, bacterial blight is recognized by brown blotches encircled by a reddish-yellow ring. Control is the same as with anthracnose.

Virus diseases such as mosaics can be controlled by spraying or dusting for insects, or by planting resistant varieties.

Rust: Reddish pustules on leaves indicate the presence of rust. The leaves eventually die and fall off. There is no control except planting rust resistant varieties.

Pea aphids: These large, green plant lice suck the juices from the plant tips, eventually causing the plant to die. Control is to dust or spray as soon as aphids are noticed. A hard rain or strong jet of water from the hose will knock many of them off.

Pea weevil: The larvae of the pea weevil are brownish grubs with black, white and grey markings. They burrow into the pods of peas. If peas are being dried for storage or seed, weevils could be a problem. If, however, peas are stored at freezing or below, the weevils cannot develop. Control is to spray or dust with a recommended pesticide, and to burn pea vines after harvest.

Yellows: Vines turning yellow can be caused

Above: The vine on left is an example of pea yellows disease. *Below:* Enlarged photograph of adult lady bug stalking pea aphids.

by root rot or by a virus that is spread by aphids, which produces yellow stunted plants and curled or misshapen pods. Control of aphids is essential. Immediately diseased plants are seen, they should be removed from the garden and burned.

Fusarium wilt: This soil-borne fungal disease causes stunted growth with a downward curling of leaves. The most effective prevention is to plant treated seed, practice crop rotation and locate peas in well-drained soil.

Root rot: Root rot is caused by several soil-borne fungi that may live in the soil for many years. It causes the vines to turn yellow, then brown at the roots and eventually die. Control is the same as for Fusarium wilt.

LILIACEAE: The Lily Family
Includes Asparagus

Asparagus: *Asparagus officinalis*

The tender spring shoots (or sprears) of this delectable perennial vegetable were known and cultivated by the Romans at least as early as 200 B.C. Cato's cultural directions would still serve us well today.

Early settlers brought plants to America, where they thrived in our cold climate. No garden with space available is complete without asparagus.

Asparagus can be grown from seed, but for the small quantity required for a home garden, I would recommend good-quality, one-year-old crowns. These should have at least ten vigorous roots, each not less than 6 inches in length. Early spring is the time to start an asparagus bed.

The location of the asparagus bed must be chosen with care, as the plants will produce for at least twenty years. The ground should be well-drained and sunny, and warm up early in the spring. The proximity of large trees, or of young trees likely to grow rapidly over the next few years, should be avoided as the roots will deprive the asparagus of essential nourishment. When allocating an area, the number of crowns required depends on the size of the family. Fifteen plants for each member should be sufficient, but if a freezer supply is needed, add ten more plants per person.

Allow 3 feet between the rows, and set the crowns 12 to 24 inches apart. Where space is limited, prepare a bed 4 1/2 feet wide, with 18 inches separating two rows. Plants should be 16 inches apart in the rows.

Asparagus grows best in a neutral or slightly alkaline soil. A soil test will determine whether lime is needed and, if so, this is best applied in the fall. Digging and manuring must be thorough, and should be done well in advance of planting time, preferably in the fall. When reworking the ground in the spring, add bone meal as well as commercial fertilizer (20 pounds of 5:10:10 per 1000 square feet).

The roots should be planted immediately they arrive in late April or early May. Mark each row with a garden line to make sure the trench is straight when dug out with a spade. The trench should be wide enough to take the outspread roots, and deep enough to cover the crowns with 4 inches of soil in a clay loam, or 6 inches in a sandy loam. Do not completely fill the trench at planting time; gradually do so as the plants start to grow.

Take care not to damage the fleshy, strip-like roots. These break very easily when being handled. After planting give the bed a thorough soaking.

It is most important to keep the asparagus bed free from weeds; regular attention is essential. Quack grass will become a serious problem if allowed to get out of control.

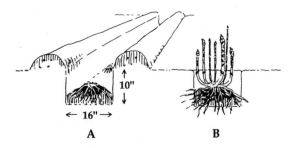

A. The asparagus trench should be about 16 inches wide, and 10 inches deep. The crowns are placed 16 inches apart, with the roots of each crown spread out around a small mound so that the roots slope downwards.

B. When the asparagus plants are three years old and well established, spears can be harvested by either cutting or snapping off.

An asparagus bed takes several years to establish. However, once it begins to flourish it is very rewarding. Here you see "tips" emerging from the cold ground in early spring. These tips can be cut (or broken off) when about 6 to 8 inches high. On a warm spring day they grow almost that much, so a daily harvesting is possible.

The asparagus season ends after six to eight weeks and, except for weeding, the bed can be left virtually unattended for the season, although it will appreciate a good top dressing of manure. This picture shows a plant in mid-summer and gives an idea of the area and size to which it grows.

At my home in Ireland, we applied a light sprinkling of agricultural salt (pickling salt) during the summer, unless seaweed was available. We still follow this practice. Salt is now not generally recommended by the experts, and I am told its sole value is as a weed killer. Seaweed is not available in our area, so we now apply a mulch of well-rotted compost which helps control weeds and provides nourishment. Hay is another common form of mulch, but it often harbours weed seeds. Clean straw is also excellent.

Do not cut any spears until the plants are three years old. Then take only a limited quantity. Once the bed is well-established, six to eight weeks of harvest is sufficient, depending on the season. After harvesting is finished, the tops must be allowed to grow. These can be cut down during the fall garden clean-up, or may be left until spring to catch snow which insulates the ground.

Early each spring apply a complete fertilizer, 5:10:10 at a rate of 5 pounds to each 25 feet of row. Work this into the ground, taking care not to damage the tender young shoots. After harvesting, give a light application of 10:10:10 fertilizer, or spread well-rotted manure around the plants. The latter is likely to encourage weed growth, but it is the practice we prefer.

When harvesting with a knife, care must be taken not to damage the tips of adjacent spears still below the soil. Many people maintain they increase the yield of asparagus by snapping the sprears off, rather than cutting. Grasp the spear in the hand, bend it downwards, and the entire spear that snaps off will be tender enough to be eaten.

Note: You will find that some plants produce large, fat spears, while others a far greater number of spindly ones. The former are female plants which, when mature, will produce seeds in the fall. The latter are the male plants. Both are equally good to eat and each plant will produce approximately the same weight of crop.

Problems and Controls

Asparagus does not suffer many ailments. The asparagus beetles are the most common problem. There are two species, one orange with black spots, the other metalic with six yellow spots. Both are about 1/4 inch long. They cause the spears to have a grub-chewed appearance and growth may be distorted or stunted. Adult beetles overwinter in debris or under old boards, emerging in spring as soon as the asparagus plants send up new growth. The females lay their eggs on the tips of shoots, and both the adults and the emerging larvae feed on the foliage and stems. About two weeks later the larvae burrow into the ground to pupate. These, in turn, hatch and the cycle repeats itself. Several generations occur each season.

Asparagus beetles can be controlled by either dusting repeatedly with Diatomaceous earth or rotenone, or by spraying with a recommended insecticide.

Asparagus beetle

Asparagus rust: To eliminate this problem, it is a good idea to grow rust-resistant varieties of asparagus. If spears show signs of orange, rust-coloured blemishes on the stem or foliage, immediately cut the infected shoots and burn or send to the garbage. Diseased material should not be put in the compost. Cut the plants close to the ground in the fall and compost the refuse.

MALVACEAE: The Hibiscus Family
Includes Okra

Okra: *Hibiscus esculentus*

Okra, which is often referred to as gumbo, is a tropical plant native to Africa. It is not a popular vegetable for short season home gardens because it is very frost-tender. Although it can be grown, it is not reliable in zone 4; the crop results depend on the season.

We have grown okra in our garden only as an experiment, and for the attractive flower. We did not find that the harvested crop gave us a good return for the space it occupied or the labour involved. However, in locations where the growing season is long, growing okra might be more rewarding. Okra occupies about the same amount of space as bush beans and can attain a height of approximately three feet, depending on the variety. The cultural requirements are similar to those of bush beans. The immature pods are used as a vegetable or to thicken soups or stews. The pods must be harvested at least every other day, otherwise they become tough and woody, and the plant will stop producing.

We do not recommend okra for gardens where space is limited.

Okra is not, however, bothered by any major pests or diseases in our colder climate.

POLYGONACEAE: Buckwheat or Knotweed Family
Includes Rhubarb

Rhubarb: *Rheum rhabarbarum*

A native to many parts of eastern Asia, rhubarb is believed to have derived its name from the Russian "Rhu" (now the Volga) River upon whose banks it grew, and from "Barbarum," from the barbarian districts beyond the confines of the Roman Empire. Rhubarb was first noticed in England in 1773, but was not in use as a culinary plant until the 1820's. In Victorian times rhubarb was known as "pie-plant".

Most early records make reference to the strong purgative properties of the plant, but this has been largely bred out of the varieties we grow in our gardens nowadays.

Rhubarb is a very hardy perennial and deserves a sunny, permanent location in every home garden. When well-cultivated it will produce a crop for many years, often twenty or more.

The preparation of the soil is approximately the same as for asparagus. Dig a deep hole at least 2 feet square and 15 inches deep. Fill the bottom of the hole with well-rotted manure or compost. Add some topsoil and a handful of bone meal, mix well, and replace an inch or two of topsoil before planting the roots.

There are several varieties of rhubarb: the tart, green one for relishes, and the pink

A healthy bed of rhubarb. They do best in a separate bed or at one side of the garden where they will not be disturbed by annual cultivation.

stemmed "strawberry" or "ruby" for desserts. The varieties Valentine and Crimson Cherry Red are both sweet and have solid red stems.

Roots may be purchased from a nursery garden or obtained from friends who are dividing their clumps. Most rhubarb clumps need only be divided every ten or fifteen years, but may be divided more often for propagation purposes. Each root planted must contain at least one strong bud, preferably two or three, which when planted should be just barely covered with soil. After planting, water thoroughly, then mulch. Under favourable conditions, each root will develop into a strong plant in one year.

Thereafter, top dress the plants each spring and fall with well-rotted manure. If manure is not available, apply one pound of complete fertilizer to each plant in the spring. We mulch the plants to control weeds and conserve moisture. This makes it necessary to pull the mulch back before spreading the manure. Rhubarb is a gross feeder and is not easily overfertilized.

No stalks should be harvested until the second year, and then only a small quantity. From the third year on, the stalks may be pulled, never cut, on attaining the proper size. Harvest for approximately eight weeks, and from then on, more carefully as long as the plants are kept growing vigorously. Plenty of water is essential.

When pulling up the stalk, grasp it firmly near the base and give it a sideways jerk. It will come away cleanly from the crown.

Two or three strong plants are usually enough for the average family, but double this quantity if you want to freeze a year's supply.

Note that only the stalks, or petioles, are edible. The leaf blades have been known to cause severe poisoning when eaten by humans or livestock.

Rhubarb is not generally bothered by insects or diseases. Spindly stalks are the result of insufficient fertilizing or a lack of sun and moisture. Always remove flower stalks by cutting close to the ground. Allowing flowers to set seed drains strength from the plant.

Above: Rhubarb roots need dividing every ten or twenty years. These knarled orange-coloured roots can be dug out and simply divided by cutting with a sharp spade. This can be done either in early spring or late fall. *Below:* A May 24 weekend work party prepares rhubarb for the freezer.

To prepare for the freezer, simply wash and dry young stalks, and cut into one-inch lengths. Fill plastic bags, seal and freeze.

SOLANACEAE: The Nightshade Family
Includes Eggplant, Pepper, Tomato, Potato, Garden Huckleberry, and Ground Cherry

Soil Requirements for Eggplant, Peppers and Tomatoes

All these plants require the same soil preparation. They will grow in a wide range of soils as long as the soil is warm, has a high water holding capacity and is fertile. The pH should be 5.5 to 6.5.

Whenever possible, add well-rotted manure or compost to the soil. Most soils also need additional fertilizer: 30 to 40 pounds of 5:10:10 per 1,000 square feet.

Work the ground deeply to ensure good friable conditions in which the plants can develop stong root systems. When setting transplants out in the garden, an application of transplant starter solution is beneficial. One cupful to each plant is recommended, using 2 tablespoons of 5:10:5 to one gallon of water or a commercial transplant equivalent.

After the soil is really warm, and the moisture level is deep, we apply a mulch. This is not essential, but it saves both weeding and watering. All three plants need full sun and protection from wind.

Eggplant: *Solanum melongena*

The eggplant, or aubergine, is not as easy to grow successfully as the tomato or pepper. It is native to India and the Far East. Because eggplants are very frost tender do not be in a hurry to get them out in the garden. They do best in a long hot summer. Eggplant seed must be started indoors eight to ten weeks ahead of planting-out time. It requires warmer conditions than the pepper, if possible 70° to 80° F (21° to 26° C) at night, 80° to 90° F (27° to 32° C) during the day. Be careful not to place the flats too close to the source of heat; this might cause damage to the roots. Reduce the temperature slightly after the

seedlings have developed. Keep the soil moist but not soggy.

Harden the plants slowly; they are very temperamental. We always allow them about three weeks in the cold-frame, gradually increasing the length of time that the lid is open. They must be given shade from intense sun shining through the glass, and extra protection at night if the temperature drops. Their exposure to the elements is gradual but, with luck, they will have spent their last week in the frame with the lid open day and night. They should now be sufficiently hardened to be set out in the garden. If you only need a few plants, it is much simpler to purchase them from a reputable grower. Make sure that you know which variety you are buying,

Close-up of young eggplant showing strong root growth emerging through nylon mesh of Jiffy-7.

A high gloss on the eggplant fruit is an indication of ripeness.

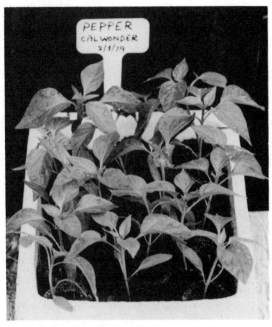

Peppers grown from seed in Jiffy-7's, ready to be planted out.

as the ultimate size of the plant depends on the variety. Many hybrids are smaller and can be planted more closely in the rows. In general, the cultivation and planting of eggplant is the same as for peppers.

Eggplant are heavy feeders and benefit from additional fertilizing. We apply a balanced liquid fertilizer high in phosphorous and potash, giving each plant a good soaking every two or three weeks. If the plant has been mulched, pull back the mulch before fertilizing, then replace it.

Crop rotation is extremely important. Never plant eggplant where any member of the nightshade family was grown the previous year. Harvest the fruit by cutting with clippers or a sharp knife. Select young fruit while the skin is still very shiny purple. If eggplants are over-ripe, the skin will be dull with brown streaks, seeds will have formed and the flesh will be pithy and bitter. We prefer to eat eggplant fresh from the garden rather than frozen. Five or six plants give an ample supply to most families.

Sweet Peppers: *Capsicum annuum*
Hot Peppers: *Capsicum a. frutescens*

The garden pepper is now a very popular plant for the home garden. If you can grow tomatoes, you can grow peppers. A native to Central and South America, peppers are known to have been cultivated by the Aztecs. Early explorers introduced them to Spain and Portugal, and they are now grown in all parts of the world where the growing season is sufficiently warm and long. Climatic conditions at the time of flower development have a strong influence on fruit set. Periods of high temperature and low humidity, temperatures below 55° F (13° C) or strong winds will cause blossoms to abort and fall off.

In short season areas peppers must be grown as transplants, starting the seed indoors in March. By mid-May, the plants should be about 8 inches tall and have sturdy, strong stems. They are then ready for hardening, prior to being set-out in the garden.

If you plan to grow only three or four plants,

Peppers ready to harvest.

provide ample fruit for both fresh summer dishes and the winter supply in the freezer. Peppers are vulnerable to many of the same ailments as potatoes, tomatoes and eggplant.

The cultivation of hot peppers is identical to that of sweet peppers. Hot peppers can be eaten fresh or dried for winter use.

Tomatoes: *Lycopersicum esculentum*

The tomato, like its cousin the pepper, is native to the tropical Americas and was introduced to Europe at about the same time. In Elizabethan England tomatoes were called "love apples" and were grown in the flower garden. For many years the tomato was believed to be poisonous. George Washington Carver (c. 1864-1943), the famous American botanist and son of Negro slaves, is reputed to have eaten tomatoes publicly before a horrified crowd. This act helped dispel the poison myth, and today the vitamin-rich fruit is one of our main sources of vitamin C. In the United States it ranks second to potatoes in economic value. Tomatoes are now the most widely grown of all vegetables in the home garden. Some people who have only a balcony or verandah grow tomatoes in tubs, pots or hanging baskets.

There are well over a hundred so-called varieties offered through the seed catalogues. These may vary in days to maturity, habit of growth, size of plant, colour, size, shape of fruit and resistance to disease. A small type of plant does not necessarily produce cherry tomatoes, any more than a large plant produces large fruit. When selecting seed, it is advisable to know the ultimate size of the bush and what type of fruit it will produce.

Tomatoes are divided into two main groups: determinate and indeterminate. The determinate, or bush, tomato stops growing when the end buds set fruit, usually at about 3 feet in height. These are the early crops. The indeterminate tomato grows almost indefinitely because the end buds do not set fruit. In our area their growth is arrested by frost. Indeterminate tomatoes are grown in

purchase them from a dependable grower, and look for sturdy plants. Spindly, tall plants will not grow into productive bushes. Do not set the plants in the garden until the soil has warmed up and the night temperature is above 60° F (15° C). In our area this is usually the first week in June. If necessary, give the plants some protection for the first few days. As the plants will become strong bushes about 2¹/₂ feet high, allow 3 feet between the rows and 2¹/₂ feet between the plants in the rows. Usually, it is not necessary to stake peppers, but if the branches should become heavy with fruit, support may be required.

Never work around the plants when the leaves are wet, and never smoke tobacco near them. If you do smoke, wash your hands before handling pepper plants. This helps prevent the spread of a viral disease, tobacco mosaic.

Sweet red peppers are the green pepper when it has ripened. We always leave some early fruit on the bushes, allowing them to ripen. Red peppers have a far higher vitamin C content than green peppers; they are sweeter too. We grow ten sweet pepper plants, which cages or are trained on stakes.

There are some varieties now being offered in Canada and northern U.S.A. whose seed can be planted directly in the garden, after all danger of frost is past. However, it is more usual to grow tomatoes as transplants; the choice of varieties is far greater. Tomato seeds germinate in six to fourteen days and should be started indoors six to eight weeks prior to planting-out time. The days to maturity given in seed catalogues are from the time the plants are set out in the garden. Tomatoes can be set out a little earlier than eggplant and pepper, even though they are also very frost-tender, and the slightest frost will damage the young plants. It is better to wait until the soil is warm than to take any risks. If you must set them out early, give them some protection until they become established.

Tomatoes prefer full sun and fertile, well-drained soil. They tend to ripen earlier in sandy soil, but will produce a larger crop in clay. When setting out transplants, plant at a 45° angle with half to two-thirds of the stem under the ground. The plants will straighten up in a day or two. This allows roots to grow along the stem, giving added support and a greater root system for nutrient up-take. Watering with a transplant solution gets tomatoes off to a good start.

Tomatoes are heavy feeders and benefit from regular applications of either liquid manure or a complete fertilizer during the early stage of growth; then, after fruit has set, with a high phosphorous and potash compound. Never permit the soil to dry out. Smokers

When planting out sturdy plants, set 2/3 of the stem in the soil (with leggy plants, 3/4 of the stem). Lay the plant at an angle. Within a few days it will straighten out. Remove any leaves that would be below the soil. Wrap a paper collar around the stem to prevent cutworm damage.

should be warned that they could transmit tobacco mosaic to the plants and should always wash their hands before entering the garden.

Tomatoes are vulnerable to a number of pests and diseases, especially "wilts", transmitted by insects. Grow varieties that have been bred for their resistance to disease. In seed catalogues the letters "V" (Verticillium), "F" (Fusarium), "T" (Tomato Mosaic Virus) and "N" (Nematode) denote such varieties. The letter "H" indicates that it is a hybrid.

Whether growing your own or purchasing transplants, look for stocky, strong-stemmed plants. If you are a newcomer to the area, inquire as to which varieties have been proven satisfactory there. Avoid purchasing leggy plants that are already in bloom or have set fruit. You may get an early ripe tomato, but the ultimate crop will be poor.

Tomato supports

Many varieties of tomatoes grow very tall and need support to prevent the stems from breaking and to keep the fruit off the ground. For many years it has been customary to prune tomato plants, leaving one main stem. With this technique a stout stake is needed and must be driven into the ground prior to planting the transplant. As the plant grows, it is tied to the stake and the shoots that grow in the axils of the leaves pinched out.

We have found this technique to be time consuming and now grow all our tomatoes in homemade page-wire rings. This method eliminates pruning. As the plant grows, it supports itself inside the ring. We secure the rings firmly to the ground by stakes. Harvesting through the open mesh is simple. Garden centres now sell tomato rings ready to assemble.

Old car tires: It was through information passed on at a Horticultural Society meeting that I first learned how useful old car tires can be in the garden. I have since heard that in windy areas along the Prince Edward Island coast tomato plants are frequently seen growing inside old car tires. The tires

Above: Flat of tomato seedlings.   *Right:* Close-up of
tomato plant in Jiffy-7 showing root system.
Below: Tomato plants in wire cages.   Straw mulch covers
the ground.   *Below right:* Close-up of cherry tomatoes,
commonly used in salads.

Tomato cages using page-wire fencing.

not only protect the plants from the wind, but also retain heat, hastening the maturity of the fruit. Several tires can be stacked around the plant as it grows.

Potatoes: *Solanum tuberosum*

The potato is native to South America, probably Peru, and was brought to Europe by the Spaniards early in the sixteenth century. Sir Walter Raleigh is generally credited with its introduction to the British Isles in 1586. There is little doubt that it was he who brought the potato to Ireland after he was granted large estates there. It is surprising to find another two centuries were to elapse before the potato gained further attention.

Today, it is among the world's leading crops.

Potatoes are one of the cheapest sources of carbohydrates and contain appreciable amounts of vitamins and minerals, especially when eaten skin and all. There are few vegetables more delicious than early potatoes freshly dug from the garden. We rate freshly picked corn and newly dug potatoes in the same class. Only those who have tasted them will understand what we mean. So-called "new" potatoes in the supermarkets bear no comparison. We dig only as many as we need for each meal; even 24 hours seems to alter the flavour.

A few early potato plants deserve a place in the garden. The main crop for winter storage is easy and inexpensive to purchase in the fall. We do not recommend growing a main crop of potatoes unless ample space is available.

Most garden soils are suitable for potatoes, but the best results are obtained from a slightly acid, well-drained soil rich in humus. The texture and colour of the tubers will vary according to the type of soil in which they are grown. Always rotate the potato patch, remembering that potatoes, tomatoes, peppers and eggplant belong to the same family and are grouped together for rotation purposes.

Always plant certified seed unless you are quite certain that your own crop was absolutely healthy. We prefer seed potato to be

Right: Egg-sized seed potatoes show at least one eye that has already sprouted. *Below:* Seed potatoes sprouting in trays in the basement.

small 1½ to 2 ounce tubers from a good, clean crop. If these are not available, larger potatoes can be cut into chunky pieces, leaving two eyes on each. After cutting, these should be dusted with a fungicide, (we use powdered sulphur) and then left for several days in a warm, dry place to heal the wound.

We find we get the best results from small seed potatoes which are sprouted before planting. This is done by placing the tubers, with the"rose", (the end with the most eyes) facing up in a flat preferably lined with peat moss. The tubers should not be crowded. Opinion varies as to how much light should be given, but we prefer to leave them in a darkish place where they will sprout anyway. The temperature should not be above 40° F (4° C). The length of time for sprouting depends on the temperature, anywhere from three to six weeks. Great care must be taken when planting-out not to damage the sprouts. By exposing the seed tubers to the sun for about one hour, the sprouts will wilt and be less brittle. The extra time taken is well spent, for there should be a significant increase in the yield of crop. It is often recommended that the seed tuber should have only two eyes sprouting, the rest should be rubbed off. We find that this is not important because the weight of crop from each plant will be the same; the ones with only two sprouts left having fewer, larger tubers. Potatoes should be planted out as soon as the ground dries up sufficiently to work, and there is little danger of a killing frost.

There are many different methods of planting, but the rows are always 3 feet apart and the tubers 12 inches apart in the row. One way is to dig holes and plant tubers 4 inches deep. Another is to dig a trench 12 inches deep; work in well-rotted manure or compost; replace a little soil; plant the potato and cover with an inch or two of soil, adding more soil as the plants grow. However, some authorities warn that the use of fresh manure in the ground the year before potatoes are sown, is conducive to scab.

Ruth Stout, in her book "A Green Thumb

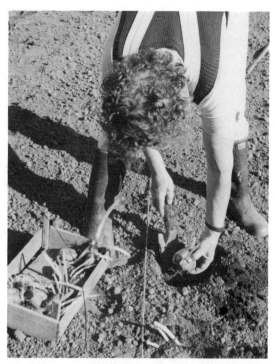

Above: Sprouted tubers being planted out.
Below: Potatoes being grown under hay mulch. The ridges are made by the growth pushing up from below. More hay may be required to prevent tubers developing green shoulders.

Without an Aching Back," has a completely different method. She just spread the potatoes on the ground and covered them with old hay! We have tried this method and it really works. Our only problem was in not spreading the hay deeply enough. We had a number of green potatoes, the result of exposure to light. Green potatoes are poisonous, as are the fruits or seed pods of the potato.

When potatoes are planted in the ground without a mulch, regular cultivation will be necessary to keep the weeds under control. As the plants grow and the tubers develop, hill up the earth around the tubers. This is usually done twice during the season. After flowers have formed on early potato plants, it is time to start harvesting. We do not dig the entire plant. Instead, we scratch away some soil and look for tubers large enough to eat, leaving the rest undisturbed to continue growing. Main crop potatoes should be left in the ground until the tops die down and the skins become firm. A light frost will not damage the tubers. We dig our main crop early in October.

Dig the crop with a fork on a warm, dry day when the soil is not wet. Leave the potatoes on the surface for an hour or so to dry,

then bring them indoors and store in a cool place where they will not freeze. The ideal temperature is 36° F to 40° C (2° to 4° C), seldom possible in modern houses.

Garden Huckleberry: *Solanum nigrum*

The garden huckleberry, an annual, produces quantities of large, blue berries all along the branches. It is only used cooked and sweetened because the raw berries are extremely tart. Four plants should be ample for a family. The seeds should be started indoors or in the hot-frame six weeks prior to planting out. A distance of 4 feet between plants is necessary for they will become large spreading bushes. Although the fruit may turn blue in August, it is seldom ripe until September, and anyone picking it too early will be disappointed with the results.

This is an easy fruit to grow and, although not susceptible to many pests or diseases, is sometimes attacked by flea beetles or succumbs to mildew. A combination spray or dusting does the trick.

The fresh fruit can be put directly into the

Left: After digging, the potatoes dry in the sun before being brought into storage. *Below:* A healthy garden huckleberry transplant grown from seed. I plant two of these approximately 3 feet apart. They will provide all the fruit we need.

Ripe huckleberry.

freezer and used when needed during the winter. Our family is particularly fond of Huckleberry Crumble served hot with whipped or sour cream.

Ground Cherry: *Physalis pruinosa*

The ground cherry, or husk or strawberry tomato, as it is sometimes called, is a close relative of the ornamental Chinese lantern. The fruits of this annual are produced inside a paper-like husk. They are golden in colour and about the size of cherry tomatoes, but are much sweeter than tomatoes.

Some of our neighbours have had successful crops from direct outdoor seeding. Not so in our garden; we have to grow them as transplants.

Cultural requirements are similar to tomatoes. The ground cherry plants will attain a height of about 3 feet. They will not require staking.

Problems and Controls

Colorado potato beetle: This common pest overwinters in the soil emerging in the spring to lay her eggs on the undersides of leaves. In about a week, red, hump-backed larvae hatch to spend the next three weeks voraciously eating the foliage of the plants. They then burrow into the soil, pupate and re-appear as yellow, hemispherical beetles that have black spots on the heads and five black stripes on each wing sheath.

In a small garden the egg clusters and beetles may be hand-picked and crushed. In larger gardens regular dusting or spraying with an insecticide may be necessary. Another control is to sprinkle bran over the plants when the dew is still wet on the leaves. The beetle will gorge itself on the bran, fall to the ground and become dehydrated.

Flea beetles, leaf hoppers, and aphids: All these insects may spread bacterial diseases, viruses and spindle tuber. They can be controlled with spraying or dusting.

Cutworms: Cutworms can destroy newly set out transplants. Some species of cutworms will even attack young potato plants.

When necessary, apply paper collars at ground level to protect tender stems. When you find stems that a cutworm has severed,

Adult Colorado beetle.

dig down around the plant to find the culprit and destroy it.

Wireworms: These pests often attack potato tubers by tunnelling into them and rendering them inedible and unfit for storage. The best control is to work the ground several times both in the fall and spring, exposing the larvae to the elements. Birds, (especially guinea fowl, which we have) eat the larvae.

Pepper maggots: These half-inch white grubs are the larvae of a yellowish striped fly. They are sometimes found in the fruit of pepper plants and can be controlled, if noticed, by dusting or spraying with an insecticide at weekly intervals, after the fruit has set.

Tomato fruitworm: This is the same insect as the corn earworm. They are not a common problem, but if you notice holes in the fruit, spray or dust with insecticide.

Tomato hornworm: Hornworms are large, ugly worms that usually measure from three to four inches in length. They are bright green with eight yellow stripes and a "horn" that protrudes from the rear end. This pest pupates over winter in the soil and emerges in early summer as a large hawk or hummingbird moth with a wingspan of up to 5 inches. The females lay single, spherical yellow-green eggs under the leaves. In about a week the caterpillars hatch and begin feeding.

They are ravenous feeders and can defoliate a plant very rapidly. As they are seldom numerous, the simplest control is to pick off by hand, any that are found. You can spot them in the area where defoliation has occurred and by a pile of mouse-sized feces.

The natural predator of the hornworm is a parasitic wasp which lays her eggs on the insect's back. When you see a hornworm carrying these eggs, you should not destroy it. The young wasps will kill this hornworm and mature to fly off and attack others.

Hornworm

Whiteflies: Whiteflies are sucking insects found on the leaves and stems of plants. They are usually noticed when a plant is disturbed, when they fly out in a cloud. To control, spray at four to five day intervals with rotenone or insecticidal soap. Also, a strong jet of water from the garden hose is surprisingly effective.

Slugs: These pests have never been a serious problem in our garden, but we know from our viewers that they can cause severe damage, and be a perfect menace in the garden. They feed from early spring until late fall.

There are commercial slug-baits available, but the simplest control is to place shallow dishes of beer around the garden in which the slugs will drown. A simple trap can be made by inverting half grapefruit rinds on the soil surface. Be sure to check them daily. The salt treatment mentioned earlier also works.

Virus diseases: Diseases such as mosaics and leaf roll are transmitted by insects, which, after feeding on infected plants or weeds, move on to healthy stock, taking the disease with them. In general, these diseases can be identified by mottling, yellowing, curling and crinkling of the leaves. To prevent spread of

Wireworm being extracted from potato with tweezers.

viruses, it is essential to control weeds and insects: there is no cure for infected plants.

Early blight: The symptoms of early blight in potatoes include small, circular or oval brown-black spots on the leaves which gradually increase in size, forming concentric rings. The rings readily identify the disease. It is a fungal disease that overwinters in discarded potato debris and is spread the following spring by wind, rain and insects. Early blight is not often a serious problem and can usually be controlled by burning old plants after harvest, or by treating plants with a fungicide at ten-day intervals during the growing season, especially when the weather is hot and humid.

Late blight: On the other hand, late blight on potatoes is extrememly serious. This fungal disease occurs when the weather in late summer and fall is wet and cool. It can attack the crop very suddenly, and the unwary home gardener might mistake the symptoms for the effects of an early frost.

A very clear description of "The Blight" is given in Desmond Guinness's and William Ryan's book "Irish Houses and Castles". It includes an extract from the diary of Miss Frances Cobbe of Newbridge Co. Dublin in which she states,

"I happen to be able to recall precisely the day, almost the hour, when the blight fell on the potatoes and caused the great calamity. A party of us were driving to a seven o'clock dinner at the house of our neighbour, Mrs. Evans, of Portrane. As we passed a remarkably fine field of potatoes in blossom, the scent came through the open windows of the carriage and we remarked to each other how splendid was the crop. Three or four hours later, as we returned home in the dark, a dreadful smell came from the same field, and we exclaimed, 'Something has happened to those potatoes; they do not smell at all as they did when we passed them on our way out'. Next morning there was a wail from one end of Ireland to the other."

Late blight can be controlled by burning old plants after harvest and spraying or dusting

Late blight on potatoes – internal symptoms.

with a recommended fungicide. It is most important to repeat this treatment every seven to ten days until September.

Kenebecs and Sebagos are moderately resistant to late blight.

Potato scab: Potatoes attacked by scab are unattractive to look at, but the eating quality is not affected. Scab is a soil-borne bacterial disease that favours alkaline or neutral soils, but seldom occurs in acid soils with a reading of pH 5.6 or less. To prevent scab, do not apply fresh manure to the soil where potatoes are to be grown and, if necessary, apply sulphur to reduce the pH level.

Black leg: A bacterial disease that overwinters in plant debris and stored tubers, black leg causes a black ring to girdle the stalk at ground level, with the result that the plant gradually wilts and dies. The tubers develop a soft rot near the stem. Control is by planting certified seed.

Black scurf: This is a fungal disease that is common to potatoes everywhere. The home gardener can identify it by the black lumps that look like dirt on the mature potatoes. It does not wash off easily. In severe cases the plant produces clusters of small, misshapen potatoes, and the crop is of little value. The fungus lives indefinitely in the soil, making crop rotation of little value in controlling black

Black scurf, the "soil" that does not wash off.

Fusarium wilt of tomato.

scurf. The scurf will be less prevalent if the seed potatoes are planted only about 2 inches deep after the soil has warmed up. Harvest the crop as soon as the potatoes are mature.

Bacterial ring rot: The symptoms of bacterial ring rot include a wilting and slight rolling of lower leaves during the day, and a yellowish ring on the tubers about 1/4 inch below the skin surface. These tubers will not keep in storage. Control is by planting certified seed.

Anthracnose: Small, dark, sunken spots on ripe fruit indicate anthracnose. The spots may eventually cover a large portion of the fruit.

Verticillium wilt: This disease is recognized when the older leaves of the plants turn yellow and wilt. The plants seldom die, but growth will be poor because the older leaves are constantly dying and dropping off.

Fusarium wilt: Similar to Verticillium, Fusarium can be diagnosed by the black-brown interior of a cut stem.

The latter three fungi mentioned, live in the soil. To protect your crop from infection, plant disease-resistant varieties, and always observe crop rotation practices and good garden hygiene.

Blossom end rot: A disease of tomatoes, blossom end rot may be one effect of environmental conditions. The blossom end of the fruit exhibits a dry, firm rot which provides an opening for secondary infection. A deficiency of calcium in the soil and hot, dry weather combine to produce this condition.

Sun scald: Overpruning of staked tomato plants, and the resulting overexposure of the fruit to the sun, is the most common cause of sun scald on tomatoes.

Blossom drop: Periods of low humidity and high winds result in blossom drop in peppers. If enough of the growing season remains, the plants will re-blossom and set fruit.

UMBELLIFERAE: The Parsley or Carrot Family
Includes carrots, celery, celeriac, parsley, parsnip-rooted parsley, and parsnips

Carrot: *Daucus carota*

The carrot is one of the most popular and widely grown of vegetables, mainly thanks to the work of a French plant breeder, Vilmorin-Andrieux, whose efforts in the late 1800's led to the development of today's varieties.

Although carrots can be grown in a wide range of soils, they do best in either a deep, loose, sandy loam or loam or muck high in fertility and moisture-retaining capacity. The ground should be worked to a depth of 9 to 12 inches and be free from stones and clods; these could cause misshapen roots. Not everyone has ideal conditions. If carrots must be grown in a clay soil, add and work in as much humus as possible prior to planting. Avoid strawy manure and raw compost because these tend to cause misshapen roots

covered with fibrous side rootlets. The selection of seed will depend to a certain extent on the type and depth of soil in the garden.

Carrot varieties are available in a wide range of sizes and shapes. If your soil conditions are perfect, you can grow long, tapering carrots. If hard clay conditions prevail, stumpy, short or round carrots would be preferable.

Carrot seed is slow to germinate, usually taking two to three weeks. Some radish seed planted with the carrot will germinate rapidly, marking the row and breaking the soil surface, thereby assisting the more delicate young carrot plants to emerge. The radishes can be harvested before the carrots require the space.

Sow the seed half an inch deep in rows 12 to 15 inches apart in a sunny spot in the

Two varieties of carrots and a row of beets planted on the same day. Note how they all produce different growth.

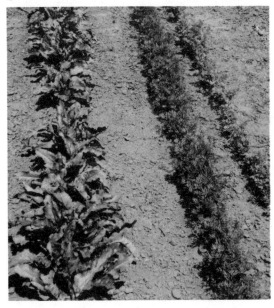

The same rows as shown at left a month later.

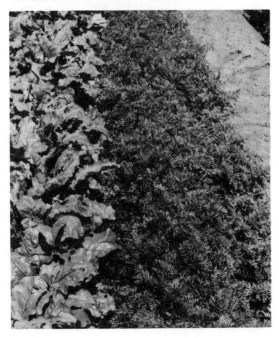

garden. A method we use when planting carrots alone is to place a board over the row after seeding, and remove it at the first sign of germination. As soon as the plants are 2 to 3 inches high, we start thinning them out. Eventually, we thin to a spacing of 1¹/₂ to 2 inches apart. If large storage carrots are desired, thin again. Experience will teach the gardener how and when to thin.

As carrots are at their prime when young, make successive plantings every two to three weeks. The first seeding is done as soon as the ground can be worked, the last in early August. The main crop, or June seeding, is the best one to plant for winter-storage carrots.

Many gardeners place a board between the rows to step on while working. This prevents the soil from becoming too compacted. As I have seen many other equally satisfactory methods used in friends' gardens, I feel all practices should be used as guidelines, and the one found best suited to the individual gardener adopted.

Thinning carrots for the table. The remaining main crop is left to mature for winter storage.

Carrots are not often subject to pest and disease problems. If you notice anything amiss, it is more than likely either the carrot rust fly or carrot yellows.

Celery: *Apium graveolens dulce*

Celery is a superb crop for eating raw or cooked, and when well-grown few other vegetables equal it in crispness and flavour. It is not easy to grow in the average home garden, but for gardeners prepared to devote a little extra time in preparing the ground, the results are well worth the effort.

Celery, in its wild state, grows in the marshy areas of northern Europe. We must, therefore, try to simulate these conditions. It requires moist, rich soil, but not waterlogged. Light or clay soil must be adapted by a generous application of well-rotted manure, compost, leaves or other organic material. Rich living conditons and continual thirst-quenchings are of prime importance. The most satisfactory plan is to dig a trench 10 to 12 inches deep and 15 to 18 inches wide, running north and south. The soil taken out can be spread evenly on the surrounding ground. In areas where the topsoil is shallow, dig out only to the depth of the topsoil. If this leaves a very shallow trench, dig out several inches of subsoil and remove it from the garden. In both situations the bottom of the trench is then broken up deeply, using a fork or spade and plenty of organic matter or manure incorporated. A couple of inches of topsoil is then returned, and a sprinkling of bone meal applied. These are then worked in lightly. The bone meal should be applied as long as possible in advance of planting.

We had difficulty in growing celery until a soil test revealed a shortage of boron. This was remedied by an application of borax worked into the trench prior to planting-out.

For the home gardener who only grows 10 or 12 plants, it is easiest to purchase a small flat of seedlings from a nursery. For those gardeners needing larger quantities, celery must be started indoors as a transplant, starting ten to twelve weeks ahead of planting-out time. In our area we plant-out in late May or early June. The young plants are set out 9 inches apart in the centre of the trench in a single line, planted at the same depth as they were growing in the flats. Leave them very firm in the soil, and give them a thorough soaking. Celery must never be allowed to dry out and, when watering, always soak the trench thoroughly so that the moisture gets down below the roots.

Celery is a very heavy feeder and benefits from an application of liquid fertilizer every two or three weeks. We use liquid manure when available, or a fish-based fertilizer. The plants will grow rapidly. Side shoots which will arise from the roots must be watched for and removed by breaking away. If this is neglected, much of the strength of the plant will be wasted.

There are new varieties of celery on the market which do not require blanching; however, we still find all celery more tasty when blanched. Store-bought celery is usually unblanched and therefore green. It has a stronger flavour than blanched celery, and the fibre or strings in the stalks are tougher.

The entire blanched celery plant is like the heart of an unblanched plant. Blanching celery is a common practice in Europe and we would recommend that home gardeners in North America try it. When the deep trench method is used, the simple way to blanch the plants is by filling in the trench around them with peat moss. The peat moss will be incorporated with the soil after the crop is harvested. Another method especially good for shallow trenches is quick and simple. Place a board on either side of the row when the plants are large and well-established, leaving only the tops of the plants sticking out. Before doing this, bunch the stalks of each plant together, holding them firmly with a couple of strong rubber bands or strips of old nylon stocking. We have found this method vastly superior to earthing up with soil or wrapping in strong paper.

Harvesting a few outer stems during the

Above: A row of well-established celery seedlings growing in a trench. *Below:* Black heart of celery, usually the result of a boron deficiency.

growing season will not damage the plants in any way. As celery takes 90 to 100 days to mature from planting-out time, the main crop will be ready from September to freeze-up. Remove a board and dig a plant as required. Mature celery can withstand a light frost. Plants can be dug in the fall, keeping the root system intact, and replanted in a box, then stored in the cool room or root cellar for

To blanch, place boards on either side of row when plants are well established, exposing only plant tops.

Above: Harvesting a celery root. First remove the blanching board and dig deeply with a spade.
Below: Blanched celery showing the strong root system. Note the rubber band which held the petioles (stems) together.

about a month.

We have found this method a lot of work, so we grow only what we need to eat fresh from the garden.

Celeraic: *Apium graveolens rapaceum*

Celeraic is a turnip-rooted celery very popular in Italian cooking. The cultural requirements are the same as for celery except it need not be planted in a trench and no blanching is necessary. The edible part is the root, which is used for soup and stew flavouring, grated raw in salads or cooked in the same manner as other root vegetables. The leaves may also be used to flavour soups. Celeriac roots are very easy to store and will keep for several months under the same conditions as beets, carrots, and turnips.

The seedlings should be planted in the ground at the same depth as they were growing in the seed-bed. As the turnip-like roots develop, trim or pull off the outer petioles.

Celeriac is a cool weather crop and, like celery, responds to an ample supply of water and fertilizer.

Parsley: *Petroselinum crispum*

Parsley is one of the most popular garden herbs and is very high in iron and vitamin content.

Parsley grows well in any good garden soil; however, because the seed is slow to germinate, either start the seed indoors in March or sow outdoors as early as possible in the spring.

A few radishes sown with the parsley seed will mark the row. As the parsley germinates, the radishes will mature and can be pulled. Another method which we have adopted and find most satisfactory is to place a board over the row after seeding. After about two weeks, when germination could be starting, we keep looking under the board to see if there are any signs of life. As soon as there are, we lift the board immediately. Germination using this technique is very high.

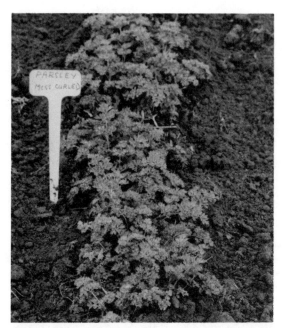
A row of young parsley plants.

Thin the parsley to approximately 6 inches between plants. Harvest by picking stalks as required. Parsley is a biennial and in warmer areas a few plants left in the ground over winter provide an early spring crop.

Also, a few plants dug up, potted and kept in a sunny window will give the house fresh parsley all winter. Parsley is relatively trouble-free; yellow leaves are usually due to dry soil.

Parsnip-Rooted Parsley: *Petroselinum tuberosum*

"Hamburg-thick rooted parsley" is grown for its root rather than leaf. Culture is the same as for carrots and parsnips, as is the cooking and serving. Excellent for soups and stews.

Parsnip: *Pastinaca sativa*

This highly nutritious plant is a native of Europe and Asia. It was introduced to North America by early colonists at the turn of the seventeenth century. A most useful crop in the home garden, it can be left in the ground all winter to provide a fresh root vegetable as soon as digging is possible in the spring. The old wives' tale that parsnips become poisonous if allowed to sprout in the spring is completely false. Sprouting only causes a decline in flavour, making it advisable to harvest the whole crop before sprouting begins.

The general cultivation of parsnips is much the same as for beets and carrots, but because the tapering root of the parsnip will grow to a depth of around 3 feet, much deeper cultivation is required. For this reason, if the parsnips can be grown in the area previously occupied by leeks, the ground will already have been loosened to a reasonable depth.

The soil should contain some lime, be rich in humus or well-rotted manure preferably worked into the soil the previous fall, and free of stones which would prevent the straight growth of the root.

Although the seed is usually viable for two years, it is best to purchase fresh seed each year to assure good germination. The seed is extremely slow to germinate, so mark the row by also planting some radish seed in the drill or by placing a board over the row and removing it at the first sign of germination, anywhere from 15 to 25 days.

Plant as early as possible in the spring in a furrow half an inch deep, leaving 2 feet between rows; cover the seed very lightly with a little soil, sand or vermiculite and tamp it down. The seedlings often have difficulty pushing through dry soil, so try to keep them well watered.

After the seedlings are about 2 inches tall, thin to 4 to 6 inches apart. The roots will not be mature until September. The flavour is greatly improved after several frosts and when eaten freshly dug.

The roots will keep in plastic bags in the refrigerator or cool room for several months. Check occasionally for excess humidity. They can also be cooked and frozen.

Parsnips are relatively disease-resistant, but can be subject to the same problems as other members of the carrot family.

A row of parsnips in the fall showing the lush foliage. Note the grass clippings mulch laid over newspaper.

Freshly dug parsnips which have wintered outdoors.

Problems and Controls

Carrot rust fly: This shiny green fly with black eyes, a yellow head and one-fifth of an inch long attacks all members of the carrot family. In late spring the female fly lays her eggs near the crowns of plants. Carrots, parsnips and celery are the most susceptible. The larvae are yellowish-white worms, about one-third of an inch long, which tunnel into the outer layer of the roots. Floating row covers are the simplest method of controlling the fly.

Wireworms: These wiry, hard-skinned, copper-coloured worms are about an inch in length. They attack members of the carrot family by burrowing into the roots. If you notice just a few, place a sliced potato on the soil surface. The potato will attract the wireworms, and they can be destroyed along with the potato.

Carrot weevil: Carrot weevils are snouted, beetle-like insects that attack the fleshy roots of the carrots, leaving great gouges, and rendering a carrot unattractive and inedible quite quickly. When good garden hygiene and crop rotation are practised, carrot weevils are not a serious problem.

Slugs: These pests are far worse some seasons than others. When control becomes necessary, use slug-bait or set out shallow dishes of stale beer in which the slugs drown.

Diatomaceous earth or wood ash spread around plants will deter slugs and snails. A little pickling salt sprinkled from a shaker or salty water is another control. Slugs can also be collected in grapefruit halves placed along the rows. These should be emptied every day.

Leafhoppers: Weeds in or near the garden plot may harbour these insects which cause the spread of carrot yellows. When they move from plant to plant, they carry the disease with them and infect the other plants they touch. To prevent contamination, control

Carrot rust fly damage.

Above: Carrot weevils.
Below: Carrot weevil damage.

Black slug attacking a celery petiole.

the weeds in and around the garden, and dust or spray if required.

Carrot yellows: The yellows is a virus disease that causes the development of hairy roots on carrots or parsnips and the purpling and twisting of the tops. Prevention consists of controlling the leafhoppers and removing and destroying infected plants.

CHAPTER 13

The Herb Garden

Chefs delight in adding herbs to enhance the flavour of many of their dishes. Some have even gone as far as to grow the fresh produce under fluorescent lights in their kitchens. We home gardeners can all enjoy these delicious extra flavours, and with very little trouble or expense after the initial plans have been made. To make the best use of herbs, grow as many as possible within easy reach of the kitchen door. In having them so near at hand, you will find you use them constantly. It's the little snips here and there that make for easy use and experimenting while cooking. The list of culinary herbs included in this chapter is only a few of the many in general use. I hope this list will prove to be of encouragement to novice herb growers who, after tasting the results of their labours, will add yearly to their list of species.

Chives: *Allium schoenoprasum*

This hardy perennial is a member of the onion family and well worth a place in every garden. It takes up very little space and both the top and bottom of the plant can be used: the tops in salads and soups and the bulbs as mild-flavoured onions. Chives thrive in a wide variety of soils and can be used as a decorative edging to flower beds; decorative because the small mauve flowers are produced freely.

The simplest method to establish chives is by planting bulbs. A few bulbs planted in the spring will become a good-sized clump in one season. Bulbs can be purchased, or perhaps a neighbour will present you with some when he is dividing his clumps. Dividing can be done any time during the season, but always cut back the tops when replanting. If bulbs are not available, seed can be sown in April or early May and the seedlings thinned to 3 inches apart. In the fall, pot some up and grow indoors for winter use.

Garlic Chives: *Allium tuberosum*

Garlic chives have a wide, flat leaf and a tall, white flower. The leaves have a mild garlic flavour and are a delicious addition to salads and soups. The cultural needs are the same as for the common chive.

Dill: *Anethum graveolens*

Dill is native to Europe, but has been naturalized in North America. Both the Romans and Greeks are known to have enjoyed it. Its properties have been considered both aphrodisiacal and soporific, and in the Dark Ages it was associated with black magic. Today we use dill as a culinary herb. The young green leaves in the spring enhance salads and sauces, and, later on, the seeds give flavour to our dill cucumber pickles and many other preserves and winter dishes.

Dill is an annual and should be planted as soon as the garden can be worked. Thin the seedlings to about 6 inches apart. It does best in a well-drained, sunny location and will attain a height of about 3 feet.

In our garden we find that so many seeds scatter each season and emerge the next

Chives.

Garlic chives.

spring among the rows of vegetables that it is never necessary to plant a row of dill. The seedlings are very easy to identify with their feathery leaves, and enough can be left undisturbed to supply the household. Dill does not transplant well.

Horseradish: *Amoracia lapathifolia*

Where space is not a problem, a 3 by 3 foot horseradish bed will provide an ample supply for the family. Once established it is hard to eradicate, for every small piece of root left in the ground will grow the next season. Horseradish is a member of the mustard family. The plants grow to about 3 feet in height and are vigorous and moisture-loving. The large dock-like leaves are not edible. All the value lies in the roots, which are ready for lifting in September or October. We prepare our year's supply by grating the cleaned pieces of root in the blender with vinegar, then bottling it. Horseradish, if grated on an open grater, will make the eyes weep in the same manner as a strong onion does.

To establish a bed, plant pieces of root of any length, as short as 3 inches or as thin as a

pencil. If these are broken, the top should be cut squarely, and a bud will form after planting. They should be planted upright in holes one foot apart. Make the holes about 10 inches deep, with a stick or crowbar. Drop

Harvesting dill. In our garden it seeds itself and has no special place allotted for growing.

Horseradish root. This specimen has branched out more than usual. Ordinarily we only get one main root on each plant.

the roots in so that they go right to the bottom. The better quality the soil is, the larger the roots will become. Try to prevent the bed from drying out in a hot season.

Lovage: *Levisticum officinale*

Lovage is a perennial member of the carrot family. It is a native of the Mediterranean countries and was brought to America by the early settlers, who grew it in their herb gardens for both medicinal and culinary uses.

One clump of lovage is ample for a household. The plant grows to a height of about 4 feet, with leaves that have a celery-like appearance as well as flavour. Stems and leaves are used in soups and stews, either chopped or in a bouquet garni. Freshly chopped young leaves add a celery flavour to salads.

The leaves may be dried for winter use, but more flavour is retained when they are chopped and frozen.

Propagation is by seed sown in spring or by root division.

Lovage thrives in a wide range of soils, provided there is good drainage as well as moisture retention during summer months. It is extremely easy to grow, seldom has any problems, and is an excellent herb for the home garden.

Marjoram: *Origanum majorana*

Indeed, sir, she was the sweet
Marjoram of the salad, or rather
the Herb-of-Grace.

All's Well That Ends Well
Shakespeare

Marjoram, or sweet marjoram, is a popular herb that is easily grown from seed. Although it is a perennial, due to our severe winters it is treated as an annual in northern climes. We grow a small clump in the herb garden alongside the summer savory and the sweet basil.

The leaves must be harvested before there is any risk of frost and hung to dry in a dark, airy place. Fresh marjoram can be obtained all winter by potting up a plant and bringing it indoors before the first frost; it will require a sunny window or fluorescent light. Marjoram will grow in any good garden loam that is well-drained. It needs full sun, and plenty of moisture, but allow the soil to dry out between waterings.

Mints: *Mentha species*

Mints are native to Europe and the British Isles. There are three main groups: culinary, medicinal and aromatic. The species usually grown in our garden is the field mint, the leaves of which are used for sauces and to spice drinks.

Mint prefers a moist soil and partial shade. It increases by underground stems or runners and, given ideal conditions, can rapidly become a pest in the garden. Whenever possible, allot it a small area on its own.

To start a mint bed, either purchase roots or get some from a generous neighbour. Once a mint bed is established, there is always plenty to give away.

Oregano, or Wild Marjoram: *Origanum*

Oregano is the trade name given to various herbs of European origin used in cooking, but in North America usually refers to wild marjoram. Some are frost-tender perennials and must be brought in before the first frost. Others are hardy. All oreganos can be grown from root divisions. We find it desirable to start new plants every two or three years.

The small oval leaves of this medium height plant may be used fresh or dried. The flavour of oregano and marjoram is rather similar.

Rosemary: *Rosmarinus officinalis*

> There's Rosemary, that's for
> remembrance; pray you love,
> remember.
>
> > *Hamlet*
> > Shakespeare

Rosemary is a frost-tender perennial herb or sub-shrub, which must be kept indoors during the winter. It is believed to have been introduced into England by Queen Philippa, wife of Edward III, the lady who pleaded with her husband to save the lives of the six burghers of Calais. Throughout history rosemary has been considered a herb of great importance, possessing medicinal, aromatic and culinary qualities.

The history of rosemary is a long and interesting one. It is a native of the Mediterranean region and, as its botanical name denotes, grows near the sea coast; it delights in sea spray. The best we "land-lubbers" can do is to give it a sandy soil containing lime and plenty of sunshine.

Oregano.

Rosemary.

Propagation can be from seed, but the easiest way is from cuttings, taken in July, of half-ripened wood pulled away from the main stems and rooted in a sandy soil. In good conditions the plants will grow to about 3 feet in height.

Summer savory.

Sweet basil.

Some culinary uses are in stuffings, bouquet garni, and rubbing on lamb before roasting.

Sage: *Salvia officinalis*

One of the most popular herbs used for cooking, sage is very easy to grow, and one plant in the herb garden will keep the family amply supplied. Although sage will grow in partial shade, to achieve optimum flavour and aroma it should be grown in full sun.

Sage can be started from seed sown as soon as the ground can be worked, or can be propagated from cuttings. These may be taken in summer and rooted in sand or in the location where the plant is intended to remain. Although sage is a hardy perennial, it has a shallow root system and benefits from a fall mulch of well-rotted compost or manure. To keep the plants tidy and obtain sufficient leaves to dry for winter use, cut the plants back in July and again before freeze-up.

Summer Savory: *Satureja hortensis*

Although there are both perennial and annual savories, the one generally grown for culinary use is an annual. By buying fresh seed each year, you avoid the risk of poor or slow germi-

nation. Sow the seed after all risk of frost is past and thin the seedlings to 6 to 9 inches apart. Summer savory enjoys rich soil and full sunshine. Feed with a complete fertilizer a couple of times during the season at intervals of about one month. The plants will grow to 12 to 18 inches in height, and when the flowers begin to form, the plants should be cut to the ground, tied in bunches and hung up to dry.

We grow a few plants in the herb garden, which provide the family with both fresh and dried leaves throughout the year.

Winter Savory: *Satureja montana*

Winter savory is a hardy perennial which thrives in poor soil conditions. We grow ours in gravel. The flavour is similar to summer savory.

Savory is our main herb for use in poultry stuffings. I use double the quantity recommended in most recipes, and always find this stuffing very popular. I also add a sprig to the stock pot for added flavour.

Sweet Basil: *Ocimum basilicum*

Sweet basil is an annual herb which is very easy to grow. Its popularity with chefs makes

French tarragon.

Lemon thyme.

it a must in every garden. There are many varieties, including one with purple leaves, and another with lemon flavour. Some mature basil plants are about 2 feet tall; others dwarf, and, being very frost tender, they should be cut for drying well before there is any danger of frost.

The leaves and flowers are used fresh in salads, and as a garnish for tomatoes, eggs, etc. The dried leaves are stored for winter use.

Lemon basil makes an especially flavourful sauce for fish.

Tarragon: *Artemisia dracunculus*

Tarragon is a popular perennial herb, which is propagated from cuttings or root divisions taken in the spring. The plants prefer a slightly acid, not too rich soil, and will thrive in either sun or partial shade. They must not be crowded, so allow plenty of room for the roots to spread. The best variety for culinary use is the French tarragon. This is not grown from seed, hence the necessity to acquire cuttings or plants. The variety offered through most seed companies is Russian tarragon, which is not as flavourful for culinary purposes. The plants will usually survive our winters, but a covering of mulch applied after freeze-up is beneficial. Tarragon can be used fresh in salads, the leaves dried for winter use, or sprigs steeped in vinegar for salad dressings and sauces.

Thyme: *Thymus vulgaris*

A member of the mint family, thyme is a low-growing creeper or bush plant mostly evergreen, or nearly so. There are a number of different varieties, all native to the islands of the Mediterranean, southern Europe and western Asia. The early settlers brought plants to America, where they have retained their great popularity both for culinary and aromatic purposes.

Thyme is a hardy perennial and enjoys our cold climate. A rock garden with a soil high in lime is the ideal, but we have found it grows perfectly in any well-drained sunny location.

Propagation may be from seed, but the best results are from cuttings or plant divisions. The common thyme (vulgaris) is the usual one grown, but if space is available, it is worth growing several varieties in the rock garden.

CHAPTER 14

Fruit

Wherever there is enough space in the vegetable garden a few small fruits provide a delectable addition to meals. Any extra fruit can be either frozen fresh or made into jam. Fruit always tastes far better freshly picked, ripened "on the vine".

Blueberries

We love blueberries. When we lived in the Laurentian Mountains north of Montreal, blueberries grew wild. They thrived in the acid soil conditions there; an absolute must for blueberries. Here in the Ottawa Valley our soil is neutral. We knew that to grow blueberries successfully we had to adjust the pH of our soil to correspond to the preferences of the bushes.

To grow blueberries, select a sunny, permanent spot. Start lowering the soil pH well in advance of planting the bushes. If possible, do it in the fall in preparation for spring planting. Maintain a pH of 5 or below. Early in the spring plant 2 year old certified bushes, about 4 feet apart. At least two varieties should be planted to ensure cross polination. There are several varieties of both high and low bush blueberries.

Watering, fertilizing and mulching with pine needles or oak sawdust, all help develop strong healthy bushes. A dose of ammonium sulphate in the spring is most beneficial.

There are very few disease or insect problems for blueberries. However, if birds are attracted to your garden, be prepared to spend time and energy protecting your blueberry crop with netting or screening.

Currants and Gooseberries

We are very fond of both currant and gooseberry jam and feel our garden is incomplete without a bush or two of each. However, as they are self-pollinating, a single plant can bear fruit. They are generally very easy to grow, require little attention and will grow in places with partial sun.

Things can go wrong, however, as we found out one year in our garden. The bushes developed anthracnose (leaf spot), and after much discussion we decided it would be prudent to dig up the entire planting and burn it. Disease is not common with currants and gooseberries, and most bushes remain healthy for many years.

In a year or two we hope to plant new stock in a different part of the garden, as far away as possible from the old planting.

Currants and gooseberries are the alternate hosts of the white pine blister rust fungus, a disease that spends part of its life cycle on the canes of these bushes. It does not harm the canes, but is often fatal to white pine. In areas where white pine grow, currants and gooseberries should not be cultivated, except the black currant variety, "Consort", which is resistant to rust.

There are three types of currants: black, red and white. The black and red are the most popular. All the gooseberries that are hardy in our area are of the cooking variety. They are too tart to eat fresh, unlike some European strains, but are excellent for pies and jams.

Both fruits freeze well without processing, and can be used during the winter as needed.

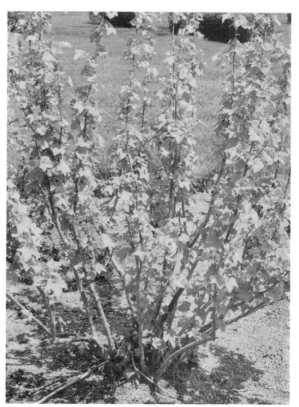

Above: Blueberry bush at the Central Experimental Farm. *Below:* Close-up of flowers on red currant.

Above: Currant bush in early spring showing pruning to allow sun to enter and air to circulate. *Below:* Branch of gooseberry bush showing fruit forming behind the flower petals.

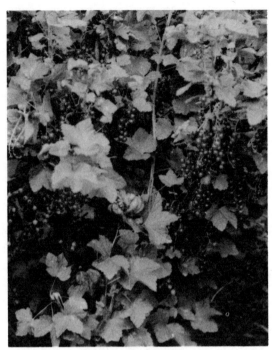
Currant bush ready to be harvested.

They are also a very rich source of vitamin C, especially black currants.

Purchase strong, well-rooted, one year old plants. These will go into production just as soon as two year old stock, and be less expensive. Be sure the plants are disease-free. Reputable growers will guarantee their stock. However, if you have a friend who grows healthy currant or gooseberry bushes, they can be propagated very simply by "layering" a branch (see glossary), or taking cuttings. After a season's growth these propagated plants are ready to move to a permanent site.

As bushes will remain productive for eight to ten years, the ground should be thoroughly prepared before planting. The soil should be rich in organic matter and the stock planted immediately it arrives in the spring. The plants should be set slightly deeper in the ground than they were when growing in the nursery. Dig the hole large enough to accommodate the outspread roots, then cover them with soil.

Tamp the ground firmly around each plant and water it if the soil is dry. Prune back the branches to a length of about 6 inches to stimulate new growth. Allow about 5 feet between the bushes, as they are all vigorous growers.

Planting can be done in either spring or fall. We prefer the spring, but if fall planting is done, wait until spring to cut back the bushes. After planting, we like to apply a heavy mulch to control weeds and conserve moisture. Hay, straw or sawdust are all equally suitable.

Pruning should be done in the fall or early spring when the bushes are still dormant. Black currants produce the best fruit on one and two year old shoots. Keep ten to twelve canes per mature bush.

We have found that both currants and gooseberries grow profusely. But unless we are rather drastic with pruning, the branches become overcrowded, restricting the circulation of air, causing many of the branches to come into contact with the ground, with subsequent rooting. Overgrown bushes make it much harder to control diseases and insects. All sickly, damaged or late leafing-out branches should be removed.

Red currants and gooseberries produce most of their fruit on two to three year old wood. Remove all older branches.

Problems and Controls of Currants and Gooseberries

Currants and gooseberries can be seriously damaged by a number of insects.

Currant borer: This borer is the larvae of a moth, rather like a small housefly, which lays her eggs in the axils of leaves. The larvae bore into the pith of the young shoot and feed there. The following spring when sickly shoots are cut, a dark hole can be seen where the larvae have burrowed into the pith. Prune and burn all sickly shoots.

Aphids: Aphids feed on the undersides of leaves and on young shoots. They are more often seen on red currants than gooseberries or black currants, and can be controlled by insecticides.

Currant fruitfly: Adult flies emerge at about the same time as the bushes are in bloom, and are a common pest and familiar to most currant and gooseberry growers. The females lay their eggs in the developing berries. Most affected fruit falls to the ground prematurely and, if inspected, a white maggot will be found in each. These insects leave the berry and spend the winter in the soil. The currant fruitfly can be controlled by insecticides.

Currant sawfly: Female sawflies lay eggs in early summer. The larvae are greenish worms with black spots, and about three-quarters of an inch long when fully grown. They are voracious eaters and can defoliate a bush quite rapidly. If only a few worms are noticed, they can be picked by hand, otherwise an insecticide spray is the easiest control.

Scale insects: Scale can be seen on dormant wood. They suck the juices from young branches, but are not often a serious problem. A lime-sulphur spray applied when the bushes are still dormant will control scale.

Powdery mildew: A common problem with gooseberries and occasionally with currants, powdery mildew is more likely to occur during warm, humid conditions. This white, powdery fungus appears in early summer on the tips of new shoots and young leaves. It is spread by spores and may affect the entire bush. Later in the season the white powdery growth turns brown and forms a covering over the affected parts of the plant. The growth of the entire bush will be stunted, and the tips of the shoots killed. Cut off and destroy all diseased branches and make sure the bush has good air circulation. Fungicide applications are an effective control.

Anthracnose (leaf spot): Brown spots that appear on the leaves in mid-summer indicate

Leaf convolutions on currant caused by aphids on lower leaf surface.

Anthracnose. These spots gradually turn yellowish-brown and the leaves fall, defoliating the bushes. Early defoliation retards the growth of the bushes and reduces the next year's crop. The fungus lives over the winter in the fallen leaves, so damaged leaves should be raked up and burned.
Fungicides should provide adequate control. Our problem, referred to earlier in this section, may have been in not recognizing the symptoms early enough.

Raspberries

An altogether delightful fruit, the raspberry is always in demand for dessert, jam and the freezer. Growing your own seems the only way to obtain fresh raspberries; they are both expensive and scarce in stores.

There are four kinds of raspberries: red, purple, golden, and black. Red raspberries are the most popular. Everbearing varieties give a fall crop in addition to the normal summer crop. This fall crop is produced on the tips of strong new shoots.

A new raspberry patch can be planted in either the spring or the fall. Always plant "certified stock", identified by the label which certifies that the stock has been inspected by government officials and shown to be virus-free. The site for the new canes should be prepared by cultivating a 3 foot wide strip for each row and incorporating well-rotted manure or compost to a depth of 9 inches. In heavy clay ground also add sand, charred woody material from the bonfire, or strawy manure when available.

To ensure that both sides of each row receive maximum sun, the rows should run north and south when possible.

The quickest method of planting is to dig out a trench the width of the spade and about 6 inches deep. Space the roots about 1½ feet apart and cover with the excavated soil. Firm the plants in by treading. Rows should be at least 5 feet apart.

Raspberries need some support. This can be provided by erecting a series of posts, either metal or wood, at 20 to 30 foot intervals along the row. Wires are then pulled tautly between the posts, the lower wire 2 feet from the ground, the upper wire about 4 feet high. The canes can be spaced out evenly and tied securely to the wires.

The size and quality of the crop depends largely on an adequate water supply. In dry weather soak the bed thoroughly once a week from spring onwards. A mulch of well-rotted manure, compost, lawn clippings or sawdust over the root area will help retain moisture.

Manure will also give extra nourishment to the plants. Food can be given through the mulch in the form of liquid manure or a complete fertilizer. This feeding should start as soon as the berries begin to swell.

Keep weeds under control. This is best done by hand, loosening the roots of the weeds with a fork. Mulching also helps control weeds.

All newly planted canes should be cut down to a good bud about 6 inches above ground level. There will be no fruit the year of planting. However, the roots will send up new growth, which will bear fruit the following year. As soon as possible after the harvest is

Our raspberries emerging from the snow in the spring. The canes stood up to the winds and weather by being well-secured to supporting wires.

over, the fruited canes should be cut down close to the ground. Weak, new canes are also cut back. The strong, new growths remaining are tied to the wires, replacing the old canes that have just been removed. These new canes will produce the following season's fruit. Cane removal after the harvest helps control disease and improves the circulation of air around the plants. No further pruning is done at this time.

In early spring prune the weak and dead tips off the canes. Shorten tall canes to a convenient height for picking. Thin out all the weak growth, leaving only the strong canes, spaced 4 to 6 inches apart in the rows.

Propagation of raspberries is by suckers which appear in profusion on either side of the rows. These can be dug up with a spade, complete with their own roots, in either the fall or spring, and transplanted. This is a particularly simple and economical method of establishing a new raspberry bed. Suckers should only be taken from thoroughly healthy plants. To propagate from unhealthy stock is to propagate trouble.

Problems and Controls of Raspberries

Aphids: Aphids attack the leaves of raspberries at any time of the season, but are most prevalent when the bushes are in their most rapid growth. This is usually early in the season and again in August or early September when new growth is emerging. Although the aphids themselves do not necessarily cause serious harm, they spread viruses which cause leaf curl and mosaic leaf. Both these viruses are serious problems, and controlling the aphids minimizes the risk of contracting disease. The first spraying should be done early in the season and a further spraying after harvesting is completed.

Leafhoppers: These are small, wedge-shaped, yellow-green insects which produce several generations each season. They are frequently seen on raspberry leaves, jumping and flying about when the canes are disturbed. They are not often a serious problem and can be controlled by spraying.

Raspberry sawfly: This fly lays her eggs early in the season, and the resulting larvae are green caterpillars which devour the leaves. Sawflies can easily be controlled by spraying or dusting with insecticide.

Raspberry cane borer: These pests can cause considerable damage in the raspberry patch. The first sign of damage from the cane borer is the wilting of shoot tips. On closer examination the gardener will see that two rings about a half inch apart have been cut around the stem, and the growth above these has wilted.

This damage has been caused by a long-horned beetle with a black body and a yellow neck about half an inch long. She lays her egg between the rings. This egg hatches into a grub that burrows a short distance down the stem and remains there for the winter. The following spring it burrows on down the

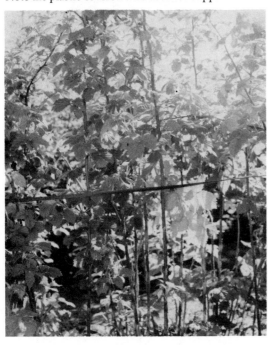

Raspberries pruned to allow light in and air to circulate. This is the best protection against disease. Note the plastic-covered wire used for support.

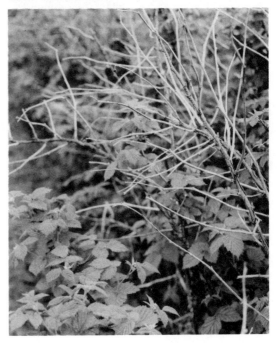

Raspberries showing an old cane that was not cut out, an invitation to disease.

Raspberry canes:
A. The clean centres are healthy.
B. The blackened pith shows that they have been
   attacked by borers.

After the harvest old fruited canes and weak new
growth are removed from the patch and burned.

cane into the root and usually kills the cane. Later, it emerges as a beetle and repeats the cycle. Some years the cane borers are far worse than others.

The best control is to cut off and burn the tops of damaged canes immediately wilting is noticed. Make the cut about 6 inches below the two rings.

Eastern raspberry fruitworm: These small worms are often found in the central cavity of the berry at harvest time. They are the larvae of a small, brown beetle that feeds on the flower-bud clusters in early spring. The larvae feed on the developing berries and remain in the berry when it is picked. Although they are harmless, they make a dish of raspberries rather unappetizing.

These beetles can be controlled by dusting or spraying with rotenone when blossom buds first appear and again when the flowers open. The beetles can also be attracted to half cantaloupe shells or containers with a honey and water mixture.

Tarnished plant bug: A great nuisance in the raspberry patch, these shiny, brown bugs, feed early in the spring on blossom buds, causing crumbly, misshapen berries. Good garden hygiene and weed control usually prevent the spread of these pests, but if they should become numerous, spraying with the recommended insecticide will control them.

Nematodes: Sometimes found in the soil of raspberry plantings, nematodes are minute, worm-like creatures that can cause damage to the roots of plants and stunt the growth of the canes.

Nematodes are hard to identify without a magnifying glass. If you notice continued poor growth for no appearent reason, consider nematodes as a possible cause. Control of nematodes is not easy, and it would be advisable to consult the nearest government agency.

Mosaic leaf: Transmitted by aphids feeding on infected plants, this virus disease can be

Raspberry anthracnose. Elongated grey spots on canes. Spur blight on cane at right.

In the fall we put out mouse poison in pop cans. These are laid on their sides along the row and in positions where birds cannot get at the treated seed.

identified by a mottled, crumpled look to the leaves. Pale green or yellow blotches appear, and the growth of the plant is stunted. Once a plant is infected, it never recovers.

To avoid mosaic leaf, purchase certified disease-free plants. Make new plantings at least five hundred feet from old planting. Control weeds and aphids and destroy any plants that show signs of disease.

Leaf curl: This is not a common virus disease. It causes leaves to curl tightly downwards and inward. The control is the same as for mosaic leaf.

Anthracnose, spur blight, cane blight, and Verticillium wilt: These are all fungal diseases that cause damage on canes, leaves and fruit. They can be controlled by spraying with fungicides.

Mice: Some years mice are a problem. They eat the bark of young canes during the winter.

Pop cans containing "mouse seed" can be set among the canes.

Strawberries

When the first colonists landed in America, they were amazed to find magnificent wild strawberry plants. The species they found is now known as Fragaria virginiana. Later, another excellent wild species, F. chiloensis, was found growing along the Pacific coast from Chile to Alaska. All the popular strawberry varieties which are now grown in our gardens in North America are descended from these two species. Strawberries are very hardy, and can be grown in all the cultivated areas of Canada and the United States.

Strawberries do best in a well-drained soil that is rich in organic material. When possible, prepare the bed in the fall prior to planting by incorporating well-rotted manure or compost. A warm, sunny location is essential for good results.

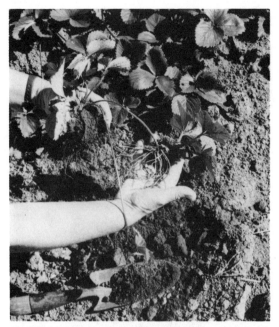

Establishing runners around a first-year "mother" strawberry plant.

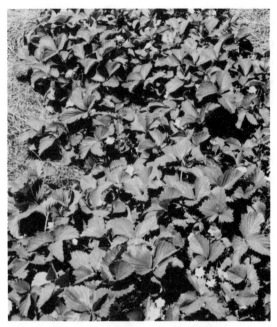

Second-year plants matted and showing a strong flowering in late spring.

Do not plant strawberries in ground previously occupied by potatoes, tomatoes, peppers or eggplant. There is a risk that the soil might harbour the fungus disease, Verticillium wilt, which would damage the strawberry plants.

Select the variety best suited to your area. There may be several which would provide you with successive crops. Always purchase certified plants and thereby minimize the risk of bringing diseased stock into your garden. Strawberries are considered a perennial. Vigorous, healthy plants will bear fruit for three or four seasons.

The time to start a new bed is in the spring as soon as the ground can be worked. This allows the plants time to establish themselves and produce runners. Remove all the flowers formed on the "mother plants" during their first season, permitting the strength to go into forming runner plants. Early formed runners are the best fruit bearers the following season. These young plants form flower buds within the crown during the latter part of the summer and in the fall. The flower buds emerge early the following spring and bear

fruit. Newly purchased plants should have well-developed crowns and plenty of strong roots. Twenty-five plants are ample for the average family and should produce 60 to 80 pounds of fruit. In Europe, strawberries are often grown as single plants, all runners being cut off. However, in North America strawberries are usually grown in the "matted-row" system.

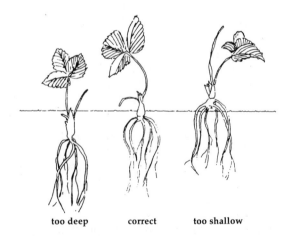

too deep   correct   too shallow

Setting out strawberry plants.

To follow this method allow at least 4 feet between rows, and set the plants 2 feet apart within the row. Each plant will send out runners which will establish themselves around the mother plant and form a thick "mat". I am still undecided as to whether the rows of single plants or the matted system is the best.

The number of plants to be set out will depend on the space available. Twelve plants will make a strawberry bed 25 by 4 feet. When setting out the plants, dig a hole with a trowel large enough to take the spread out roots. Water thoroughly and firm into the ground. Make sure the plants are set with the mid-point of the crown at ground level.

Many home gardeners like to start a small, new bed every year and maintain a three year cycle, discarding the oldest bed after it has fruited. If you observe this program, ten to twelve new plants each spring would be sufficient. You can use your own stock if you are certain that it is strong and healthy.

It is most important that the plants do not lack moisture from blossoming time until the end of the harvest. Lack of moisture causes hard, runted berries. After the harvest is over, apply a complete (10:10:10) fertilizer to the bed when the foliage is dry. Mow the plants with a rotary lawn mower, set high, or cut with garden shears. Take care not to injure the crowns of the plants. In northern areas where the season is short, it is best not to mow.

Winter protection is recommended. Freezing and thawing of the soil causes the plants to heave, breaking the roots, and low temperatures injure the roots, crowns and flower buds. Straw is the best mulch as it is usually free of weeds. One bale is often sufficient for the home strawberry patch. The straw should be applied after there have been several light frosts, and the ground has started to become frozen. The plants will then be dormant. If applied too early, the crowns are liable to rot.

Hay is not recommended for winter protection because it also brings in grass seeds. Leaves, grass clippings and garden waste can

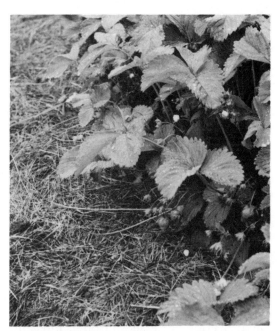

In early summer fruit begins to form while some plants are still in flower.

smother and kill the plants. If no straw is available cover the bed with "brush" cuttings, the old Christmas tree, etc. This will collect a deep snow mulch.

In the spring remove the straw from the plants as soon as new leaf growth appears. Lay the straw to the side of the patch or between the rows. It can be replaced on the plants if there is a risk of frost during blossoming or left to control weeds and conserve moisture.

Everbearing strawberries produce several crops during the season. The berries are often much smaller than regular varieties. Follow general rules for culture.

Strawberries are quite prone to root infections and to several viruses. Collectively, these contribute to the usual "decline" of the berry patch; another reason for replanting with certified stock.

Problems and Controls of Strawberries

White grubs: The larvae of the June bug, white grubs damage the roots of young strawberry plants. They are only likely to occur in soil that was recently in sod. So to avoid this problem do not plant strawberries in newly broken land.

Strawberry root weevils: Throughout most of North America, these pests can be a serious problem. The larvae feed on the roots of plants and the beetles damage the foliage. The plants will be stunted and unproductive. Control the beetles by dusting or spraying the plants with an insecticide before bloom and after harvesting. If root weevils remain a problem, remove and burn the old plants and make a new bed as far away from the old as possible.

Strawberry clipper weevils: The gardener will be aware of the presence of these very small beetles, if he sees clipped blossom stems on his plants. Control by spraying with a recommended insecticide. If the blossoms are open, spray in the evening to avoid killing bees. By then the bees will have returned to their hives.

Plant bugs: These bugs are a common strawberry pest and can be a great nuisance. They are generally the cause of runted, small, deformed berries. These insects pierce the developing fruit and suck the sap. Control by spraying or dusting before the blossoms open and again ten days later. These pests are hard to observe, and the gardener is usually aware of their presence only after he finds his berries are deformed and hard. The following season preventative action should be taken.

Spittle bugs: The presence of spittle bugs is indicated by frothy blobs on plant stems. They can do a great deal of damage in a short time. Control by spraying before the first blossoms open.

Aphids and whiteflies: These must be controlled because they are the agents that spread diseases from weeds and other infected plants.

Small, runted berries due to an attack of plant bugs. Compare the large, juicy healthy berries.

Root rot: This term refers to several soil-borne fungi that attack strawberry roots. Gardeners will notice a decline in the healthy growth of the plants, and the berries from diseased plants will be small, but not deformed. The roots start to blacken and decay, and gradually the entire root rots. The best prevention is to practise crop rotation and to avoid planting strawberries in heavy or poorly drained soils.

Fruit rot or grey mold (Botrytis): Botrytis is a fungal disease particularly prevalent in wet weather between blossoming and harvest. Infected berries usually rot just before ripening, but green fruit may also suffer. Prevention is important, because once this disease is established it is very hard to eradicate. Control is by spraying with a recommended fungicide at the first sign of blossoms.

Red stele: This fungal disease thrives in cold, wet soils and can remain viable in soil for up to seventeen years. Spores swim through soil water to spread infection. The gardener can identify red stele by noting a temporary wilt of the plant during the day followed by a recovery in the cool evenings, and by a loss of the shiny green appearance of the leaves. The plant stops growing, and by harvest time the leaves are small and the fruits are dried up. The roots become rat-tailed, and the central core or stele becomes brick-red. To avoid bringing this disease into your garden, examine new plant roots carefully for symptoms. Always purchase disease-resistant varieties.

Verticillium wilt: A soil-borne fungus that can live in the ground indefinitely, verticillium wilt is spread by cultivation, wind, and soil erosion. It does not need a wound to enter the plant, but penetrates the roots of susceptible plants. The symptoms may occur during the planting year. The outer leaves wilt and turn brown, while the new leaves curl and lose colour. Brownish-black streaks may appear along the grooved surface of the leaf stem. Eventually, more leaves collapse and the plant dies.

In fruiting years the outer leaves turn yellow or red soon after bloom. The plants wilt and die just as the fruit begins to ripen. Verticillium wilt strikes plants sporadically rather than in large patches in the plot, as does red stele. Any infected plants must be removed and burned. Once plants are infected, there is no cure, but good garden hygiene and growing resistant varieties can help prevent an occurence. This fungus also infects all solanaceous plants such as tomatoes, peppers and eggplant; therefore, strawberries should be included with these in the crop rotation plan.

Grapes

Wild grapes are found all over the North American continent, and it is from these native vines that a few of the varieties we grow today are descended. Some are cultivated, some hybrids, and some used as rootstock on which European varieties are grafted. The early settlers found that the European vines they brought with them were unable to survive our winters when grown on their own roots. Great strides have been made in developing suitable varieties for different North American zones. In some climatic regions of Canada and the United States, grapes are an important commmercial fruit crop. Gardeners in these areas will have no problems. However, for most of us easy grape growing is not the norm. People interested in growing grapes should first inquire from the nearest Research Station as to which vareities are recommended for their area.

Grape vines can form an interesting part of a garden landscape. They can be trained to

Grapevines are pruned in early spring. We grow Concord (blue) grapevines on the south and west sides of a shed. Only new growth carries leaves and fruit.

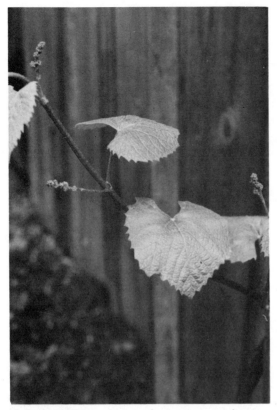

A close-up of three clusters of grapes on new shoots.

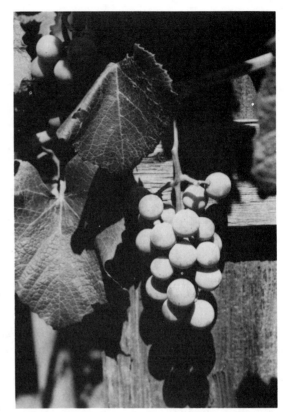

Grapes ready for harvesting.

grow over an arbour or trellis and provide a delightfully shaded nook for summer living.

Many people have found it necessary to surround their property, or perhaps the swimming pool, with a chain-link fence. Grape vines grow well on these fences. They are ornamental, grow rapidly during the season, give privacy to the enclosed area and, with any luck, provide a good crop of fruit.

Grapes require a temperate climate and, although the vines may survive the winter, they may not produce fruit. Frost in late spring can cause severe damage to the young shoots and flowers. It is essential to grow a variety suited to the micro-climate of your garden, and the length of frost-free time in your garden.

Grapes will grow in a wide range of soils as long as it is well-drained; they cannot tolerate wet feet. They also require sun and heat to mature.

We have several different varieties of grapes. So far Concord has been the most satisfactory grape in our garden. It grows profusely on a rail fence. Each spring we prune and train it along the rails and each fall it rewards us with a bountiful crop.

A new variety has recently been developed at the University of South Dakota. It is called "Valiant". This new variety can withstand extremely low temperatures and can ripen by the third week of August. It is said to have a more intense flavour than Concord and produces higher quality juice and jelly. Our climate is not suitable for growing table grapes.

Growing grapes is a study in itself, and we recommend one of the excellent government pamphlets which are available at no cost.

CHAPTER 15

"Putting By" Vegetables and Fruit

Many home gardeners grow far more produce than their families can possibly eat fresh during the growing season. With the exception of salad, none of these vegetables need be wasted but should be "put by" (or as some prefer, "put up" or "put down") for winter use.

When planning a garden, consideration should be given to using all such surplus produce and, indeed, expanding the garden to meet as much as possible the year round needs of the family. The facilities for storage will also dictate the size and type of crops you plan to grow.

Methods for putting by include freezing, canning, drying, preserve-making, salting or storing in a cool room, root cellar or a cool, dry location. There are so many ways of putting by fruit and vegetables that it is impossible to cover the subject fully here. Free government pamphlets are available on request, and many books have been written giving both old and modern methods.

The Home Freezer

The home freezer represents a considerable capital outlay, but freezing is a far quicker and safer method of putting by fruit and vegetables than any other with the possible exception of the root cellar for root crops. A freezer reduces the risk of spoilage or dangerous toxicity that can be encountered with home canned foods held in storage. Vegetables surplus to your immediate needs should be harvested while still in their prime, processed, bagged and put straight into the freezer. "Prime" means while they are young, tender and have a delicate flavour. The shorter the time between harvesting and freezing, the better the quality and nutritive value of the produce. The commercial grower is unable to compete with the home gardener for these qualities. His crops must be able to withstand mechanical harvesting and shipping.

You can start filling the freezer around May 24 with rhubarb, then continue all summer as crops mature. Leeks and Brussels sprouts harvested in November are the last crops to go into the freezer.

I have found the best bags to use for freezing are the clear, plastic ones in which milk is sold in the stores. They are very strong and can be reused several times if thoroughly washed and disinfected. A dash of disinfectant in the rinse water is a simple precaution against infection. I also prefer to package vegetables in small quantities and to use two or more packages if needed.

Canning

Not so long ago in North America, canning was the most popular home method of putting by food. Today, the freezer has replaced the canner. Very few households now have the equipment required to safely can low-acid foods at home.

Low-acid vegetables include peppers, squash, carrots, cabbage, beets, beans, asparagus, spinach and cauliflower. Unless these vegetables are being pickled (a large amount of acid added in the form of vinegar) they must be processed in a pressure cooker. This involves a considerable expenditure.

However, high-acid vegetables and fruit such as tomatoes, apples, rhubarb, and gooseberries can safely be processed in a "boiling water bath". I prefer to freeze rhubarb and gooseberries because they require no cooking, just dicing and freezing. But I find tomatoes and tomato juice far nicer put by in glass sealers. I recently acquired a hand press which has taken the tedious work out of the job of extracting juice. Visiting friends also enjoy cranking the handle, and in this way we prepare bucketfuls of juice in no time. It is also excellent for processing apple sauce, which may be frozen or bottled.

Drying

Drying is one of the oldest known methods of preserving food, dating back to pre-Biblical times. Early settlers in North America were taught the art by the Indians, and many of us use the same techniques today. Our microwave ovens and dehydrators are a far cry from the primitive methods, but are not essential for the home gardener.

Herbs are the simplest produce to dry. This is done by harvesting, washing and air drying them in a warm, dark, dry airy place. We have an attic that is ideal for this. If you don't have such a place, put the bunch of herbs in a brown paper bag and hang them up. When the drying process is complete and you have the time, the herb leaves can be crushed and stored in dark jars in a dark cupboard. Parsley can be dried this way. However, I have found the best results are achieved when I dry it in a very low oven. It keeps its colour much better.

Practically all vegetables and fruit can be dried successfully if they are exposed to low heat and good ventilation to remove moisture. Most of us have a romantic picture in our minds of pioneer kitchens festooned with strings of fruit and vegetables hanging to dry. Nowadays, we have more efficient and convenient methods. Dehydrators range from the simple, solar-powered food dryers to sophisticated electrically operated models. Home convection ovens are excellent for drying.

Vegetables must be blanched and drained before being set on the rack in the dryer. Fruit does not require blanching. Fruit leather is a chewy, candy-type food, made from fruit pulp. This pulp is spread on cookie sheets and dehydrated until it is dry enough to handle. It will be rather leather-like in appearance and consistency and can be stored in jars or bags. It has a delicious flavour and can be given to children as a substitute for candy.

As I have a freezer, I freeze vegetables rather than dry them, but for those who are not so fortunate, a homemade solar unit would make it possible to preserve surplus vegetables and fruit at very low cost. Information is readily available through libraries.

Preserves

A great variety of fruits and vegetables can go into the making of jams, jellies, relishes, chutneys and pickles. With the increased concern over additives in processed food, many families are now making their own preserves at home. I rather enjoy this job. The sight of shelves lined with jars and bottles of homemade produce is very satisfying. I am delighted to hear that men as well as women are finding it a relaxing occupation and are making preserves just for the fun of it.

When all the bulk ingredients are grown in the garden and only sugar, vinegar and spices have to be purchased, the cost of the jams and relishes is considerably lower than that of their store-bought counterparts. Also, with home preserves you know exactly what went into each jar.

Preserves are best stored in a cool, dark, dry cupboard. As we don't have this ideal situation in our house, we keep ours in the next best place, the cool room. Spoilage of preserves is readlily detected.

Salting Vegetables

The salting of vegetables is an ancient method of preserving, but with modern storage facilites, it is seldom used nowadays.

In Ireland the only salting we ever did was of green beans. These were frenched (sliced) and put in a large earthenware crock with dry salt sprinkled between the layers. They added to the variety of vegetables during the winter. However, I find frozen beans are far superior to salted ones.

Brine-cured Pickles and Sauerkraut

Brine curing cucumbers and cabbage is very popular in Europe, and an excellent way of preserving cucumbers and cabbage for the winter if you have the know-how. I would suggest to those brining for the first time that they get some lessons from a knowledgeable friend or neighbour before starting. It is easy to lose a whole batch through inexperience. This happened to me, and I had to throw out an unpleasant, mushy mess.

DILL PICKLES

After the disastrous results with the only batch of cucumber pickles I ever tried making in a crock, I returned to my old method of making "dill" pickles in quart sealers.

Sterilize four quart sealers. Place in each sealer, one clove of garlic (optional), six peppercorns, one clove and a flower of dill. Scrub and dry sufficient small halved or quartered cucumbers and pack tightly into the sealers. Bring to the boil one quart of water, two quarts of vinegar, and one cup of coarse pickling salt. Fill the sealers with this solution and seal immediately. Allow the pickles to cure for a week or longer before serving them.

SAUERKRAUT

Sauerkraut is cabbage cured in brine and fermented. It is an excellent way of preserving surplus cabbage. I have never made sauerkraut myself, so I asked my neighbour to give me her recipe. In the fall she always has large earthenware crocks of cabbage fermenting in her kitchen.

Here is the recipe: To each 5 pounds of finely shredded cabbage add 3 1/2 tablespoons of coarse salt. Sprinkle the salt over the cabbage and mix together in a large open pan. Allow to stand while you shred the next batch. It is important that the measurements are accurate, because the cabbage will not ferment properly if there is too much salt.

Pack the salted cabbage and liquid it has produced into a large earthenware crock and continue adding batches until the crock is filled to within 6 inches of the top. This allows sufficient "head" room for fermentation. The cabbage should be completely covered by brine, but if more is needed add a weak solution of 1 1/2 teaspoons of salt to one quart of water.

To make a cover, partially fill a large plastic bag or three smaller bags with water and seal or tie the tops tightly. Place the bag or bags of water on top of the cabbage. The water-filled bags will spread out to completely fill the top of the crock, excluding all air and preventing a white film or mold from forming. Check the kraut daily and, if necessary, remove any film that may have formed.

Fermentation will take two or three weeks in warm weather, four weeks when cool. When bubbling stops, tap the crock gently, and if no bubbles rise, fermentation will have ended. At this point, the kraut can either be canned or left for up to two weeks, depending on the cook's schedule. Next, pack the kraut into sterilized sealers to within one inch of the top. Cover with juice. Set the sealers in a cold water bath; the water should reach the shoulder of the jars. Bring the water slowly to the boil. Remove the jars, wipe the rims, put on the lids and process in a boiling water bath. Quart jars take thirty minutes. Remove from the canner and complete the seals unless the lids are self-sealing.

Sauerkraut can be frozen, but my neighbour tells me the flavour of canned sauerkraut is far superior.

The Cool Room

Not so long ago the "root cellar" and "cold pantry" were considered essential in all well-managed households. With technological advances, cool, damp basements gave way to dry, cozy recreation rooms, and the cold pantry off the kitchen was converted into a powder or utility room.

Many people are once again considering the advantages of having a cold room in their basement where thay can store fresh produce. This room can be very small but should be insulated against heat. There should be a window or air vent so that the temperature can be controlled at between 32° to 40° F (0° to 4° C). Freezing would damage most vegetables.

There are excellent government pamphlets on this subject. Anyone planning to store fresh produce such as potatoes, carrots, beets, parsnips, turnips, cabbages and celeriac should make sure they have a suitable cool room before either growing or bringing the produce indoors. Rotting vegetables, especially cabbages and turnips, have a most unpleasant odour that permeates the whole house.

Our cool room measures 4 feet by 8 feet and is in the northwest corner of the basement where there is a small window. Since a stone basement in a stone house is never warm, even in the heat of summer, we have not insulated the cool room walls. However, modern houses usually have warm basements, particularly in winter when the furnace is running. In this case, insulation would be essential.

Our walls are lined with shelves, some narrow for bottles and jars, others wide and deep to house containers of vegetables. The potatoes are in sacks on the floor.

In addition to storing fresh produce, the cool room is suitable for keeping home-canned goods and preserves from spoiling. One of the great features of root-cellaring is that there are no "hidden dangers" lurking, undetected in the produce, as is the case with canned or bottled goods. When fruit and vegetables are spoiled, we know from looking, smelling and touching, so there is no possibility of food poisoning.

In our household we put by enough fresh vegetables in the cold room to last until February; after that we eat frozen produce. Potatoes are the only exception. They carry us through until the ground outdoors has thawed sufficiently for us to dig Jerusalem artichokes.

Approximate length of time vegetables will remain in good condition in the cool room.
Celery: several weeks
Cabbages: until Christmas
Carrots: early May
Celeriac: early May
Beets: early May
Turnips: early May
Parsnips: until the ground is thawed sufficiently to dig those remaining in the garden
Potatoes: until the next season's early crop is ready to harvest

A Cool, Dry Location

Certain vegetables such as squash and onions keep better in a slightly warmer, drier atmosphere than the average root cellar provides. However, they do need cooler temperatures than in the average home. A cupboard on an outside wall is often suitable. These vegetables will then keep well until the following spring.

DINNER IN A PUMPKIN

Select a well shaped pumpkin as the soup tureen. The stem should still be attached to use as the handle. Cut out the lid. Clean the interior. Place the pumpkin on a large pie plate and bake in a moderate oven until the flesh is just starting to soften. Fill the cavity with either a meat based stew or a rich vegetable soup. Return to the oven and cook for about an hour. Test the pumpkin flesh with a fork every so often so that it does not overcook. If it collapses in the oven the result is a terrible mess. This is a wonderful winter dish.

PRESERVING GARDEN PRODUCE

Name of produce	Freezing Raw	Freezing Blanched*	Canning	Root Cellar 32°-39°F (0°-4°C) No. of Months	Dry Warm Cellar No. of Months	Preserves and Pickles	Drying	Salting
Artichoke – globe						•		
Artichoke – Jerusalem	leave in ground			4-6				
Apples	•	•	•	4		•	•	
Asparagus		•	•					
Beans – fresh		•	•			•		•
Beans – ripe shelled					more than one year			
Beets		•	•	6			•	
Blueberries	•		•			•		
Broccoli		•						
Brussels sprouts		•		1 on stalk				
Cabbage		•		2 on stalk				•
Cabbage – Chinese				2				
Cantaloupe	•							
Carrots		•	•	6		•		
Cauliflower		•				•		
Celeriac		•		6				
Celery				1½-2				
Corn		•	•			•		
Cucumber						•		
Currants	•	•				•		
Eggplant		•						
Garden huckleberry	•					•		
Ground cherry	•		•			•		
Herbs	• (some)						•	
Horseradish				6		•	•	
Kale		•						
Kohl-rabi		•						
Leeks	•			1-2				
Melons	•							
Onions					6-8	•	•	
Parsnips	leave in ground	•		6				
Peas		•	•				•	
Peppers	•						•	
Pumpkins		•			2-4			
Raspberries	•		•			•		
Rhubarb	•		•			•		
Rutabaga		•		3-4				
Spinach		•						
Squash		•			4-6			
Strawberries	•		•			•		
Swiss chard		•						
Tomato		•	•	until ripe		•		
Turnip		•		4-6				

* Blanched: To prepare produce for freezer by plunging first into boiling water for a required length of time, then into cold water.

One of the great advantages of growing your own vegetables is being able to harvest, prepare and serve them within the shortest possible time. The vitamin content and food value of vegetables dissipates rapidly after harvesting.

Vitamin A

An indication of vitamin A content in fruit and vegetables is the colour. It is usually present in the yellow-orange colour of a mature vegetable or the creamy colour of an unripe fruit. Examples are carrots, tomatoes, apricots, potatoes, spinach and peas. When these vegetables become dehydrated, most of the vitamin content is lost. Any shrivelled vegetables are lacking in vitamin A.

The B Vitamins

Thiamine: Unless vegetables and fruit are used immediately after harvesting, they must be stored in cool conditions. Heat in storage will destroy thiamine very rapidly. Cook in the minimum amount of liquid for the shortest period of time possible because 50 per cent of thiamine is lost by boiling. Steam whenever possible and use cooking liquid when making soups, sauces and gravies. Examples are potatoes, peas and turnip greens.

Riboflavin: This vitamin is easily destroyed by overexposure to light. Unless eaten immediately, these vegetables should be stored in the dark to prevent this loss. Examples are potatoes and peas.

Vitamin C or Ascorbic Acid

Vitamin C is one of the better known vitamins, easily obtained through fruit and vegetables. But if these are not treated properly, it is easily destroyed. With all fruit and vegetables that contain vitamin C, the motto should be: the fresher, the better.

Although some of these vegetables listed below will be cooked, the loss will not occur during cooking but because of incorrect preparation. For optimum vitamin retention, salads should be "made" immediately prior to serving; vegetables prepared immediately before cooking; and juices squeezed as needed. When these foods are not used right away, they should be refrigerated or put directly into cold storage. Examples are green vegetables such as asparagus, spinach, broccoli, Brussels sprouts, cabbage, peas, lettuce, cauliflower, tomatoes, potatoes, carrots and water cress, as well as many others. If a vegetable is a growing shoot such as broccoli or Brussels sprouts, it usually contains large amounts of vitamin C.

Protein

In a vegetarian diet it is necessary to have an adequate supply of protein-producing vegetables to substitute for the lack of animal protein. All legumes are an important source of protein. Some examples are peas, beans, soybeans, and sunflower seeds.

Carbohydrates

In the vegetable family the chief sources of carbohydrates are potatoes and the seeds of leguminous plants such as peas, beans and lentils. Bulbs, roots and tubers store sugars and starches in roots and underground stems and are therefore an important consideration in diet planning.

Iron

As a general rule, the greener the leaf, the more iron it contains.

GLOSSARY

Annual: A plant that grows from a seed to maturity, blooms and dies within one growing season.

Axil: The v-shaped angle between a branch or leaf and the main stem.

Balanced or Complete Fertilizer: A fertilizer that contains nitrogen, phosphorus, potash and trace elements.

Biennial: A plant grown from seed that flowers and fruits the second season; then it dies.

Blanch: To whiten plants by excluding light, thereby making the edible portions more tasty. Also, to plunge into boiling water for a required length of time, then into cold water, prior to freezing.

Bolt: To send up a flower stalk and go to seed. Lettuce and spinach bolt rapidly in hot weather and become useless for eating.

Broadcast Sowing: Seed scattered evenly over a planned area or bed. Not grown in rows or hills.

Bulblet: A small bulb.

Bulbs (true): A modified bud with fleshy scales. Usually underground. Examples are daffodil, lily, onion.

Carbon-Nitrogen Ratio (C/N Ratio): The relationship between the amount of carbon and the amount of nitrogen in organic matter. The ratios vary according to the different organic materials involved in composting. In general, home-garden waste will result in a mixture whose C/N ratio will be adequate for decomposition.

Clay: Minute particles of soil that pack together tightly, thereby deterring the drainage of water.

Cold-frame: A wooden or insulated box-type structure with a glass or plastic lid used to grow certain seedlings and to harden plants.

Collard: A type of nonheading cabbage popular in the southern United States because of its ability to withstand intense summer heat.

Companion Planting: Planting two or more crops together, one of which will repel insects from attacking the other.

Compost: Decomposing organic matter.

Cool Crop: Crops that prefer cool weather conditions. Some examples are the cabbage family, lettuce and peas.

Corm: The enlarged fleshy base of a stem; bulb-like but solid. Examples are gladiolus, crocus.

Crop Rotation: To change crops grown in a given area each season. Controls pests and diseases. Enhances soil fertility. Increases crop yields.

Crown: The heart of the plant from which several leaves branch or roots grow.

Damping-off: Term applied to condition of seedlings which topple over with a dark, rotted area at the surface of the soil. This is caused by a fungi and should be treated immediately to prevent rapid spreading.

Diatomaceous Earth: Diatomaceous earth is the fossilized silica shells of algae called diatoms. It is an abrasive powder which damages the insects' cuticle (skin) causing the body fluids to leak out.

Dormant: The inactive or resting condition trees, shrubs and plants assume during the winter.

Drill: A straight trench or row in which seeds are planted.

Espalier: A fruit tree or ornamental shrub which is trained to grow in a flat plane against a wall or trellis.

Fertilizer: Organic or inorganic materials usually added to the soil to provide correct usable amounts of nitrogen, phosphorus, potash, and trace elements.

Flat: A shallow rectangular or square container used for starting seeds and cuttings.

Fruit: The ripened result of a fertilized ovary in any seed-bearing plant. May be edible and even referred to as a vegetable.

Fungicide: A material to control fungal disorders of plants.

Genus: Botannical name for a group of closely related species of plants.

Germination: The development of the plantlet from the seed.

Grafting: To graft is to successfully unite a scion with a compatible root stock, plant or tree.

Growing Season: The period between the last spring frost and the first fall killing frost.

Half-hardy Plants: Plants unreliably resistant to cold.

Hardening: To gradually introduce plants raised in a controlled indoor environment to outdoor conditions.

Hardy Plants: Plants resistant to cold.

Hill: Several seeds planted in a circle. The weak ones are thinned as the growing season progresses, leaving three or four of the strongest. Squash are usually planted in hills.

Hill-up or Earth-up: Draw soil up against the growing stalks of a plant.

Hot-cap: A protective cover, usually for a transplant. Helps plant re-establish its root system without injury from sun, wind or cold.

Hot-frame or Hot Bed: A frame heated by electric cables or fresh horse manure, used as a miniature greenhouse to start seedlings early in spring.

Humus: Decaying animal and vegetable matter that should be present in all good soils.

Hybrid: A plant resulting from a cross between two or more dissimilar parents of the same kind in an attempt to obtain the best characteristics of each kind.

Inorganic or Chemical Fertilizer: a fertilizer derived from chemical sources. Not of plant or animal origin. Often water soluble.

Insecticide or Pesticide: The general terms used to describe materials, liquid or powder, which control pests causing damage to plants. They can be herbal or chemical.

Intensive Gardening: The use of raised beds, double digging, non-linear, intensive planting, and companion planting to increase crop yields and improve quality. This is accomplished in a limited space with no machinery necessary.

Intercropping: A method of planting more than one crop simultaneously in a piece of ground to increase productivity.

Jiffy-7: A compressed pellet specially designed for starting plants and seeds. Expands in water to form a small pot.

Larva: The second stage of a complete metamorphosis undergone by such insects as the butterfly. Larvae are variously referred to as caterpillars, maggots, and grubs.

Layering: A method of propagation in which an attached stem of a plant is put into the ground, covered with soil, weighted down and allowed to root.

Leaching: The action of water to dissolve and wash away valuable nutrients in the soil to a depth where plant roots cannot reach them.

Leader: The main shoot of a plant or tree. If the leader is damaged, the nearest sideshoot can be trained or will naturally take over as the new leader.

Leaf mold: Composted leaves used as plant food and/or mulch.

Leggy: A seedling that has grown tall and

weak. A result of overcrowded flats, lack of sun or too much nitrogen.

Legume Inoculation: Seeds of legumes that are inoculated with nitrogen-fixing bacteria allow the plant to make greater use of the nitrogen in the air to increase yields and quality. Especially valuable in green manuring. (See nodules).

Legumes: Pod-bearing plants such as peas or beans.

Loam: A good soil consisting of sand, clay, silt and humus.

Mother plant: A plant, usually brought in from the garden towards the late summer, from which cuttings are taken during winter and spring. Examples are rosemary and oregano.

Muck Soil: Poorly drained areas that are, in fact, natural compost heaps. Properly managed, they will support most crops.

Mulch: A layer or layers of organic material placed on top of soil to conserve moisture, to insulate, and to control weeds. Black plastic is another form of mulch.

Necrosis: Dead plant tissue indicating disease.

Nematode: Microscopic worm-like creatures that, when present in the soil, may cause damage to the root systems of plants.

Nitrogen: An element which promotes strong vegetative growth; good dark-green colour.

Node: The points on a stem from which buds, branches and leaves originate.

Nodule: Tiny, round swellings on roots of inoculated leguminous plants that contain bacteria, capable of changing atmospheric nitrogen into forms available to plants.

Off-shoot, or Off-set: A lateral shoot growing from the main stem of a plant; or a shoot growing from the base of a plant or shrub; usually to one side. These frequently develop their own root systems and can easily be severed from the mother to start a new plant.

Organic Fertilizer: Of plant or animal origin, usually insoluble in water. Must be broken down by micro-organisms before nutrients are available to plants. Some soluble products are now available.

Osmosis: The process of diffusion whereby plant roots absorb food from the soil's nutrient solution.

Parasite: A plant or animal that lives on or in another living creature and derives its sustenance from it. The host may be killed as a result of this relationship.

Pathogen: A living organism that causes disease.

Peat Moss: The partially decomposed remains of sphagnum moss. May be added to growing mediums or as a mulch or soil conditioner.

Perennial: A plant that continues its life cycle for many years.

Perlite: A sterile, lightweight material used in growing and planting mediums to increase soil porosity. Usually used instead of sand.

pH: The symbol for potential of hydrogen used to express the acidity (sourness) or alkalinity (sweetness) of soil.

Phosphorus: An element which helps promote maximum fruit formation. Aids seedlings to re-establish after transplanting.

Pinch Back or Pinch Out: To remove growing points in order to promote bushy growth.

Pollination: The process by which pollen is transferred from the male to the female part of the flower, or from the male flower to the female flower. The result is fertilization and ultimately fruit.

Potash: An element which promotes stronger stems and roots. Deepens flower colour. Helps produce starch and sugar.

Propagation: To reproduce. To have offspring either from seed or by asexual means (grafting, cutting, budding, layering, root division, etc.). The resulting plants always "come true" if asexual techniques are adopted.

Resistant Varieties: Varieties of plants that are naturally able to ward off certain diseases and insects.

Rhizome: An underground stem often enlarged by food storage, for example: the iris.

Rotenone: An organic insecticide.

Sand: Large irregularly shaped particles of soil which do not pack tightly, thus permitting water to drain through freely.

Scallion: Young onions grown from seed and pulled before the bulb has formed.

Set: Immature bulbs, such as onions, stored over winter to be replanted the following year.

Setting of Fruit: The term used to describe the successful fertilization of blossoms. It is indicated by the swelling of the ovary, or the beginning of fruit formation.

Shallot: Small, multiplier onions grown from sets or small cloves.

Silt: Particles of soil between sand and clay in size.

Soil: The top layer of the earth's surface containing minerals and organic materials that will support plant life.

Species: Botannical word describing a group of closely related plants. Species will breed true from seeds.

Subsoil: The layer of soil beneath the topsoil (or loam). If the topsoil is shallow, small amounts of subsoil and humus can be incorporated occasionally with the topsoil in order to obtain a better depth of workable garden. A packed subsoil may also be the cause of poor drainage.

Succession Planting: Also known as catch-cropping, this term refers to the practice of planting a second crop on the same area of ground either before or right after the first crop has been harvested.

Tender: Plants not resistant to cold or extreme heat.

Thinning: The process of removing some plants in a row to leave room for the rest to grow.

Till: To work or prepare soil for growing crops.

Tilth: The quality of the soil tilled.

Trace elements: Those mineral elements essential to plant growth that are needed in minute quantities.

Transplant: May be a seedling or tree. In the vegetable and flower garden it usually applies to annual plants that must be started indoors early in the season and planted out when the weather is suitable.

Tuber: A thickened portion of a subterranean stem or branch provided with eyes (or buds) on the sides. Examples: dahlia, Jerusalem artichoke, potato.

Tuberous: Bearing or producing tubers.

Vermiculite: A sterile, lightweight mica product which absorbs water and is used in planting and rooting mixtures.

Viable or Viability of Seed: The length of time a seed retains its ability to germinate. May be days or hundreds of years.

Variety: A subdivision of species which may or may not breed true.

Whip: A shoot or stem of a woody plant, usually without branches.

Zone: Maps are available showing hardiness zones based on the average annual minimum temperature.

FURTHER READING

While researching the technical aspects of this book, I found that there was an abundance of material that discussed the many facets of home vegetable gardening. A number of these were most helpful; others were not. It would be impossible to list all the pamphlets and books consulted, so I have named only those that I feel would be helpful to the novice gardener for further reading.

My primary source of information has always been the government pamphlets that are put out by the federal, provincial, and state departments of agriculture. Readers may obtain a list of publications from the Department of Agriculture and Food, and then send away for those titles that they desire. There are also numerous periodicals and magazines concerned with the home vegetable garden that are readily available on magazine racks or in local libraries.

For general information about gardening see:

The Organic Gardener's Handbook of Natural Insect and Disease Control; Barbara W. Ellis and Fern Marshall Bradley, eds.; Rodale Press; Emmaus, Pennsylvania; 1992.

Rodale's All-New Encyclopedia of Organic Gardening; Fern Marshall Bradley and Barbara W. Ellis, eds.; Rodale Press; Emmaus, Pennsylvania; 1992.

"Food problems are becoming more and more acute as the demand for food increasingly overshadows the supply. Primitive peoples depended upon food resources which are now neglected. Other sources of possible human nutrition have doubtless remained untouched, and the time may come when a comprehensive utilization of food plants will be essential to human sustenance. It is believed, therefore, that the information so ably brought together by Dr. Sturtevant cannot fail to become increasingly useful."

This extract from a letter of June 1, 1919, written by W.H. Jordan, then director of the New York Agricultural Experiment Station at Geneva, New York, is ample introduction to an extremely interesting book, *Sturtevant's Edible Plants of the World*, U.P. Hedrick, ed., Dover Publications, New York, 1972. Although quite technical in many aspects, this book is very descriptive and easy to read.

Wyman's Gardening Encyclopedia, 2nd Edition; Donald Wyman; MacMillan; New York, New York; 1987. This publication is a comprehensive collection of information concerning plants, cultivation, fertilization and pesticides. It tends to be rather technical but is good for reference and I find myself frequently reaching for it.

W. Atlee Burpee Seed Co.
300 Park Avenue
Warminster, PA, 18974
(215) 647-4900
(215) 647-0838 (Fax).

The Cook's Garden
Moffitt's Bridge,
Box 535, Londonderry VT.
05148
(802) 824-3400
(802) 824 3027 (Fax).

William Dam Seeds
Box 8400
Dundas, Ontario
Canada, L9H 6N1
(416) 628-6641
(416) 627-1729 (Fax).

Dominion Seed House
114 Guelph St.
Georgetown, Ontario
Canada, L7G 4A2
(416) 564-SEED (7333)
(416) 564-8038 (Fax).

Gurney Seed and Nursery
2nd and Capital
Yankton, SD, 57078
(605) 665-4451
(605) 665-6435 (Fax).

Johnny's Selected Seeds
Foss Hill Rd.
Albion, Maine, 04910-9731
(207) 437-9294
(207) 437-2165 (Fax).

J.W. Jung Seed Co.
335 South High Street
Randolph, WI, 53956
(414) 326-3121
(414) 326-5769 (Fax).

Lee Valley Tools
12 East River Street
Ogdensburg, NY, 13669
1-800-461-5053. (Tool Specialists)

Lee Valley Tools
Box 6295, Station J
Ottawa, Ontario
Canada, K2A 1T4
(613) 596-0350
(613) 596-6030 (Fax)
1-800-267-8767.
(Tool specialists)

McFayden's
Box 1800
Brandon, Manitoba
Canada, R7A 6N4
(204) 726-0759
(204) 725-1888 (Fax).

A.E. McKenzie Co., Ltd.
30 Ninth Street
Brandon, Manitoba
Canada, R7A 4A4
(204) 725-7333
(204) 728-8671 (Fax).

Nichols Garden Nursery
1190 North Pacific Highway
Albany, OR, 97321
(503) 928-9280
(503) 967-8406 (FAX).

L.L. Olds Seed Co.
Box 7790
Madison, WI, 53707
(608) 249-9291
(608) 249-0695 (Fax).

Ontario Seed Co. Ltd.
330 Philip Street
Waterloo, Ontario
Canada, N2J 3Z9
(519) 886-0557
(519) 886-0605 (Fax).

G.W. Park Seed Co.
Hwy 254 N.
Box 31
Greenwood, SC, 29646
(803) 223-8555
(803) 941-4239 (Fax).

W.H. Perron & Cie Ltee.
2914 LaBelle Boul.
Chomedey, Laval, Quebec,
Canada, H7P 5R9
(514) 332-2275
(514) 682-4959 (Fax).

Richter's
Goodwood, Ontario
Canada, L0C 1A0
(416) 640-6677
(416) 640-6641 (Fax).
(Herb specialists)

Stokes Seeds Ltd.
Box 10, St, Catherines, Ontario
Canada, L2R 6R6
(416) 688-4300
(416) 684-6101 (Fax).

Stokes Seeds Inc.
Box 548
Buffalo, NY, 14240
(716) 695-6980
(716) 695-9649 (Fax).

Thompson and Morgan, Inc
Box 1308
Jackson, NJ, 08527
(908) 363-2225
(908) 363-9356 (Fax).

T & T Seeds Ltd.
111 Lombard Avenue
Box 1710, Winnipeg, Manitoba,
Canada, R3C 3P6
(204) 943-8483
(204) 956-1994 (Fax).

Vesey's Seeds Ltd.
York, P.E.I.
Canada, C0A 1P0
(902) 368-7333
(902) 566-1620 (Fax).

INDEX

CANADIAN PLANT HARDINESS ZONE MAP
Based on USDA Plant Hardiness Zone Map

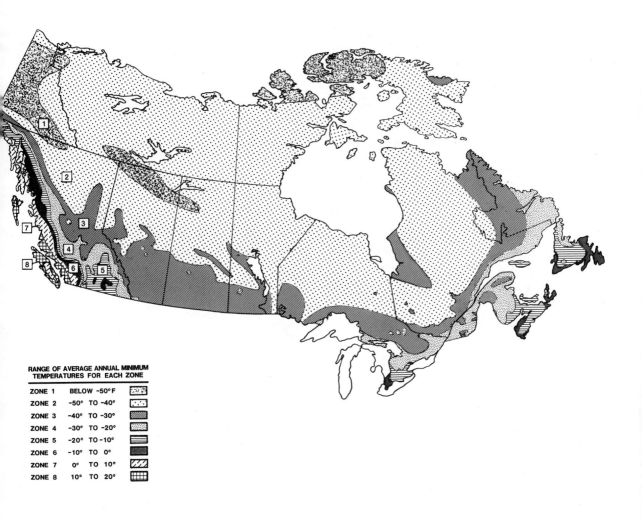

RANGE OF AVERAGE ANNUAL MINIMUM TEMPERATURES FOR EACH ZONE

ZONE 1	BELOW −50°F
ZONE 2	−50° TO −40°
ZONE 3	−40° TO −30°
ZONE 4	−30° TO −20°
ZONE 5	−20° TO −10°
ZONE 6	−10° TO 0°
ZONE 7	0° TO 10°
ZONE 8	10° TO 20°

AVERAGE FROST DATES

	Last Spring Frost	First Fall Frost		Last Spring Frost	First Fall Frost
Vancouver	Mar 31	Nov 3	Sudbury	May 12	Oct 2
Yellow Knife	May 27	Sept 16	Timmins	May 28	Sept 13
White Horse	June 8	Aug 30	Toronto	Apr 20	Oct 29
Calgary	May 25	Sept 15	Thunder Bay	May 30	Sept 12
Edmonton	May 6	Sept 24	Windsor	Apr 26	Oct 21
Regina	May 24	Sept 11	Montreal	Apr 19	Oct 14
Winnipeg	May 23	Sept 22	Quebec City	May 10	Oct 15
Kingston	May 7	Oct 10	St John	May 2	Oct 21
Niagara Falls	May 3	Oct 23	Halifax	Apr 30	Oct 19
Ottawa	May 8	Sept 30	Charlottetown	May 16	Oct 14
Sault Ste Marie	May 24	Sept 29	St John's	June 1	Oct 11

USA PLANT HARDINESS ZONE MAP
Based on USDA Plant Hardiness Zone Map

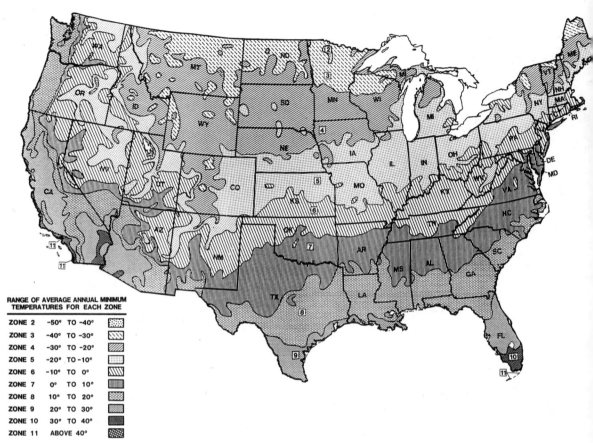

RANGE OF AVERAGE ANNUAL MINIMUM TEMPERATURES FOR EACH ZONE

ZONE 2	-50° TO -40°
ZONE 3	-40° TO -30°
ZONE 4	-30° TO -20°
ZONE 5	-20° TO -10°
ZONE 6	-10° TO 0°
ZONE 7	0° TO 10°
ZONE 8	10° TO 20°
ZONE 9	20° TO 30°
ZONE 10	30° TO 40°
ZONE 11	ABOVE 40°

AVERAGE FROST DATES

	Last Spring Frost	First Fall Frost		Last Spring Frost	First Fall Frost		Last Spring Frost	First Fall Frost
Albuquerque, NM	Apr 13	Oct 28	Harrisburg, PA	Apr 9	Oct 30	Portland, OR	Mar 6	Nov 24
Asheville, NC	Apr 12	Oct 24	Hartford, CT	Apr 22	Oct 19	Providence, RI	Apr 13	Oct 27
Atlanta, GA	Mar 21	Nov 18	Houston, TX	Mar 14	Nov 21	Pueblo, CO	Apr 23	Oct 14
Baltimore, MD	Mar 28	Nov 19	Indianapolis, IN	Apr 17	Oct 27	Raleigh, NC	Mar 24	Nov 16
Bangor, ME	May 1	Oct 4	Jacksonville, FL	Feb 16	Dec 16	Rapid City, SD	May 7	Oct 4
Birmingham, AL	Mar 19	Nov 14	Kansas City, MO	Apr 6	Oct 30	Reno, NV	May 8	Oct 10
Bismarck, ND	May 11	Sep 24	Las Vegas, NV	Mar 16	Nov 10	Richmond, VA	Mar 29	Nov 2
Boise, ID	Apr 23	Oct 17	Lexington, KY	Apr 13	Oct 28	Salt Lake City, UT	Apr 13	Oct 22
Boston, MA	Apr 5	Nov 8	Little Rock, AR	Mar 17	Nov 13	San Francisco, CA	Jan 7	Dec 29
Buffalo, NY	Apr 30	Oct 25	Los Angeles, CA	Jan 3	Dec 28	Santa Fe, NM	Apr 24	Oct 19
Burlington, VT	May 8	Oct 3	Lubbock, TX	Apr 1	Nov 9	Savannah, GA	Feb 27	Nov 29
Caribou, ME	May 19	Sep 21	Memphis, TN	Mar 20	Nov 12	Seattle, WA	Mar 14	Nov 24
Charleston, SC	Feb 19	Dec 10	Milwaukee, WI	Apr 20	Oct 25	Shreveport, LA	Mar 8	Nov 15
Charleston, WV	Apr 18	Oct 28	Minneapolis, MN	Apr 30	Oct 13	Sioux City, IA	Apr 27	Oct 13
Cheyenne, WY	May 14	Oct 2	Montgomery, AL	Feb 27	Dec 3	Sioux Falls, SD	May 5	Oct 3
Chicago, IL	Apr 19	Oct 28	Nashville, TN	Mar 28	Nov 7	Springfield, IL	Apr 20	Oct 23
Cleveland, OH	Apr 21	Nov 2	New Orleans, LA	Feb 20	Dec 9	Springfield, MO	Apr 12	Oct 30
Concord, NH	May 11	Sep 30	New York City, NY	Apr 7	Nov 12	Syracuse, NY	Apr 30	Oct 15
Dallas, TX	Mar 18	Nov 17	Norfolk, VA	Mar 19	Nov 16	Tampa, FL	Jan 10	Dec 26
Denver, CO	Apr 26	Oct 14	Okla. City, OK	Mar 28	Nov 7	Texarkana, AR	Mar 21	Nov 9
Des Moines, IA	Apr 24	Oct 16	Omaha, NE	Apr 14	Oct 20	Trenton, NJ	Apr 4	Nov 8
Detroit, MI	Apr 21	Oct 20	Philadelphia, PA	Mar 30	Nov 17	Tucson, AZ	Mar 19	Nov 19
Duluth, MN	May 22	Sep 24	Phoenix, AZ	Feb 5	Dec 6	Washington, DC	Mar 29	Nov 9
Eugene, OR	Apr 13	Nov 4	Pittsburgh, Pa	Apr 20	Oct 23	Wichita, KS	Apr 5	Nov 1
Grand Rapids, MI	Apr 23	Oct 30	Pocatello, ID	Apr 28	Oct 6	Wilmington, DE	Apr 18	Oct 26
Gt. Falls, MT	May 9	Sep 25	Portland, ME	Apr 29	Oct 15			